MW00620451

.75t

The Russian Presidency

Society and Politics in the Second Russian Republic

Thomas M. Nichols

palgrave

For Linda

THE RUSSIAN PRESIDENCY

Copyright © Thomas M. Nichols, 1999. All rights reserved. No part of this book may be used or reproduced in any manner whatsoever without written permission except in the case of brief quotations embodied in critical articles or reviews.

First published in hardcover in 1999 by St. Martin's Press

First PALGRAVE™ edition: September 2001
175 Fifth Avenue, New York, N.Y. 10010 and
Houndmills, Basingstoke, England RG21 6XS
Companies and representatives throughout the world.

PALGRAVE is the new global publishing imprint of St. Martin's Press LLC Scholarly and Reference Division and Palgrave Publishers Ltd (formerly Macmillan Press Ltd).

ISBN 0–312–22357–9 hardcover
ISBN 0–312–29337–2 paperback

Library of Congress Cataloging-in-Publication Data
Nichols, Thomas M., 1960-
The Russian presidency : society and politics in the second
Russian Republic / by Thomas M. Nichols.
    p.   cm.
  Includes bibliographical references and index.
    ISBN 0–312–29337–2 (paperback)
    1. Presidents—Russia (Federation)   2. Political culture—Russia
(Federation) 3. Russia (Federation)—Politics and government—1991-
I. Title.
JN6696.N5   1999
352.23'0947—dc21   99–29167
                                                                    CIP

A catalogue record for this book is available from the British Library.

Design by Letra Libre, Inc.

First paperback edition: September 2001
10 9 8 7 6 5 4 3 2 1

Printed in the United States of America

Contents

Preface to the Expanded Edition

The Russian Presidency was written between 1995 and 1998, and first appeared in bookstores in the winter of 1999 . . . December, to be precise. Although completion of the book was at times delayed by the turmoil in Moscow (among other, less grandiose obstacles), by 1998 it seemed that the Russian political scene had settled down to the point where it was possible to draw conclusions about Russian institutions and the immediate future of Russian democracy.

On New Year's Eve 1999, I turned on the television just in time to see Boris Yeltsin resigning. Needless to say, over the ensuing days and weeks, colleagues and friends familiar with the book asked how this sudden turn of events affected my assertion that Russia was, for all its problems, a stable presidential democracy.

It's a fair question.

On the face of it, Yeltsin's move seemed like exactly the kind of end-run around the democratic process his critics had always feared. Putin's arrival seemed to confirm the very worst expectations of the most pessimistic observers of Russian politics. Would Putin pardon Yeltsin, and make the ex-president a power behind the throne? Would the elections in 2000, even if they were held, be anything more than a formality? And was Putin, with his KGB background and dour demeanor, the sort of figure Russia-watchers for the past decade had held their breath waiting for, the inevitable "Comrade Crackdown" who was going to take Russia's messy democracy by the throat and impose order and discipline, perhaps to the cheers of impoverished, disaffected Russians?

These fears are unfounded, not least because they do not take into account the popular limits to presidential power even in Russia. Ordinary Russians have gotten used to democracy, in the sense that they have become used to saying what they will, to gaining information from multiple sources, to communicating with each other, and—however limited it may be by economic circumstance—to doing pretty much as they please. (As a

Russian friend said to me in 2000, Russians fear the tax police more than the secret police, making them not so different from Americans in this regard.) The idea that Putin, even if he were so inclined, could block access to the Internet, seize millions of telephones and fax machines, black out CNN, silence local government across the Federation, and rule as a twenty-first century Russian autocrat, is too much to accept—but even more fantastic is the idea that Russians would allow him to do any of these things. (Even the attempt to capture independent NTV television, although so far successful, generated significant protest.)

It is important to bear in mind that the election of Vladimir Putin, or someone like him—young, healthy, confident—was probably unavoidable, and it says more about Boris Yeltsin personally than it does about Russian democracy. Yeltsin, whatever his merits or flaws, came to be seen as an ineffectual old man: corrupt, unpredictable, and perhaps even emotionally unstable. It should be no surprise that Russians admire the apparently unflappable Putin. This, of course, does not mean that Putin is in fact the panacea many Russians think he is, but rather only that their enthusiasm is understandable. Celebrating a candidate who remedies the perceived shortcomings of his predecessor is a tradition in presidential politics; Americans might recall the way Jimmy Carter was received after the days of scandal under Richard Nixon, or the adulation that surrounded the optimistic Ronald Reagan in the wake of the gloom of the Carter White House.

Russia, then, despite the damage done by Yeltsin's dramatic exit, remains a democracy. After Yeltsin's departure, life went on; elections to the Duma were held, the presidential election took place fairly, even if Putin was the heavy favorite from the outset. The institutions described in the earlier edition of *The Russian Presidency* not only remain in place, but are becoming more deeply rooted in Russian political life. Putin and others have started to reconsider the future shape of those institutions, but this, I would argue, is actually a healthy sign, in that it shows that Russia's political elites have accepted that structures of presidential democracy are permanent, rather than expedient, and need to grow and change if they are to remain relevant.

It is still possible, I suppose, that by some feat of political sleight-of-hand, Putin will manage to undermine the institutions put in place since the Soviet collapse, and turn the Russian Federation toward some sort of dull, bureaucratized authoritarianism, a kind of neo-Brezhnevism in which citizens are basically left alone if they do not annoy the government or ask too much of it. But to fear this outcome is to assume that this is what Putin *wants* for his country, and that his fellow citizens are willing to accept it. Both of those propositions seem unlikely. Putin, whatever his past, seems committed to fundamental democratic processes; more important, what Putin or any Russian president thinks or wants is now only part of the story. The strongest barrier to a resurgence of repression is not one particular law or set of laws, but rather Russians themselves, who under the institutions of the past decade have come to regard their own freedoms as their due, as part of a normal life.

Order and stability are tempting, but democracy and freedom are powerfully addictive. Russians, I believe, have come to understand that there is no reason they cannot have both.

Thomas M. Nichols
May 2001

Preface

This study has its origins in questions that arose after the events of October 1993, when Boris Yeltsin's tanks and the armed militia that was once a parliament went to war in the streets of Moscow and gave dramatic meaning to the concept of "legislative-executive relations." The destruction of the Supreme Soviet seemed to fulfill the worst expectations of many in the West who had argued since 1991 that it would be only a matter of time before Russia fell back into old habits, and that the experiment with democracy would be little more than an odd footnote in an otherwise unbroken record of autocracy. I am forced to admit that I was part of this chorus of pessimism, and in late 1993—despite the fact that I felt Yeltsin had no choice but to crush the attempted coup of Ruslan Khasbulatov and Aleksandr Rutskoi—I expected little more than that Russia would then descend into some kind of muddled and mild authoritarianism.

But soon after the October 1993 attack on the legislature, it seemed that democratic reforms were moving forward rather than backward. More interesting, this seemed to be taking place in direct contravention of an overwhelming academic consensus that held, in effect, that further democratic consolidation was nearly impossible given the institutions put in place by the December 1993 constitutional referendum (an event that itself was a surprise, given the wide expectation that Yeltsin would keep direct presidential rule in place for as long as possible). Russia was not supposed to be a democracy, and it was certainly not supposed to be a *presidential* democracy. It was no longer enough merely to assert that Russian democracy was a sham: with each successful election, with every day that passed in which Russian politics became more "ordinary," the failure of previous predictions became more obvious and a more coherent explanation of Russian political development became more pressing.

For the second time in less than five years, the conventional wisdom among Western social scientists had gotten an important, even vital question wrong. (Russia wasn't supposed to be a democracy, but then the

USSR wasn't supposed to collapse, either.) Somehow, the tanks of October had led not to autocracy but to democratic renewal. Why?

The answer presented in this book is a simple one. Russia is a mistrustful society: seven decades of Soviet policies aimed at alienating citizens from each other in order to discourage any kind of independent association among them taught the Soviet citizen that political participation was usually pointless and often dangerous. This legacy of mistrust is what makes parliamentarism impossible and presidentialism indispensable in modern Russia. The experiences of the Soviet period left Russia without the social infrastructure to create the parties and organizations that normally sustain a parliament, and the Russians have therefore turned to presidentialism as the one form of democratic organization on which they can all agree. These arrangements have served Russia well, helping to dampen social anxiety about a possible reversion to the authoritarian past and providing a measure of stability and accountability while Russian society recovers from the wounds of Soviet rule.

I call this current presidential regime the "Second Republic." While this is not a term the Russians themselves use, it is meant to make a distinction between the arrangements brought into being under the 1993 constitution and the "First Republic," the conglomeration of institutions left in the wake of the Soviet collapse in 1991. While purists might argue that the very first Russian republic was the one proclaimed in the interregnum between the Tsar's abdication and the Bolshevik coup in 1917, I believe that the Soviet experience was sufficiently traumatic and transformative to justify considering 1991 as the start of a completely new era in Russian politics.

This book, then, is about the social foundations of modern Russian politics. It is not about the ins and outs of the daily political struggles in Moscow, nor is it an analysis of the administrative details of Russian presidential government. Indeed, readers will find that the emphasis on Russian social conditions means that much of the book is devoted to the failings of Russian parliamentarism, rather than to any kind of triumphalism about the putative achievements of the presidency (or the president). To explain the emergence of presidentialism in Russia and its success in preserving the Russian democratic experiment, it is important to understand why the pre-1994 regime failed, and why there is no alternative to presidential democracy in Russia today.

Of course, no one can be sure that Russia's political institutions will not be swept away by a political earthquake of the magnitude of those in 1989, 1991, or 1993. Nor is it clear that the current system is the final stage of

Russian political development. But even if the system were to fall tomorrow in some strange or violent scenario, the experiences of only the past decade are themselves unexpected enough to merit further study and to force us to reconsider our conceptions both of postcommunist politics and of the part political institutions play in them.

This project began with support from the William H. Spoor Dialogues on Leadership, a program at the Nelson A. Rockefeller Center for the Social Sciences at Dartmouth College. The Spoor Dialogues normally consider questions of presidential leadership in the American context; it was the Center's director in 1994, George Demko, who first suggested enlarging the mandate of the Dialogues Program to encompass such issues in a comparative context, and I am grateful to him for his early and continuing encouragement of this project. I was quite fortunate to have excellent research assistance from three outstanding students while at Dartmouth and I thank Cara Abercrombie, Marina Lakhman, and Maria Popova for their conscientious work.

Crucial support that allowed completion of this project came from the National Council for Soviet and East European Research, whose Special 1996 Research Competition grant provided not only for time to write but also for research in Moscow in early 1997. The initial result of the work conducted with the assistance from the National Council was a monograph published in the Carl Beck Papers series at the University of Pittsburgh. My thanks to series editor Ron Linden, and especially to the anonymous reviewers who served as referees for the Beck series. Their comments and questions (as well as those from later readers of the Beck Papers) forced me to think more carefully about several issues that would make their way into the book, and their thoughtful and meticulous review improved both the Beck manuscript and the present work. I also wish to thank the Davis Center for Russian Studies at Harvard University for allowing me to spend 1998 as an Associate at the Center, where I was able to put the final manuscript in order.

Of course, I would also like to extend my thanks to the many Russian politicians and staff members who were willing to speak with me, including Boris Nemtsov, Anatolii Greshnevikov (who showed me many courtesies and was of great help during my visit to the Duma), Sergei Baburin, Konstantin Borovoy, Vladimir Grigoriev, and many of the Duma's staff members. I know that their conclusions would not necessarily be mine, but I am grateful for their willingness to speak with me at length.

I also wish to thank the many friends and colleagues who offered helpful criticism and advice. I owe a great debt to two colleagues in particular.

Dirk Vandewalle went well beyond the requirements of professional courtesy to read several versions of various chapters, and he unfailingly provided incisive and useful comments. Professor Sergei Baburkin of Yaroslavl University was not only a careful and insightful critic, but his assistance in Moscow was invaluable to my research there. Thane Gustafson, William Fuller, and John Allen Williams provided comments on the initial design of the project, and Gordon Silverstein, James Shoch, and Dean Spiliotes were kind enough to indulge me in several conversations about presidential politics, institutional theory, and constitutionalism. I am grateful to my colleagues in the Strategy Department's faculty seminar program at the Naval War College for their comments on the latter stages of the project, and to my teaching partners in the Strategy Department in 1998 and 1999, Commander Tim McElhannon and Commander Lisa Squire, USN, for their patience with me on those occasions when my mind seemed to be in Moscow rather than Newport.

Finally, I owe the greatest thanks to my wife, Dr. Linda Titlar. This project, for various reasons, was delayed at times over the course of more than four years, and she has patiently listened to me as I forced her to endure more conversations about social trust, presidentialism, democracy, and other topics than anyone should have to, especially at home. (When one political scientist marries another, dinner conversation can get rather arcane.) Her enthusiasm never flagged, even when mine did. She was a constant source of encouragement, advice, good sense, and love. For all this, and so much more, this book is dedicated to her.

Thomas M. Nichols
Newport, Rhode Island
July 1999

A Note on Names and Sources

Translations, unless otherwise noted, are mine. I've used standard Russian to English transliteration for documents; however, I've left names of well-known people as they are typically used in the Western press (such as Yeltsin, Zhirinovsky, Zyuganov, rather than El'tsin, Zhirinovskii, Ziuganov). Original sources were in some cases—television and radio broadcasts, for example—unavailable other than from the Foreign Broadcast Information Service (FBIS) or other media. Citations to FBIS, Radio Liberty research materials, and certain news agency wire reports have no page numbers or other bibliographic data since they are no longer paper publications and are available only in electronic format.

Introduction

The Paradox of Russian Presidential Democracy

Everywhere it is stressed that if there is a president, a presidency . . . then we are in for dictatorship.

—*A Russian People's Deputy, 1993*

"This Ruinous Vicious Circle"

"Was Russia really doomed to bloodshed?" Boris Yeltsin posed this question to himself in the pages of his journal on October 1, 1993.[1] For days, members of the Russian Federation's parliament had been holed up in their chamber in defiance of Yeltsin's decrees suspending the constitution and ordering them to disband. The president was resolute that a parliament no longer existed in Russia; the lawmakers had in turn impeached Yeltsin and were now armed and vowing to die. Pressure on the Russian Army became intense as both sides laid claim to their loyalties. What began as a political standoff had become, in Yeltsin's words, "a crisis of statehood," in which he felt it had become his duty "to break this ruinous vicious circle."[2] After two weeks and several collapsed negotiations, the president's military and security forces opened fire on the legislators. Hundreds were killed and wounded in the very heart of Moscow, and several national political leaders, including the chairman of the parliament and Yeltsin's own vice president, were marched out and taken in chains to prison.

Russian democracy was for a time pronounced dead. For some, Yeltsin had finally thrown off the disguise of a democrat, as habits learned in his years as a senior member of the Soviet Communist Party reasserted themselves and his authoritarian background triumphed over a flirtation with representative democracy. For others, it was clear that the institutions of Russian government, too hastily cobbled together from the wreckage of a Soviet superstate that had been too quickly destroyed, were inadequate to the task of maintaining a republic. In either case, there could be but one outcome: dictatorship.[3]

The Paradox of Russian Presidentialism

The imposition of the "firm hand" and the consequent establishment of a new Russian autocracy did not take place. What emerged from the ashes of the White House in 1993 was a new Russian Republic, a rough democracy that has since been tested by crises ranging from elections to civil war. Russia today remains a damaged nation: crime abounds, federal power is uncertain and uneven, and the economy lurches in fits and starts. But basic civil liberties, open and fair elections, and a free press stubbornly remain in place. The Russian Federation, despite its myriad problems, remains a democracy, an outcome that would have been dismissed as all but inconceivable by observers in both the East and West.[4]

The quick recovery of Russian democracy after 1993 is especially puzzling to scholars of democracy and political change. If it is remarkable that Russian democracy has survived at all, it is even more surprising that it has survived as a presidential republic, a form widely held as the least conducive to democratic development. Not only did the Russians choose to retain a presidency after 1993, they actually enshrined an even stronger version of that presidency in a second republic after the violent failure of the first, and if the idea of a renewed Russian democracy seemed improbable in 1993, the idea of a viable Russian *presidential* democracy seemed impossible, virtually a contradiction in terms. Simply put, Russian presidential democracy is a paradox that has confounded the expectations not only of Russia-watchers but of a broader community of academic and policy specialists, as well.

How did Russian democracy survive the trauma of 1993, and why did the Russians return to presidential republicanism despite the sad experiences of other regimes and the dire warnings of constitutional scholars? By any standard, the Russian presidency is vested with immense powers; why has it failed to decay into an authoritarian instrument? And does the presidential system in Russia actually work, or has Russia escaped disaster in spite of its political institutions rather than because of them?

This book seeks to answer these questions by placing Russian political institutions in their social context: Russia (as will be discussed in the next chapter) is a society marked by a lack of trust and a consequent lack of the associationalism needed to create the parties and other institutions that mediate the relationship between state and society. Under these conditions, parliamentarism tends to deteriorate into a pitched struggle for the ultimate weapon of parliamentary supremacy, and the presidency emerges as the only institution that has both the standing and the power to keep fractious parties and politicians from extinguishing each other in political combat. The nature of lawmaking in the presence of divided powers also helps to prevent revanchist legislation, but even more important, the separated institutions of the presidential system go far to allay fears that any one group or coalition could quickly, if at all, capture the state and its considerable coercive instruments.

The Russians themselves understand the nature of their society and have consciously chosen the presidential system as a compromise that is accepted by most of Russia's political forces as a form of common self-protection from each other, or from antisystem elements that would, many Russian politicians believe, simply extinguish democratic movements if left unchecked.[5] Most Russians, even those who in principle would favor a more open parliamentary system, would agree. There is a widespread belief among Russian citizens (an accurate one, as this book will argue) that Russian society is simply not capable of supporting the parliamentary alternative even if it is in theory preferable as more "democratic." Two Russian legal scholars captured this ambivalence when they wrote that "the parliament, the voters and society as whole must grow into a parliamentary republic," and that in the meantime, a president can protect all groups from dangerous minorities just as Charles De Gaulle "saved French democracy from the excesses of certain irresponsible Frenchmen."[6] While trust is lacking at all levels of society and a dedicated minority of "certain irresponsible Russians" and their leaders might plunge the nation back into dictatorship, civil war, or even global conflict, Russian voters have reasonably chosen a cumbersome and complex political system that assures them (and their representatives) that power cannot fall into hostile hands without warning, without struggle, or without publicity.

This is more than just a desire for order. It is true, as Rousseau wrote, that "a tranquil life is also had in dungeons," and there will for a time be a small (and, due to age, declining) number of Russians who will always prefer Leonid Brezhnev's tranquil communist dungeon to the chaotic freedom of post-Soviet Russia. But most Russians do not want Boris Yeltsin or any other president to govern as a dictator and provide security at the expense of freedom; indeed, as will be seen in later chapters,

Russian voters are wary of presidential power and believe in a system of checks and balances. Their concerns about the president pale, however, in comparison to their fear of some of the groups in parliament, and given their choice (as they were in 1991, 1993, and 1996) they would rather leave the presidency in place than risk the parliamentary alternative at this point in Russia's young democratic history. The presidency, for all its flaws, was a logical choice for the Russians, and one that has helped, rather than hindered, Russia's democratic consolidation.

Before continuing on to consider the role of the presidency in the survival of Russian democracy, it is important to pause here and to contend with the most obvious and controversial objection to the "paradox" of Russian presidential democracy—that it is no paradox at all, because Russia is not a democracy.

Russia as a Democracy

The charge that "Russian democracy" is a misnomer is important to answer, if only because it was as often heard in the West as it was in the streets of Russia itself in the 1990s. At best, many Russians would say, the Russian Federation has had a "nomenklatura democracy," a system that mimics the modern republic but in reality only operates to the benefit of the former Soviet elite and remains unaccountable to the electorate. The system, in this view, muddles through without much opposition because the state eschews repression while spreading around some of the spoils of the economic system in a social contract that exchanges "unaccountable power for untaxable wealth."[7] Even those less critical of the Russian system have treated the post-1993 situation as something of a fluke, an interlude of "conservative stability" that has more to do with the disarray of Moscow's political class than with democratic values per se.[8]

Western criticisms, for their part, often consist of curious statements accepting that Russia exhibits the attributes of democracy and then rejecting the possibility that Russia *is* a democracy. "Russia mounts elections and tolerates a free press," Stephen Holmes has written, "but it does not have democracy."[9] Gerald Easter argues that "many institutional features of democracy [currently] exist in Russia," but that "democratic consolidation appears well out of reach."[10] This kind of dismissal of Russian democracy is not uncommon, and reflects the presumption among many that the Russian Federation is undemocratic until decisively proven otherwise. "It's getting to the point," an exasperated Western diplomat in Moscow told the

Wall Street Journal in late 1996, "where you wonder what this country has to do to prove it's a democracy."[11]

Of course, the legacy of the Soviet past, and the dexterity with which members of the old regime repositioned themselves in the new Russia, remain cause for concern. Skepticism about "Russian democracy" was especially warranted in the first two years of the Russian transition, while battle was still underway between extremist forces (including admitted Soviet restorationists) and reformers, with no clear victor in sight. Even now, the ultimate test of a stable democracy—the peaceful transfer of power from one ruling group to another—has not been passed, although the willingness of the regime to accept the legislative victory of the communists in 1995 was a telling sign in this regard. But the plain fact remains that whatever the successes of the current regime, it will always be a republic built quite literally on the ashes of its predecessor, and it is understandably difficult for observers in both East and West to accept that any kind of democracy has finally arisen after a millennium of autocracy.

At some point, however, skepticism must give way to common sense. Several years have passed since Yeltsin's destruction of the Supreme Soviet, and Russia's free (if rowdy) elections, aggressive media, and liberalized political life cannot now be dismissed merely as a façade for a kinder and gentler authoritarianism. Even Russia's opposition politicians are less prone now to use loaded language like "authoritarian" to describe the system, and as more time goes by and more elections take place, many find themselves in something of a bind when trying to portray the system as undemocratic. One legislator—a member of the White House resistance in 1993 and still serving in the Duma at this writing—described Russia to the author in 1997 as having only the "beginnings" of a democracy, but then admitted that his own base of voter support was quite strong, and that he had been fairly and popularly reelected three times since 1990.[12] Even a more implacable foe of the government, Deputy Duma Speaker Sergei Baburin, has acknowledged that while he sees the Russian system as imperfect, if given the chance he would seek only changes in "nuance" rather a drastic reconstruction of Russian institutions. This is a far cry from his more radical days in the opposition, and reflective as much of his probable desire to run for the presidency (and therefore to keep it strong and intact) as it is of the routinization of political conflict in Moscow.[13]

Many of the arguments rejecting the notion of Russian democracy reflect an exceptionalism that applies to Russia criteria that many other "democratic" nations might well fail to meet if subjected to similar scrutiny. As David Remnick pointedly remarked in 1997:

> We demand to know why, for example, there are no developed political parties in Russia; somehow we fail to remember that it took the United States (with all its historical advantages, including its founders) more than sixty years after independence to develop its two-party system, that in France nearly all the parties have been vehicles for the likes of Mitterrand or Chirac. The drama of 1991 so accelerated our notion of Russian history that expectations became outlandish; and now that many of those expectations have been disappointed, deferred, and even betrayed, it seems as if we have gone back to expecting only the worst from Russia.[14]

This exceptionalism not only subjects Russia to inconsistent treatment by both scholars and policymakers, but also manages to remove the Russian case from any kind of context. (To take but one example: why is the Russian campaign finance scandal of 1996 somehow worse or more revealing than the comparable American scandal?[15] After all, Russians might well argue that at least the money used in their scandal wasn't imported from the army of a hostile foreign power.) Irregularities in campaign finance, abuse of power, and corruption among high officials and other scandals are not unknown in the United States or its European allies, but such events are not commonly used as prima facie evidence that the Western nations are not democracies.

One answer to this is that the Western democracies are more resilient and more experienced at handling internal crises than Russia, and that there are institutional and cultural safeguards in place that prevent the damage from spreading too far into the system. Moreover, it could be argued that Western politicians who try to short-circuit those safeguards (such as Richard Nixon, for example) pay a serious price and rarely succeed, and that it remains unclear whether any Russian president could be stopped in a similar way. This is a sensible rejoinder, particularly because there is no sure way to tell just how much damage the Russian political system is capable of absorbing before it collapses. All regimes have a breaking point—the United States and its democratic brethren have all come to the edge of a political abyss at various points in their history—and modern Russia's capacity for political stress remains unclear. But the recognition that scandals and crises are more anxiety provoking in a young and disorganized democracy like Russia does not then lead to the conclusion that Russia is therefore not a democracy.

More generous critics of the Russian system might argue that Russia is not an authoritarian system but rather an "unconsolidated" democracy, in which "democracy in its most generic sense persists" but political life "never gels into a specific, reliable, and generally accepted set of rules":

These countries are "doomed" to remain democratic almost by default. No serious alternative to democracy seems available. Elections are held; associations are tolerated; rights may be respected; arbitrary treatment by authorities may decline—in other words, the procedural minima are met with some degree of regularity—but regular, acceptable, and predictable democratic patterns never quite crystallize.[16]

This description reflects a basic truth about the Russian political system: Russia is an ancient nation but a young state, and its political practices and constitutional mechanisms are new and in some ways untested. It may well be too early to say that current Russian political patterns will endure, but that in itself says nothing about whether those patterns are democratic or authoritarian. (It also raises the question of what arbitrary age a regime's institutions must reach before they are blessed by Western social scientists as having "crystallized.")

It is, of course, possible that the current republic will prove to be merely a transitional arrangement. But this is not the same thing as saying that Russia is therefore inherently an undemocratic state or that the republic is therefore a sham. The Russian system manages to meet and in many cases to exceed these "procedural minima," and it would be overly critical (to say nothing of condescending) of Russia or other young democracies to charge that it is only by "default" that they manage to hold free elections, support free association, and protect civil liberties, as if these were not in themselves acceptable criteria for a democracy. It is also unhelpful to think of Russian democracy itself as an expedient, some sort of accident left in place until someone thinks of something better, since this produces little more than the unfalsifiable argument that Russian democracy is merely an interlude between phases of autocracy. In any event, even if we are to add the mildly pejorative label of "unconsolidated" (at least for now) to "Russian democracy," it is still a situation that defied expectation and demands explanation.

None of this is to condone the daily conduct of Russian politics, but rather only to point out that messy politics are not necessarily undemocratic politics. To say that the Russian civil administration is corrupt, that Russian streets are haunted by crime, and that Russian political institutions are ruled by powerful politicians and special interests is to say only that Russia, for better or worse, is plagued with some of the worst problems that normally afflict most democracies. Indeed, many of these problems are the unintended consequences of political and economic liberty: If Moscow and St. Petersburg in 1999 look more like, say, New York or

Chicago in 1939, that is hardly an indictment of Russian democracy, but rather only a reminder that establishing a modus vivendi between unregulated capitalist democracy and public order is no simple task.

Democracy in Russia is not particularly efficient or well-organized, and it is certainly not attractive. Neither is democracy in France, Peru, Greece, South Korea, and a host of other nations that today need not endure prolonged debate over their general orientation or stability, whatever their spotty pasts. Russian democracy, however unlovely it may be, is still recognizable as such, and this fact in itself creates part of the puzzle that this study seeks to explain.

Overview

What follows is not meant as a comprehensive history of the Russian presidency—it is clearly too early for that—but is rather an attempt to explain both the origins of the Russian presidency and the survival of Russian democracy under a presidential system.

To understand the Russian paradox, it is necessary to understand the nature of the objections to presidentialism in general. Chapter 1 examines these objections in more detail and presents an alternative understanding of the role of presidential institutions in divided societies such as Russia. The fragmentation of Russia did not begin in 1991; the Soviet regime consciously sought to divide and atomize society for seven decades as a means both of mobilizing the population for its own purposes and of preventing any unauthorized political or social activity that might provide an alternative to Communist Party rule. By 1989, these policies had made the USSR ungovernable by any means short of force. As a last resort, the Soviets created a national presidency, an office that served as both a model and a lesson to the presidencies that would follow in the republics. Chapter 2 discusses the establishment of this Soviet office and Mikhail Gorbachev's efforts to use it to stop, or at least to slow, the accelerating disintegration of the Soviet Union.

As Gorbachev was maneuvering himself into his short-lived USSR presidency, Boris Yeltsin was engineering his own rapid return from the political exile into which Gorbachev had forced him in the late 1980s. This comeback culminated in Yeltsin's election to the leadership of the Russian Soviet Federated Socialist Republic (RSFSR), his first "presidency." Actually, Yeltsin was a parliamentary executive: as chairman of the RSFSR legislature, he was nominally the republic's leader. But as the Russian public lost faith in the central Soviet government's ability to forestall outright social warfare, Yeltsin's post soon eclipsed the Soviet presidency in terms of both popular support and practical strength, and was finally transformed by referendum into an actual executive presidency. Chapter 3 discusses this first Russian experiment with presidential democracy, a strange amalgam of Soviet, presidential, and parliamentary practices that was unviable from the start. The fate of what I have termed the "First Republic" is interesting in itself, as it was the exact reverse of what might have been expected under a presidential system. Rather than a grab for power by a strong president against a weak legislature, the October 1993 violence in Moscow was the result of a parliament trying to seize power by calling for civil war against a legitimately elected president.

Chapter 4 recounts the reconstruction of Russian national politics after 1993 that led to the current Second Republic, in reality the first truly "post-Soviet" government. No sooner had most Russians (and Westerners) breathed a sigh of relief over Yeltsin's refusal to assume imperial powers than a new threat arose: Vladimir Zhirinovsky's fascistic Liberal Democrats and Gennady Zyuganov's retooled Russian communists stormed into the new legislature with a greater share of votes than anyone in the Kremlin had expected. The failure of these groups to capture the system, the eventual fall of Zhirinovsky's star, and the growing stabilization of Russian politics despite the ideological hostility between the president and his parliamentary opposition are important parts of the story of Russian presidential democracy.

It was widely feared that the 1996 presidential elections could well break the fragile back of the Russian system. Communist challenger Zyuganov, after all, entered the race with what seemed to be an immense lead, and there was dark talk in Moscow (some of it from Yeltsin's ham-handed advisors) about canceling the elections and declaring presidential rule. Mysterious suitcases of cash, assaults on candidates—Gorbachev was physically attacked by angry voters—and the obvious abandoning of any pretense of objectivity by most of the Russian media were among several incidents that raised the question of whether truly fair elections could be held, if they were even held at all. Chapter 5 is a brief exploration of the 1996 election, the results of which showed not only that the elections were fair, but that the voters understood the logic of the presidential system and acted to keep it intact and in moderate hands in yet another of the unexpected outcomes in the post-1993 era of Russian politics.

In 1999, Boris Yeltsin—battered by scandal, Russian economic woes, and a resurgent Chechen rebellion—appointed an unknown bureaucrat (and former KGB officer) from St. Petersburg as prime minister, an act that in retrospect seems either quite clever or quite desperate. Yeltsin then resigned, clearing the way for Vladimir Putin to win an abbreviated presidential campaign against a slew of disorganized candidates. Did Yeltsin's engineering of Putin's sudden rise to prominence do more harm than good to the presidency, and to Russian democracy in general? Chapter 6 considers the last days of the Yeltsin administration, and the beginning of the new Putin era. So far, it seems that the presidency is having as much of an effect on Putin as the man is on the office, a healthy sign in a nation where institutions are so young. While it is admittedly early yet to draw a final conclusion on Putin or his effect on the Second Republic, so far it appears that the constitutional arrangements put in place in 1993 not only continue to function, but helped to effect a calm, democratic transfer of executive power.

The final chapter of this book explores the prospects for the strengthening of Russian democratic institutions, and considers the possibilities of a Russian Third Republic, a constitutional reorganization that may well take place within the next decade, if not sooner.

Chapter One

Presidentialism and the Politics of Mistrust in Modern Russia

And of course the president declares that he was chosen by the people and he is subordinate to, and answerable to, no one but the people. Well, except maybe also to the Lord God . . . when He's not asleep. And that's that, the circle is closed!

—*Russian parliament member Vladimir Isakov, 1993*

I don't trust anyone, and I am not planning to vote. The only thing I know about elections is that we will be on alert the day of the polls.

—*A Russian police officer, 1995*

Presidentialism and Its Discontents

Are presidents dangerous? That is, are they actually a threat to the republics they are sworn to protect? A string of failed presidential regimes in various regions of the world since 1945—failed in the sense that they were or became authoritarian states—led to a "sharp polemic" among scholars "on the subject of whether presidential or parliamentary democracy is the 'better' form of representative government," in which most scholars have by now come out "quite squarely behind parliamentarism as the preferred alternative."[1] Indeed, to say that academics and constitutional engineers are pessimistic about the capacity of presidentialism to strengthen democracy in Russia or anywhere else is something of an understatement: recent critics, as one scholar has written, are "unrelievedly negative" in their assessment of the consequences of presidential arrangements and their "inherent vices."[2]

The belief that presidential institutions are inherently dangerous is not the recent product of a late-twentieth-century dispute among scholars, however, nor is it specifically related to the reconstruction of politics in the former Soviet region. The fear of presidents has a long history among both observers and practitioners of democratic government, with some of the harshest charges ever leveled against presidents heard not in troubled capitals such as Abuja or Jakarta or Moscow, but in Washington and Paris, the two great capitals of presidential democracy. "Array the stories of the [U.S.] presidents in succession," one American observer has written, "and the blunt disruptive force of this institution instantly comes to the fore."[3] Edward Corwin's classic study of the American system describes even so revered a figure as Abraham Lincoln during the Civil War as "a dictator even exceeding the Roman model," and duly notes Senator James Kent's 1834 evaluation of President Andrew Jackson as "a detestable, ignorant, reckless, vain and malignant tyrant," the product of a foolish experiment in "American elective monarchy."[4] In France, President François Mitterrand once referred to the establishment of his own post by Charles De Gaulle as "a permanent coup d'état," and warned shortly before his death that French political institutions "were dangerous before me and could become so after me."[5]

This ambivalence about presidents is to some degree an ambivalence about the practice of democracy itself. The creation of a presidency as an institution outside of the legislature is a kind of calculated risk, an attempt both to weaken government by dividing it but also to salvage some measure of effectiveness by placing some of the state's immense powers in the hands of one person. A single and independent executive is therefore always Janus-faced, representing everything that is both fearsome and virtuous about democracy. The president is the embodiment of the nation while yet remaining free during his term to act against the national will; as chief executive, he is a bulwark against a faceless legislative or majoritarian tyranny while yet remaining a potential source of personalized tyranny himself. Complicating this anxiety about the power of the presidency is the unwillingness of most societies to curtail it. Quite the contrary: presidents remain powerful figures because modern republics have embraced the ambivalent role of the executive as a way of protecting the state when legislatures become too incoherent or judges too imperious. As Harvey Mansfield writes:

> Machiavelli himself might remark that by adopting executive power, liberal constitutionalists have admitted that they could not do without him. Their

constitutions would not work without a branch whose function could be accurately described—though you might never hear it described that way—as getting around the constitution when necessary.[6]

Little wonder that the office itself inspires mixed feelings, especially in new democracies like Russia where the citizen may feel a certain unease about what amounts to a gamble that the president will be less dangerous than the turbulent legislature. This unease, however, is far more pronounced among scholars, who are far less inclined to advise such a throw of the dice.

The Case against Presidentialism

The simplest brief against presidentialism begins by noting the inescapable fact that most of the world's existing democracies are parliamentary in form, and that so many presidential regimes have collapsed into authoritarianism. Beyond this initial correlation, however, an enumeration of the world's regimes tells us little: categorizing states according to this parliamentary-presidential taxonomy not only produces some strikingly odd comparisons—the United States and Cyprus? Australia and Jamaica?—but it does not in itself say anything about causality.[7] Moreover, upon closer inspection it becomes clear that presidential "failures" tend to cluster in Latin America and Africa and parliamentary "successes" tend to cluster in Western Europe, which is hardly surprising since *all* types of democratic failures tend to cluster in the third world and corresponding successes tend to cluster in Europe and North America. (The aggregated data also submerge a fascinating fact in a larger sea of numbers: the most recent examples of democratic failures in Europe—Greece in 1974 and Turkey in the 1980s—took place in *parliamentary* regimes.) In any event, as Mansfield notes, formal quantitative analysis can only go so far, for "in modern politics, the executive stands for what is singular, individual and particular. Any science that does not recognize those qualities but insists on counting, aggregating, and formalizing will not comprehend executive power."[8]

In fairness to critics of presidentialism, they do not rely simply on a quantitative correlation, but make more assertive arguments in which they contend that the democratic failures in presidential systems are directly traceable to the very characteristics that define a "presidential" system.[9] Because these types of systems produce executive power through an electoral mandate separate from, and independent of, that of the legislature, they are assumed to be overly powerful, insufficiently accountable, and, ultimately, socially divisive. Presidencies are by design powerful offices that can be occupied only by one person at a time; therefore, as Maurice Duverger long ago warned, the personalization of presidential power is "an inevitable temptation" that can be resisted only by an incumbent with "much strength of character."[10] Presidential systems rely on independent mandates for each branch of representation; therefore, as Juan Linz warns, they rest on an unstable basis of "dual democratic legitimacy," in which "a conflict is always latent and sometimes likely to erupt dramatically."[11] Presidential elections are winner-take-all affairs; therefore, as Arend Lijphart warns, because only one candidate and one party can win, "everybody else loses," a bruising result that makes politics "exclusive instead of inclusive."[12] Presidential regimes are "rigid," governed by fixed terms and unable to adapt to sudden changes in the political landscape; therefore, as Alfred Stepan and Cindy Skach warn, presidents and their legislatures can end up "stuck" with one another, with the executives "condemned to serve out their terms" in the face of a hostile parliament.[13] When a crisis or confrontation emerges—and one almost inevitably will, according to antipresidentialist critics—presidential governments do not "fall" so much as they merely "hang," leaving only the heavy hand of authoritarian rule to break the impasse.

Thus the entire presidential system, in this view, from elections to governance, mitigates against compromise, against deliberation, against cooperation, against efficiency, against democratic behavior itself. The separate mandate, rather than binding the president to the will of the people, may serve to convince him of his special, even extraconstitutional rights. The fixed term of office, rather than protecting the executive from the vagaries of popular passions or legislative impulse, may become the unassailable platform from which the president launches his institutional assault against the other branches of government. And presidential elections, rather than clarifying or even magnifying the victory of the winner, may end up generating more political wreckage and popular division than they prevent.

The most troubling aspect of these charges (even leaving aside the issue of regional bias) is that this "mechanistic, even caricatured view of the presidency" results in a brief against presidentialism that is flatly tautological.[14] If presidents suppress democratic institutions, then they have given in to the inherent authoritarian temptations of the office. If they do not engage in undemocratic behavior, they nonetheless *want* to but have failed only because they are somehow effectively held in "check" for the moment—and the office is still an inherently dangerous and tempting one.[15] This is much like the reasoning that was once applied to the armed forces, when it was assumed that the military was, by the very fact of its existence, inherently dangerous to civil government. (Or, as S. E. Finer once wrote, "instead of asking why the military engage in politics, we ought surely ask why they ever do otherwise.")[16] A trial lawyer might recognize this as the "means plus opportunity equals motive" fallacy, the idea that the ability to commit a crime leads logically to the desire to commit a crime. Whatever the institutional capacity of the office, however, the fact of presidential power does not explain why some presidents undermine democratic processes and others do not, any more than the fact of military power explains why some military officers intervene in politics while others do not.

The seeming inevitability that unifies all this pessimism about presidentialism emanates from a set of shared presumptions—specifically, that political institutions are essentially autonomous, that they possess a logic of their own, and that they produce certain political outcomes once they are set in motion.[17] The problem for the student of executive power lies not with assumptions about institutional autonomy, but rather with the way in which those assumptions have been adapted to antipresidentialist arguments. Positing power as an overriding institutional goal, a resource that all presidents will seek to maximize, provides the basis for a leap from the reasonable idea that presidential institutions *matter* to the more tenuous conclusion that executive institutions in particular are somehow *determinant*.[18] The institutional critique of presidentialism confuses the reasonable question of whether and to what extent institutions act in their own interest (for clearly, on occasion, they do) with the more troubling issue of whether institutions predestine political outcomes.

The United States and France have been accepted as being somehow idiosyncratic, although why they have escaped the maladies that should theoretically afflict presidential systems is left largely unexplained. (France, in particular, with its turbulent history of constitutional instability and a near-coup in 1958, should be the truly puzzling case; Linz, for his part, claims only that "the jury is still out" on the success of the Fifth Republic.)[19] To these two great exceptions, Russia must now be added, casting doubt on the whole antipresidentialist critique. The Russian case in particular strongly contradicts many of the central expectations of the antipresidential consensus, and this should lead us to consider Valerie Bunce's question of "whether the oft-posited relationship between institutions and political practice should not be reversed in the East European context." In postcommunism, Bunce suggests, "political institutions seem to be more a consequence than a cause of political developments."[20] At the very least, it raises the question of whether it is reasonable to assume "that the risks and opportunities associated with a particular set of political institutions will be the same regardless of different social conditions . . . [or] that the set of desirable institutional capacities is the same in all countries."[21]

If presidentialism is the result of political and social conditions rather than their cause, what kind of societies would be most likely to choose presidential arrangements and even thrive under them? Stephen Holmes (responding to Linz) has suggested "the dangers of presidentialism surely vary according to the intensity and kind of social conflict a political system has to manage," and that "a popular president can be very useful for sustaining some public confidence in elected bodies, and combating the feeling, especially widespread among citizens who feel harmed and left behind by reform, that they are unrepresented by the political elites."[22] This is another way of raising the question of how parliamentarism could take hold in a divided society; Linz agrees that his parliamentary alternative needs to be supported by "strong, well-disciplined parties," but this begs the question of where such parties come from in the first place.[23] Holmes sensibly predicts that strong presidencies "will emerge where society is not well-organized enough to produce through elections a parliament that, in turn, is coherent enough to support a single-minded government capable of taking tough economic and other decisions."[24] In other words, presidentialism is likely to emerge as an attractive alternative when society is divided or incoherent.

But what does it mean for society to be "disorganized" or "incoherent," and how do these conditions affect the choice and performance of institutions? The answer lies in an accessible (if not perfectly measurable) aspect of social life that explains much about the behavior of presidents, the performance of parliaments, and the viability of democracy in general: the level and quality of social trust.

Russian Presidentialism and the Politics of Mistrust

The study of the Russian political system is a study in the politics of mistrust. To govern Russia is to govern a society that is characterized by the almost complete lack of social trust, in which no group is willing to risk the consequences of a decisive political victory by any other group. Russian citizens expect little from each other, almost nothing from government institutions, and the very worst from organized political parties and movements. Participation in politics is not so much an act of citizenship as it is of self-defense; loosely affiliated groups seek representation primarily to avoid coming by default under the baleful domination of some other group. Hostile intentions between social blocs are simply assumed to exist, a prophecy that is as often correct as it is self-fulfilling. One Russian political analyst, commenting sadly on a 1995 fistfight on the floor of the Duma (a free-for-all that included the spectacle of ultranationalist Vladimir Zhirinovsky sucker-punching a female deputy) captured the essence of this concern when he wondered "just how much savage malice and uncontrolled hatred is stored up in other figures, leading other sorts of parties, and laying claim to direct the entire Russian government, to the highest power in their reach." Acknowledging that governments can and should change, he lamented that while "power might be different [tomorrow]—democratic, communist, liberal, conservative . . . it shouldn't be frightening."[25]

This fear is the motivating force of Russian presidential democracy. Russian presidentialism has played a crucial part in the transition from Soviet communism to Russian republicanism precisely because *presidentialism is more likely than other arrangements to preserve processes of democratic consolidation in societies that are characterized by a lack of social trust*. The divided powers of presidential systems make changing the legal status quo difficult, and dramatically reduce the possibility that any one group or bloc can capture the government in toto, thus raising the confidence of the citizen that politics is an ongoing process rather than a one-time dash for power. Even a major victory in such a system does not translate into an immediate ability to reorganize political life, and losers can expect to survive to fight another day. By contrast, "a classic, highly competitive parliamentary system . . . takes the dangers of political uncertainty to their extreme: if the other side comes to power, they can pass whatever laws they want," even those that might "subvert or completely destroy everything the first party has put into place."[26] In a low-trust society, where other groups are seen as not merely competitors for power but malevolent opponents, this supremacy of unified parliamentary power may be too much risk for the citizen to bear. Put another way, the less trust citizens have in each other, the more anxiety they will have about the ease and speed with which the coercive instruments of the state can change hands. Presidentialism mitigates that anxiety by making that process slower and more difficult.

Where trust is lacking, the critique of presidentialism is turned on its head and the putative institutional failings of presidentialism emerge as positive virtues. Presidencies are indeed powerful offices; therefore, they serve not as irresistible temptations for one person, but as a restraint on the plethora of parties that seek as their primary goal the extinction of other political forces. Presidential systems rely on separated mandates; therefore, rather than creating a dilemma of "dual legitimacy," they ensure that the entire national government cannot be thrown into chaos or brought down in one fell swoop. Presidential elections pit a very few candidates against each other for very many votes; therefore, they force candidates to broaden their appeal and diversify their platforms in order to capture a national mandate. (They also ensure that the president's mandate to govern is not diluted by power-sharing—or policy-sabotaging—arrangements with implacable opponents.)[27] Presidential systems are governed by fixed terms; therefore, the end of the election cycle is not the beginning of a prison sentence for political leaders but rather a welcome respite from the continual conflict of electioneering. If trust is the prism through which these arrangements are viewed, then in every instance the institutional effect of presidentialist arrangements that might be considered as unnecessarily complicated or divisive can be reinterpreted as a form of protection for the citizen whose central fear is the possibility that the regime might fall into hostile hands.

The irony of modern Russian politics is that democracy has emerged from a millennium of autocracy only to find that its best hope of survival lay with a system of strong executive power. Placed in its social context, Russian presidentialism (and, for that matter, its short-lived Soviet predecessor) is less a paradox than an object lesson in the political management of mistrust. Rather than an incipient dictatorship, to the fearful citizen the presidency represents a fixed period of controlled conflict in which the monopolization of public authority by any one group is virtually impossible. The Russian presidential system is, from a legal standpoint, riddled with flaws, but it is the only arrangement that is acceptable to a population—and to a political elite—that is plagued by pervasive social anxiety.[28]

The Problem of Trust in Russian Society

"If decade after decade the truth cannot be told, each person's mind begins to wander irretrievably," Aleksandr Solzhenitsyn wrote in *Cancer Ward*. "One's fellow countrymen become harder to understand than Martians." The Russian Federation is not a presidential system because the government does not trust the people, or because the people do not trust the government: it is a presidential system because the Russian people do not trust each other.

The absence of social trust in Russian society is a problem that can be traced directly to the policies of the Soviet regime. A number of sociological studies have noted that communist methods of rule produced throughout

Eastern Europe "a social vacuum between the private world and public life, a lack of trust toward others and an unusual importance attached to the intimate circles of family and friends."[29] The hallmark of the Soviet system was the purposeful destruction of "social capital," the informal networks of engagement and reciprocity that breed the kind of trust, cooperative behavior, and voluntary relationships of civic associationalism that are the infrastructure of a democratic society.[30] The very basis for these relationships was eradicated by Soviet policies designed to destroy previous social groupings: the village, the church, or any of the other myriad entities—even the family—that were thought (correctly) to be obstacles to the regime's goal of transforming and reordering social life.[31] This totalitarian project ruptured these preexisting social, cultural, and familial bonds, "atomizing" society in order to reconstitute the polity as a collection of individuals in a narrow, vertical relationship with the Party-state. The point was not merely to repress, but actually to decimate autonomous social structures.[32]

These policies proved to have deeper roots and to be more lasting than the regime they were meant to protect. The most important lesson taught, and the most enduring lesson learned, from this period was that participation in political life was at best pointless and at worst lethal. John Lowenhardt has aptly termed this the Soviet Syndrome, "a deadly mixture of symptoms that paralyzes normal political intercourse."[33] In fact, this "syndrome" represented more than political paralysis; it represented a pervasive anxiety, a continuing alienation from social interaction. One Russian academic has described Soviet social life as "a unique organic alloy of existential fear and idiotic enthusiasm" whose legacy even now is a *homo sovieticus* for whom public life is seen as Hobbesian, and who can therefore "readily and without regret . . . inflict pain and suffering on another" without clear gain, even while understanding that he himself may be the next victim of such pain and suffering.[34]

This is, of course, only part of a complex, composite picture of a people who were forced to engage in cruel, dispassionate, or merely self-absorbed behavior as a daily matter of survival.[35] Still, it reflects an understandable practice of holding friends close, family closer, and all others at arm's length. (Friends, once identified, were quickly embraced, which may explain what so many foreigners found puzzling about Soviet-era social life: the coarseness with which Soviets treated each other in public, and the warmth with which they treated each other in private.) But even the retreat to the family or close friends was by no means a reliable escape in a system devoted to destroying any bonds of affinity outside the sanction of the state. As one Russian writer has put it, "even in the holiest of holies—your own family—

there would be no trusting relationships, no secret conversations," lest one's child, "guided by a 'higher truth,'" turned out to be an informer, while outside the family people "would keep themselves even further from sin: they would avoid dangerous conversations, and break off friendly relations because of even trivial suspicions."[36]

This is not to say that Soviet citizens did not interact with each other publicly and regularly. But familiarity is not the same thing as trust, and forced interaction is not the same thing as "spontaneous sociability."[37] Public activities in the Soviet period were removed from a voluntary context and left as desiccated vessels of state-approved activity. This produced what T. H. Rigby has called the "mono-organizational society," in which "the public arena, emptied of spontaneous political life" is nonetheless "noisy with contrived activity."[38] But underneath the state-sponsored rallies, the state-sponsored youth clubs, the state-sponsored vacation groups and all the other sham communitarian activities that characterized Soviet social life, the alienation and fear bred by the system meant that Soviets were individuals *bound into* groups, not individuals *associating in* groups—a crucial difference from the perspective of creating social capital and building social trust.

Even the abatement of terror after the 1950s did little to alleviate the Soviet citizen's fear of his fellows or to strengthen his willingness to participate in public life, and for good reason: as Jacek Kuron pointedly put it, the social monopoly of the state in the Soviet Union and Eastern Europe was such that if citizens gathered to "discuss freely a matter as simple as roof repairs on a block of apartments, it [became] a challenge to the central authority."[39] The regime went to absurd lengths to interfere with unofficial association among ordinary citizens: an internal 1980 KGB memorandum to the Central Committee, for example, promised to find the "instigators" of a meeting at Moscow State University in memory of slain Beatle John Lennon and to prevent "all participation" in "this unauthorized meeting."[40] In addition to Lennon's fans, the Soviets remained vigilant in suppressing or controlling such dangerous groups as yoga devotees, karate enthusiasts, and stamp collectors well into the 1980s.[41] By the late Brezhnev period the dominant leitmotif of Soviet public and cultural life was disengagement and self-absorption. Older Soviet citizens tended to see politics as dangerous (for obvious reasons), and younger ones, while they did not see civic engagement as quite so risky, certainly saw nothing of value in it.[42]

The marketplace might have been expected to provide some common ground for the kind of daily interaction important to the accumulation of social capital. But the Soviet marketplace was merely one of the points of contact in the daily tug-of-war between the citizen and the state for scarce resources, rather than an open arena of free exchange between individuals. The one functioning market that did exist in the USSR, the black market, actually corroded trust and depleted social capital, for it was fraught with legal and material risk, and was supplied by what was then the Soviet criminal class. The result, according to a recent study, is that the shadow economy "trained large parts of the population in illegal activities, creating human capital specific to illegality and a social morality supportive of activities outside formal legality." In other words, the black market—that is, the one that worked—taught the Soviet citizen that exchanges of goods were risky, furtive, and potentially lucrative for those willing to break the law, and it is unsurprising that pollsters found "widely felt exasperation [among] many citizens that successful businessmen must be criminals."[43]

Still, in the late 1980s, when the Gorbachev regime decided to allow the growth of the so-called *neformaly*, or informal groups, loose networks (including stamp collectors, sports fans, karate buffs, and yoga teachers) reaggregated with startling speed. There is no firm agreement on how many of these groups existed at any given time, but rough Soviet and Western estimates place the number at some 30,000 registered organizations in 1988, doubling within a year and then trebling to 90,000 by 1990.[44] By 1991, most of these groups had disintegrated or faded away in the kaleidoscopic reordering of society that represented not the reformation of a civil society, but a kind of endless round-robin of associations among individuals who, in the end, remained "free agents" in both a social and political sense, unattached and independent of social movements and organized political activity.[45]

While the sudden growth of the *neformaly* did not lead to the formation of more stable social or political groupings (every attempt to create even the loosest kind of "Russian popular front" from these groups in this period failed), it did illustrate two important facts of social life that would have an impact on the creation of the post-Soviet Russian Republic.[46] One the one hand, it showed the degree to which Russian society had been truly atomized by force, and raised the hope that the process might be reversible; given even the slightest opening, millions sought to join larger groupings (thus casting doubt on the idea that the isolation of Russian social life was either voluntary, or some sort of cultural norm). On the other hand, it showed that the temporary and shifting reaggregation of individuals would not simply produce something called "civil society" or any of the consequent political institutions associated with the concept. The rapid growth of the "informals" was like the snapping back of a tightly-stretched rubber band, a dramatic release of tension. The liberalization of the late-1980s restored something like a normal environment for association, but it could not ex nihilo create normal associations in and of itself.

All of this, in retrospect, could be seen as almost comical—the idea of an ongoing struggle between the KGB and yoga clubs or karate dojos seems especially ripe for satire—were it not for the scars of lasting social mistrust left among Russians. The absence of functioning social networks and the consequent lack of intermediate organizations in the Soviet period left the average citizen unprepared for, and with no extended network of support in, the tenuous and uncertain conditions associated with political and economic freedom. Post-Soviet Russia emerged as an "hourglass society," in which there are strong links only among relatives and friends, no intermediate institutions (of the kind normally associated with "civil society") and a heavy superstratum of disorganized and unrespected governmental bodies.[47]

At the top of this hourglass, governing elites went to war with each other, and "how it all ended" in 1993, former Duma speaker Ivan Rybkin writes dolefully, "is well known" (and discussed in more detail in chapter 3).[48] But the bottom of the hourglass is not all that stable either. It is unsurprising that family relationships were the quickest to recover from the damage of the Soviet era, but it would be a mistake to treat other patterns of mistrust as merely ephemeral. Tempting as it is to ascribe the sterility of the social environment to the immediate atmosphere of repression under the Soviets, the emptiness of social life in Russia is hardly a passing anomaly. Russian Academy of Science (RAN) sociologists found "weakening of feelings of closeness to practically all groups and communities in a period of only a single year [from 1992 to 1993]" including slight drops even among friends and family (although the level of identification with those groups, and with coworkers, remains high). The RAN study ascribed this ongoing "disorientation" in Russian society to the previous policies of "herding" groups and individuals into state activities, and they conclude that Russians continue to have difficulty coping with other citizens outside of the narrow "stereotypes and categories" imposed by the previous regime. Most disturbing was that the RAN survey found slight increases of identification with only three groups: "those who don't like to stand out," those who think that "what matters most is luck," and "those who aren't interested in politics."[49] These feelings of mistrust and alienation deepened as society devolved into a free-for-all that many Russians describe as "*bespredel*" or "without boundaries."

If all this seems to bear more than a passing resemblance to the "amoral familism" found in Edward Banfield's classic study of southern Italy, it is no accident. Banfield's "Montegrano" and Soviet Russia were both populated by citizens who sought to "maximize the material, short-run advantage of the nuclear family" based on the sensible assumption that "others will do likewise."[50] But there was a crucial difference between the Soviet and the "Montegrani:" for the Soviet, cooperation with others was not just fruitless in a material sense, but was, perhaps, even dangerous. Mistrust in Russian society and politics lingers not as the vestigial product of an evolutionary process among content and isolated villagers, but rather as the echo of a cruelly Darwinian strategy of survival under a regime that, acting as a kind of perverse Leviathan, artificially created a war of all against all while enforcing a façade of national unity.

Measuring Trust and Its Impact on Politics

From the *Federalist Papers* to postwar studies of democratic culture and into the current era of global democratization, observers of democratic politics repeatedly reach Judith Shklar's wise conclusion that liberal democracy requires more trust than any other political system known to man.[51] Nearly 40 years ago, Gabriel Almond and Sidney Verba wrote in *The Civic Culture* that the "role of social trust and cooperativeness cannot be overemphasized"; they then presciently warned that although constitutional engineers have "designed formal structures of politics that attempt to enforce trustworthy behavior . . . without these attitudes of trust, such institutions may mean little."[52] Despite this striking and direct acknowledgment of the role of trust in democratic societies, the question has rarely been linked explicitly to the problem of representative institutions. To be fair, in part this is because in the first two decades after *The Civic Culture* appeared, there were few new democracies worthy of the name, but it is also because trust is an elusive quality, difficult to find and measure. "The accumulation of social capital," Francis Fukuyama has written, "is a complicated and in many ways mysterious cultural process. While governments can enact policies that have the effect of depleting social capital, they have great difficulties understanding how to build it up again."[53]

To call this process "mysterious" may seem unhelpful at first, but it emphasizes the fact that "trust," like other concepts in the study of politics (such as "deterrence" or "legitimacy") is a quality that is known to exist but is always most conspicuous in its absence. The fact that it defies precise measurement does not mean it is not important, nor does it preclude making an approximate evaluation of its relative lack or abundance in a given society.

The closed nature of the Soviet regime made it almost impossible to get at the problem of trust in the pre-perestroika period, but in the years since Russian sociologists have made up for lost time. Not surprisingly, they are keenly interested in the problem of trust and have carried out consistent polling on the issue since they were first allowed to do so in the late 1980s. These polls, combined with the kind of snapshots taken by the increasingly free mass media after 1989, provide the social backdrop to the events surrounding the creation of the First and Second Republics. These Russian efforts have been supplemented by a growing body of data and literature provided by Western scholars who have begun to emulate their Russian colleagues in asking similar questions about trust and political attachments.[54] While we do not have the complete studies of the kind carried out intermittently over the past 40 years in the United States (or even more consistently in the same period in West Germany), the fact is that we never will; we do, however, have several studies that are comparable, for example, to the well-regarded late 1995 Kaiser study of trust in America.[55]

One measure of the level of trust in Russia, and an indication in itself of the degree to which the Soviet regime destroyed the basis for generating social capital, is the nearly complete lack during the Soviet period of the kind of dense, unofficial, horizontal networks—hobby clubs, social associations, fraternal organizations and the like—normally indicative of voluntary associationalism. The Soviet regime was explicitly designed to destroy any such relationships and to prevent the emergence of new ones. Indeed, it is something of a misnomer to speak of the Soviet destruction of "civil society"; rather, it was a more fundamental attack on society itself, on the individual and the daily interactions between human beings from which the larger groupings of civil society arise. It is now clear that the state had been more successful than anyone realized at destroying them and preventing their reemergence. Not only had the regime razed the fields of voluntary associationalism, it had plowed salt into the furrows as well.

The Russian case is therefore especially amenable to the study of trust and politics. By any yardstick, the Russian Republic embarked on a course of conscious institutional creation under conditions of the almost complete lack of accumulated social capital. Moreover, we can identify the sources of the damage done to Russian society that depleted social capital to this virtually nonexistent level, and follow the impact of that damage as it reverberates through the first years of a new democracy. Thus, the emphasis on trust provides an explanation of Russian presidential democracy that links modern Russia coherently to its Soviet past, sidestepping the unresolvable issue of "natural" or "historic" Russian dispositions (thereby avoiding as well specious arguments about inevitability). Of course, the conditions surrounding the collapse of the Soviet Union may well mean that the generalizations produced here may be applicable only to the former Soviet republics and their Eastern European holdings (that is, only to the postcommunist world), but that in itself is a constructive step away from what has so far been an unsatisfying attempt to import to the region questionable lessons learned under very different circumstances in Latin America and Africa.

The Implications of Trust

In societies suffering from a lack of generalized, transitive trust, people not only have overwhelming personal reasons to choose presidentialism over parliamentarism, but under such conditions it may well be that presidentialism is in fact the best hope for consolidating democracy. This conclusion rests on three hypotheses that should lead to a reconsideration of previous approaches to building democracy in the postcommunist world.

First, a widespread lack of trust creates a clear social preference for presidential arrangements, since mistrustful voters will reject the risky arrangements of parliamentarism; that is, presidentialism is the result, not the cause, of social fragmentation. (This in turn suggests the corollary that successful parliamentarism is likely the result of a stable society, and not its cause.) Second, because it lessens uncertainty and prevents rapid change, presidentialism paradoxically mitigates larger social conflicts even as it exacerbates the daily tensions of legislating and sharpens the tone of legislative-executive conduct. Put another way, presidential systems eliminate parliamentary supremacy as a possible spoil of electoral victory and thus force opposing groups into fixed terms of coexistence, thereby shifting conflict away from the great social confrontation of an election to the more prosaic and cumbersome arena of lawmaking. Finally, if it is parliamentarism that presents unacceptable risks and dampens citizens' willingness to participate in civic life, and presidentialism that allows for the emergence of more participation and the growth of more civic attitudes, then we would expect to find a growing normalization of politics in Russia, a stability that is creating rather than destroying the kind of social environment conducive to democratic consolidation.

These hypotheses carry several implications. From the point of view of building institutions and maintaining a young democracy, the most important implication here obviously lies not with the strength of presidents but with the weakness of parties, and consequently much of this book is about the problems of Russian parties and the Russian legislature rather than the presidency itself. Effective parliamentarism, by its very definition, requires cohesive parties, and this in turn requires strong patterns of associationalism and trust across society. Societies lacking the networks through which social capital is accumulated lack the basic structures of trust and association that make party politics (and therefore parliamentarism itself) possible; people simply do not associate enough to create true parties themselves, nor do they have enough trust in people they do not know to trust the parties offered to them by others.

This explains why the Russians would choose presidentialism, with all its risks, over the parliamentary alternative, despite the best advice of the constitutional engineers (who look primarily at legal structures rather than social conditions). Legislatures typically mirror the divisions in the societies they serve, and in a fragmented and distrustful society parliaments are likely to be viewed as chaotic and frightening. In the Russian case, even at moments of extreme parliamentary-presidential conflict, such as the October 1993 standoff, the Russian public remained by a large margin in favor of maintaining Yeltsin and the presidency (which they knew to be two different things) for reasons, as will be seen later, that are directly linked to issues of trust and social cohesion. Thus, presidentialism in Russia is not a "mistake," an experiment, or an authoritarian hoodwinking of the public, but rather a deliberate act, a compromise among elites who, like the public that elected them, see it as the system most likely to protect all of them from each other.

Here, Russian presidentialism emerges not as an optimal choice, but rather as a compromise, an arrangement that keeps all parties in play from one election cycle to another. Democractic theorists may lament the "rigidity" of fixed terms of office, but those terms, combined with the existence of the president and his veto, means that the government cannot collapse on a moment's notice and then be reconstituted as a temporary coalition designed to eradicate particular parties or movements from politics. Many Russian legislators themselves, when asked directly about which system they preferred, are quick to note their disagreements with the president or his ministers but then candidly admit that without the presidential system many of their own parties would be forced into extinction and the Russian federal system, along with Russian democracy itself, would probably disintegrate.[56]

These concerns are well-founded. Russia's antisystem parties, given the opportunity, would have done away with the presidency early on as a means of doing away with the Second Republic and their own enemies within it. In order to have even a reasonable chance to capture power in Russia, such antisystem parties need both to neutralize the independent executive and to secure at least a parliamentary plurality. But both the separate elections of the two branches and the first-past-the-post arrangements that elect half the legislature prevent the diffuse support for such groups from coalescing into a dominant, national-level force in either presidential or parliamentary elections. The communists, for example, may always be able to win seats in the Duma, but they can probably never—at least without dramatic changes in their program—win the presidency, or an outright parliamentary majority.[57]

Another intriguing aspect of the emphasis on trust is that it provides an alternative explanation for legislative-executive conflict. Russian elections have been relatively calm events, compared with the daily conduct of the legislature, which at times lapses into actual violence. If the emphasis on trust is correct, parliamentary confrontation and gridlock should be traceable to the mistrustful intrigues of elite groupings that reflect the bitter divisions in the electorate itself, rather than to presidential mischief. Indeed, it seems that because they cannot win everything at once at the ballot box, Russia's political antagonists take their war with each other (and with the executive) into the legislative arena. Research on Eastern European parliamentarism outside of Russia already points to this pattern, with parties (such as they are) acting the part of the would-be autocrat as they seek to extinguish each other or to further extremely particularistic interests rather than to govern by grappling with national problems. One study charged that newly emerging parties in Eastern Europe have in most cases tried to establish a "tyrannical majority," a simple parliamentary majority that is "without any effort, taken for granted, and without any consensus being built with the minority in the parliament."[58] The elites leading these parties "have been thinking in terms of a 'final victory' and have tried to push out their competitors from politics as 'enemies.'"[59] Likewise, other evidence suggests that presidents in fact do play a restraining role, much to the chagrin of legislators: "in several instances presidential intervention [in Eastern Europe] has provided a needed corrective . . . thereby impeding incipient authoritarian tendencies [of parliaments in the region]."[60]

Some of the most persuasive testimony to this paradoxical effect, in which elections are more civil than the legislatures they create, has come from Russia's most rabidly oppositionist parties. Knowing that they cannot cobble together enough of a national mandate to capture all the institutions of a separated presidential system, they participate in legislative elections in hopes of changing or destroying the system itself. During the 1995 Duma campaign, for example, Viktor Tiulkin, a leader of the extremist Russian Workers Party (RWP) said at a rally in St. Petersburg "we will go to the Duma. We will fight for complete victory over [St. Petersburg mayor Anatoly] Sobchak, Yeltsin and all the other bastards."[61]

Despite this kind of disturbing rhetoric, this is actually a positive development in a new democracy; it means that political rivals are taking their battles to the parliament rather than the streets, and playing by commonly accepted electoral rules rather than resorting to illegal or violent means.[62] People like Tiulkin may want to smash the system from within, but getting inside the system legally is difficult, and destroying it once there even more so. When opposition politicians play by common rules, they are legitimating the system, however grudgingly, even if in the short term they engage in legislative pyrotechnics and try to provoke heated legislative-executive conflict.

Russian presidentialism, then, is not an obstacle to be overcome on the road to democracy. Rather, it is an obstacle for Russia's most dangerous political forces to overcome in the attempt to head back along the road to authoritarianism. It is an ungainly and difficult system that slows legislation while forcing deliberation, an arrangement that prevents sudden, dangerous changes, occasionally at the expense of slowing the kind of energetic reforms needed to reconstruct the shattered Russian economy. It is, to paraphrase Winston Churchill, the worst of all systems, save for any of the alternatives; it is, so far, the best protection Russia has against the groups on the far left and far right who would take Russia back to its past.

Judas! Judas!

During the 1994 trial of General Valentin Varennikov (the only member of the August 1991 "Committee of Eight" who refused an official amnesty and demanded a trial), Mikhail Gorbachev was summoned to testify in person. His car was greeted daily at the courthouse with protesters taunting him, shouting "Judas! Judas! Soviet Union! Soviet Union!"[63] Despite this, Gorbachev felt it his duty to run for president in 1996; he had, after all, once been president of the Soviet Union itself. In the end, he polled less than one point of the popular vote, and was physically assaulted at least twice while stumping for Russia's top post.

This was a far cry from 1990, when he was given the Soviet presidency practically by acclamation. Gorbachev's elevation to the first separate executive post in Soviet history was an act of desperation, an attempt to stave off the disintegration of the state, and his failure to prevent the collapse of the Soviet Union is still seen by many as an act of either cowardice or perfidy. We turn now to this period, and to the circumstances surrounding the emergence of Yeltsin and Gorbachev as the warring presidents in the last days of the Soviet Union.

Chapter Two

The Creation of the Soviet Presidency:
Social Chaos and Executive Power, 1989–1991

Either we create presidential power or chaos triumphs. This is our choice.

—*an unnamed "government source" in Pravda, 1990*

Social Chaos and the Soviet Presidency

Although Boris Yeltsin was elected president of the Russian Soviet Federated Socialist Republic in June 1991, he took office under the shadow of another presidency barely older than his own. Little more than a year earlier, the Soviet Congress of People's deputies had elected Mikhail Gorbachev the first "president of the USSR," a new office that represented the first independent executive post in Soviet history. Although it may have seemed another step on the road to a changed, democratic Soviet Union—a newly formed legislature had chosen the nation's first independent president—it was in fact an act of desperation. Until 1990, the theory and practice of governing the Soviet Union had been predicated on the explicit rejection of the very idea of separated powers, or even of classical models of parliamentarism.[1] But that was before perestroika had gone awry, and Soviet society had descended into chaos and violence. Gorbachev's post was created as a reaction to this turmoil and growing fear, conditions that would be bequeathed to the Russian presidency (and its counterparts elsewhere in the Commonwealth of Independent States) when the Soviet government finally imploded. The Soviet president was the first, but not the last, in this region, and the lessons of Gorbachev's doomed experiment would not be lost on Yeltsin or the Russians as the

Union crumbled about them and power made its inexorable way from the president of the USSR to the presidents of the republics.

This acceleration of social disorder spurred the emergence of a rough system of separated powers in the final years of the Soviet period.[2] The fall of Gorbachev as Soviet president coincides with Yeltsin's return from political exile, just as the collapse of the Soviet presidential system was paralleled by the rise of the Russian and other republican presidencies. The Soviet presidential experiment is important not only in terms of the institutions it left behind in the Russian Federation, but also in terms of how it affected the Russians and the politicians who would emerge as their new leaders.

The Failure of Perestroika

Perestroika was a paradoxical approach to reforming the USSR, and a lesson in the law of unintended consequences. The paradox lay in the fact that perestroika, as it was originally conceived by Gorbachev and his advisors in late 1985 and early 1986, relied heavily for its success on the very thing it was supposed to create: Gorbachev's plans to restore order in the workplace and morale in the streets required precisely the kind of civic, disciplined, lawful, and cooperative society (a society, in other words, rich in accumulated social capital) that the Soviet Union lacked in the first place. The unintended consequences arose from the regime's basic misunderstanding of the forces it had unleashed. Soviet reformers found that their main problem was not that perestroika had failed to reinvigorate public life, but rather that it had succeeded too well, by opening the public arena to a torrent of movements over which the regime quickly lost even the semblance of control. The atomization of Soviet society in the previous six decades meant that beneath the surface of Soviet repression was not a nascent civil society waiting only for the right moment to emerge, but rather a loose hodgepodge of small underground groups reflecting conflicting and often extreme views and interests. Little wonder that the period between 1986 and 1990 is characterized by Russian researchers as one of "mass disorder in the USSR."[3] Far from uniting society or creating a new basis of legitimacy for the regime, the openness associated with perestroika and glasnost actually allowed for the vocal expression of complaints, and for the settling of scores old and new.

Gorbachev and his advisors did not understand the contradiction built into their own thinking about reform, or how that contradiction led to the Communist Party's eventual loss of control over Soviet society. In part, this was because they had no firm idea of what their own policies were intended to produce even in the near term. The late Soviet historian and Yeltsin aide Dmitrii Volkogonov charged that "to the very end, the phenomenon of perestroika was not fully understood by its creators (or its executors)" and that Gorbachev was never able to "answer, either in a philosophical or a practical sense, the question: what was the goal of perestroika?"[4] Because there was no clear sense of direction to perestroika, the reforms themselves managed to fail even as greater freedoms and openness spiraled wildly out of control.

Perhaps most maddening to the regime in this period was that there was clear agreement among the Soviet public in principle that change was needed and that the Union was worth saving, but no one was quite willing actually to do anything about it. Soviet polls showed broad support among ordinary workers for perestroika throughout the late 1980s, but on closer inspection Soviet sociologists also found a disturbing undercurrent of a "secret prejudice against change," which reflected many citizens' belief that their own lives would not improve no matter what policies were enacted, and that therefore the status quo was better than uncertainty.[5] One Soviet report noted that despite overwhelming support for the concept of perestroika, it was "quite another thing to take an actual part in changes and to strive for results"; as a British observer later noted, in an atmosphere of "considerable apathy and indifference . . . people expected perestroika to be introduced by decree, without their active participation."[6] The Gorbachev leadership failed to realize that perestroika could not simply reverse seven decades of learned passivity, and that consequently people simply didn't know how to conduct themselves outside of established routine, despite exhortations to do exactly that.[7]

This is not to say that perestroika did not energize Soviet public life. Small centers of autonomous social association had begun to coalesce during the Brezhnev era, and while these groups proliferated rapidly under Gorbachev, years of persecution had left them hesitant to play a public role.[8] These informal groups were the last great hope of perestroika, the raw material from which Gorbachev's team hoped to build a civil society that was somehow to be both independent from, and yet supportive of, the regime.[9] Even here, there was an agenda, as John Dunlop points out:

> By consciously promoting the growth and the spread of the *neformaly* . . . throughout the Russian Republic and the USSR, Gorbachev and [advisor Aleksandr] Yakovlev had sought to create a "civil society," a vibrant collection of "social movements" that would aggressively support the reformist

course of the Party leadership, while allowing itself to be used as a bludgeon against entrenched conservatives resisting change.[10]

But this represented a fundamental misperception on the part of the elite not only of the nature of Soviet society, but of the processes that had created that society. Martin Malia presciently noted in 1989 that "perestroika and glasnost have . . . only aggravated the systemic crisis they were intended to solve," because liberalizing policies (what Malia dubbed "soft communism") challenged the fundamental principle of Communist Party supremacy and therefore went "against the logic of the system they are trying to save."[11]

What Gorbachev and his advisors had failed to understand was that no man was going to join together what Stalin and his successors had rent asunder. Gorbachev's belief that liberalization would strengthen the regime was nothing less than a profound misjudging of the condition of his own society. Valerii Boldin, a Gorbachev aide later implicated in the 1991 coup, charges that by 1989 Gorbachev was simply in denial about the chaos unleashed by his own policies; he claims that Gorbachev's political paralysis, which included curtailing his domestic travels rather than face the situation in the country firsthand, crippled the ability of lower-level party organs to respond to the bewildering tempest of demands and charges engulfing them.[12] A former member of the Central Committee staff likewise accused Gorbachev of creating such turmoil in the Party ranks that "the reigning atmosphere in the CC CPSU apparatus was this: better to keep quiet than to do anything."[13] This is more than disgruntled apparatchiks settling scores. Even loyal Gorbachev advisors Aleksandr Yakovlev and Georgii Arbatov have since acknowledged that Gorbachev was so taken aback—and worse, so taken by surprise—by the chaotic and vicious nature of public debate that he soon turned away from his own policies.[14] The Soviets were fond of Shakespearean analogies, and while Gorbachev later made reference to himself as speaking like Hamlet, his press secretary Andrei Grachev perhaps more tellingly captured the sense of bewilderment Gorbachev felt when he described his boss in his memoirs as "President Lear."[15]

Unfortunately, Gorbachev's own memoirs regarding this period are both self-serving and distinctly less candid.[16] The decision to establish the presidency is treated with distressing brevity (this despite the lavish detail given elsewhere to the arcana of various Central Committee meetings), and the emphasis on foreign policy in the bulk of the book lends credence to Boldin's charge that Gorbachev turned his attention outward as the domestic situation spiraled out of control. Perhaps the fairest assessment of Gorbachev's leadership in this period is to consider him overly optimistic, as Peter Reddaway did when he wrote that Gorbachev, like Khrushchev before him, believed that in the wake of his more liberal policies "the people would be grateful, would work harder . . . would 'make socialism work' . . . Both leaders failed (or did not want) to see that within Soviet society lay the seeds of potential anti-Russian and anti-communist revolutions."[17]

In any case, the convulsions tormenting Soviet society soon made Gorbachev's commitment to perestroika as he had envisioned it in 1986 a moot point. In due time, the phrases associated with perestroika ("acceleration" and the like) quickly became little more than slogans to be lampooned by a populace more concerned with the day-to-day survival of the nuclear family than with Gorbachev's annoying efforts to get them to drink less, to work more, and, in essence, to cheer up.[18] When asked in 1990 what perestroika represented, 29 percent of Soviet citizens had no answer at all; the next largest groups were the 18 percent who believed that it was "an attempt by the ruling group to hold on to their power by a certain degree of democratization," and another 14 percent who thought it simply an "out of date and exhausted slogan."[19]

The Implosion of Soviet Society

By late 1989, the question for Soviet leaders was not whether the Soviet Union was falling apart, but rather whether it was too late to stop it. At home, perestroika had clearly failed; the economy, still geared toward funding an immense defense establishment and manned by a dispirited workforce, continued to slide toward a meltdown. Abroad, things were—incredibly—even worse. From a commanding global presence as recently as the late 1970s, the Soviet Union had tumbled back to the status of a muscle-bound and impoverished giant, a superpower that was now at the mercy of the international economy and practically incapable of projecting force beyond its immediate borders.

Predictions of ethnic and social turmoil once dismissed as impossible by both Westerners and the Soviet elite were now coming to pass with alarming speed. The Soviet version of the apocalypse was underway: instead of the orderly creation of parties, movements, clubs, and organizations that were supposed to be the result of the post-1986 liberalization, Soviet citizens regrouped into thousands of small clusters, many of them quite bizarre and openly hostile to the others. A Russian Academy of Sciences group later detailed the "political disintegration" of the USSR by noting that as of November 1, 1990, there were roughly 60,000 groups averaging between 500–600 members, whose "influence" extended over no less than 20 million adults. These included movements dedicated to

> national rebirth, national movements in support of perestroika, regional na-
> tional fronts, democratic movements of antisocialist type, antisocialist group-
> ings, organizations of antidemocratic character, workers' movement clubs, the
> movement to create independent professional trade unions, movements for co-
> operative owners and other entrepreneurs, small landowners, a movement to
> create a green party, a movement to create a social-democratic party, an anar-
> cho-syndicalist movement, groups and organizations of a christian-democratic
> character, constitutional-democratic groups and organizations, historical-en-
> lightenment *(istoriko-prosvetitel'skie)* movements, intellectuals in support of per-
> estroika, and voters' clubs and associations.[20]

Volkogonov recalls that "the very atmosphere, the climate, of perestroika was extraordinarily conflictual," and captures the fearful scale of public disorder by 1990 when he describes the USSR as "ablaze with thousands upon thousands of mass rallies."[21]

Most of the groups involved in these activities were antagonistic to each other, narrowly constituted, and bound only by a kind of generalized oppositionism. Some were motivated by intimate family concerns (such as the group representing mothers of boys slain in Afghanistan), others by naked self-interest (such as those organized around entrepreneurship), while yet more were bound by hatred, bigotry, or social resentments of various kinds (such as *Pamyat,* Moscow's skinhead gangs, or the groups of Afghan veterans who terrorized teens, gays, and others deemed weak or disrespectful). Finally, of course, were groups that engaged either in crime or politics—or, in the best Soviet tradition, both—based on ethnic and clan ties. By 1990, the economy was infested by a constellation of ethnic gangs and local mafias, leaving most major cities ripe for the shootouts that would thin criminal ranks over the next five years in a process that bore a striking resemblance to similar bloodlettings among the ethnic gangs of New York and Boston in America a generation earlier.

But even before the criminal gangs went to war with each other, social conflict among ordinary citizens broke into the open at all levels. Sacred cows were ripe for slaughter: the privileged position of the Soviet military was under assault, quite literally, as servicemen in uniform were attacked in the streets, even in the Russian republic itself. Old wounds between the city and the countryside were reopened as the economic crisis worsened, and rumors of price liberalization produced occasional bread panics. And in a throwback to the days of Lenin's New Economic Policy, conflicts appeared between blue-collar workers and the nouveau riche entrepreneurs and "cooperative" owners, some of whom were legitimate businessmen, others of whom operated with silent partners in the local political apparatus. Speculators, who bought items at foolishly depressed state prices and resold them at huge profits, were objects of special hatred. Even the official Soviet enterprises were acting irresponsibly. Conservative Politburo member Egor Ligachev tried to warn Gorbachev that liberalized pricing policies had allowed Soviet industries "literally to grab the consumer by the throat." After a late 1987 Politburo meeting, Ligachev surveyed the precarious financial condition of the country and said, "The sooner the year ends, the better, Mikhail Sergeevich."[22]

But subsequent years would be no better. Ineffectual and vacillating economic measures (ranging from micromanagement of certain enterprises to Gorbachev's on-again, off-again flirtation with liberal economists like Stanislav Shatalin) sharpened an already dire economic crisis, and even basic necessities began to vanish from Soviet shops. At the end of five years of reform, the members of an already mistrustful and anxious populace now found themselves pitted against each other in a very real competition for their daily bread. All of this prompted one Soviet legislator to wonder aloud at the end of 1989, "I keep thinking: have we bypassed the point at which a chaos-free transition to a democratic society [is] possible?"[23]

The picture of Soviet society that emerged at the end of perestroika is an unattractive one, overwhelmingly characterized by alienation, anger, and envy. Every portrait of the Soviet electorate from this period finds a combination of self-pity and harsh judgmentalism. By 1990 only 26 percent of Soviet respondents agreed that "other people should be trusted," with 36 percent adding that caution was warranted, and 38 percent remaining uncommitted, well below the 85 percent to 95 percent positive responses to similar questions in Western Europe, and below even levels found in southeastern Europe or more recently in the United States.[24] Writing in mid-1990, Soviet political analyst Aleksei Kiva laid blame for these attitudes directly with the "lumpenizing" of Soviet society under Stalin and Brezhnev:

We have been fooling ourselves for too long . . . we have to overcome in ourselves many of the things we used to see as socialist values but which were in fact the values of a poor, backward society. To take pride today in our poverty, disorganization, dullness, homogeneity, and squalid uniformity is a kind of atavism, a sign of our moral and spiritual degradation. [25]

Without a change in these beliefs, Kiva warned, "we will end up ruining and bankrupting ourselves, starving and strangling one another while continuing to be proud of our specialness and uniqueness."

Kiva was not being alarmist; a 1990 poll found that more than a quarter of Soviets believed "that what their fellow citizens lack most is diligence and thrift," even as two-thirds of the same respondents openly admitted that they were unwilling to work harder for more money, and more than half would have traded away higher salaries in exchange for easier work. [26] More telling was that loneliness was a dominant theme among respondents, with a plurality blaming their loneliness on "the very organization of our society and the lack of consideration people have for one another." However, this cry for consideration did not extend to the less fortunate, those on the margins of society, or the simply unconventional: nearly a third of the respondents favored the death penalty for prostitutes, homosexuals, and drug addicts, and slightly less than a fifth favored it for AIDS victims, the mentally ill and "rockers" (a catch-all phrase that included bikers and heavy-metal music fans). Startlingly, in a country beset by poverty and alcohol abuse, between 3 to 9 percent of the respondents nonetheless supported executing street beggars and alcoholics. When asked about the source of their own sense of self-respect, 43 percent of this group (the most common response) listed "being a parent," an unsurprising finding in a society centered on the nuclear family. More depressing was the least reported response: only 9 percent chose the answer "being a human being."

But did these responses reflect the conduct of daily life? After all, Americans in particular have been known to express distress or anxiety by giving pessimistic answers to questions about trust and personal well-being, while they continue to associate with each other in what are essentially trusting relationships. [27] The Soviets, however, in public life practiced on each other what they preached to the pollsters. Public organizations were, and are still, characterized by very short half-lives, quickly torn apart by distrust, bickering, and even violence among their leaders. Even as the loosely affiliated *neformaly* coalesced into parties in 1990 and 1991, for example, they remained parties in name only, unable to expand their membership or to gain even an informal following. Despite the increased activity and visibility of a host of new parties, rates of membership or even of expressions of general support hovered at virtually insignificant levels, a clear indication that the alienation from public life was more than rhetoric. Violence, both among strangers and within families grew after 1988, and perhaps worse, was publicized sensationally. This, coupled with an epidemic of fraud and theft, pointed not only to a worsening economy at the time, but to the fact that the complaint of loneliness and cruelty found in Soviet polls reflected daily reality for many Soviet citizens, and the fears of many more.[28]

This alienation was compounded by a sense among ordinary Soviet citizens that there was no remedy for their troubles even in the public institutions that were supposed to guard and protect them. Corruption, only thinly veiled under Brezhnev, brazenly came into the open as the heavy hand of state coercion was lifted. Local officials routinely joined hands with criminal elements; police officers, then as now, were understood to be bribable on all but the most severe matters—this, as rates of violent crime skyrocketed. Judicial remedies were out of the question, since the courts had long ago come to be seen as dilatory and partial arms of the Soviet bureaucracy, rather than functioning arenas for conflict resolution.[29] Commenting on the flood of letters to newspapers from ordinary citizens seeking action about relatively mundane issues, one Soviet jurist remarked flatly in 1990: "Let us be frank: Our courts have lost their prestige. This is why the people appeal to the newspapers for any reason at all."[30] (This was reflected empirically in a 1994 study in which the courts and the police ranked well behind the only public institution that continuously gets high marks for fairness from the average Russian citizen: the postal service.[31])

In short, by 1990, the worst of all worlds had arrived. Soviet society, given a modicum of freedom, had not responded with a collectivist effort to rebuild the state and its shattered economy. Instead, it had gone to war against itself.

The issue of nationalism and its relationship to the collapse of the Soviet Union is a topic too immense to tackle here, but from the perspective of institutions and trust it is important at least to mention the character of national and ethnic movements that arose under perestroika. At the level of national elites, it is difficult to disagree with Aleksandr Yakovlev's angry assertion: "I am convinced: nationalist movements did not crowd out communism in the union republics; rather, it was intra-elite rivalry, which dictated the use of nationalism as a means of the struggle for power . . . I call it parasitical separatism."[32] At the grassroots, the legacy of Soviet rule was distrust and disorder. All groups had suffered under the Soviet regime, but as soon as central Soviet control receded, republican and regional leaders resorted to ancient (and in some cases more recent) hatreds as a means of state-building or of merely guaranteeing personal positions. Perestroika provided both an opening and a certain amount of camouflage, and later Russian researchers were quite right that by 1989 "national fronts supporting perestroika in some republics had fallen into the hands of extremist-nationalist elements who essentially subordinated the struggle for perestroika to the struggle to exit the USSR."[33]

The Soviet elite, which now had broadened to include prominent legislators of the newly-formed Congress of People's Deputies, knew a civil war in the offing when they saw one, and they sought to head it off with a figure of national authority, trust, and conciliation: a national president. To some Soviets at the time, this seemed like undermining democracy in order to save it, and even Gorbachev himself had earlier ruled out the notion of a separate state presidency. (Yakovlev, ever the more far-seeing of Gorbachev's advisors, had already proposed that Gorbachev create an independent Union presidency as early as December 1985.)[34] When he changed his mind, he found he had unexpected allies supporting the creation of this kind of superpresidency. One was the legislature itself. The other was the Soviet public.

The Fall of the Party and the Call for Soviet Presidentialism

If the idea of a "Union of Soviet Socialist Republics" was losing meaning in 1989 and 1990, it was in no small measure due to actions Gorbachev had taken against the Communist Party in the name of reforming it, and in the end Gorbachev's decision to allow the creation of an all-Union presidency had as much to do with his own political security as with any larger issue of social trust. Until 1990, the fortress from which every Soviet leader had ruled was the Communist Party of the Soviet Union, and the only means by which leadership changed was through internal revolt or death. In 1989, Gorbachev was in fine health; it was now the Party that was clearly doddering and sclerotic. If Gorbachev were to continue to rule the Soviet Union, it would have to be from a perch more secure than the general secretary's seat in the Politburo. Although public support for this decision reflected broader social conditions, the origins of the Soviet office itself were thus also directly tied to the political fortunes of Gorbachev and his inner circle.

The creation of the presidency owed much to the fact that perestroika, again, had produced the opposite effect that Gorbachev had intended. Opening the political process to younger reformers was supposed to galvanize the Party faithful, who in response would duly turn and vote the last of the Brezhnevite dinosaurs off to the tar pits. But democratizing the political process undermined the entire rationale beneath a single-party state. Gorbachev himself recognized this potential land mine and tried to defuse it in his 1987 opus on perestroika:

> The question is put forward—by some with secret hope, by others with apprehension—whether perestroika perhaps represents a move away from socialism, or for the most part an utter dilution of its basis? Certain people in the West would have us accept this version: socialism, they say, is undergoing a deep crisis, and is leading society into a dead end . . . [But] our entire program, as a whole and in its specific parts, is based on the principle: more socialism, more democracy.[35]

A clever defense, but in the end unconvincing: either the Party would rule as a vanguard organization whose elite represented the moral compass of socialism, or it would submit itself to the judgement of the masses as a parliamentary party in the effort to create "more democracy." Gorbachev chose the latter hoping the people would confirm the former, and in doing so unintentionally set in motion events that would end the Party's political monopoly.

But even if Gorbachev had been able to explain away these ideological contradictions, he still had to contend with the entrenched Party conservatives who opposed the whole scheme. "More democracy" requires "more democrats," and to this end Gorbachev set about purging the aging ranks of the CPSU. This shakeout, representing the most severe turnover in Soviet political and administrative elites in over 50 years, was intended to invigorate a moribund organization while at the same time flushing out enemies of reform.[36] Instead, Gorbachev's doomed frontal assault divided and weakened the Party: while the upper echelons fell into bitter struggle, the rank and file opted out in droves, choosing instead informal organizations or even apolitical lives. Growth in Party membership, already slowing in the 1980s, declined for the first time in 1989 when some eight hundred thousand members quit, to be followed by over three million more in the next two years.[37] Recruiting the young was even harder. The Komsomol, already in trouble, lost fully 25 percent of its membership in 1990 alone; perhaps worse was that one-third of Komsomol members surveyed in 1989 said they would leave the country if they could, a slightly higher level of response than found overall among those aged 18–30.[38] The younger men and women who were supposed to be the future of the Party, in other words, would be the first in line to leave the USSR if they could.

Despite the steep decline in membership, the CPSU still declared itself the sole source of political authority in the Soviet Union, and the steady dissipation of that authority was even more disturbing than what could have been viewed at the time as merely transitional problems of recruitment. The erosion of Party authority was part of the overall decentralization (both physical and organizational) of the powers of the central Union government, another Gorbachev policy that had been intended to strengthen the regional reformers at the expense of the Moscow *apparat* but instead had spun out of control. It was bad enough that more and more decisions were being made outside Moscow; worse yet was that they were often made by people outside the Party. In describing the *neformaly* in 1990, Nicolai Petro found that they represented the "localization of politics," as they began "to pay more attention to local concerns and thus shift the balance of political activism from the national to the local level."[39] This set the stage for what later was called the "war of laws," in which legislation or decrees issued from the Kremlin were then promptly ignored, superceded, or publicly rejected at the republic level—with the Russian republican government right down the street from Red Square one of the most visible such offenders. Increasingly incoherent policies were stymied first by the indecision of the apparatchiks, later by the conflicting directives of the Congress of People's Deputies, and finally by the growing power of local and regional elites.

Centrifugal forces were tearing the Union apart, and the Communist Party, in the name of reform and "more democracy," had not stepped in to halt them. (Indeed, insofar as the Party could bring itself to act, it chose to oppose rather to encourage many of the nascent political organizations that might have served to stabilize the situation.) For the first time since the chaotic days of the Russian Revolution, the question arose of whether the Party could still control large sectors of daily political and economic activity within Soviet borders. In early 1990, a sociologist at the Central Committee Social Science Academy warned:

> For the first time during the years of perestroika the proportion of those who have lost faith in the party's progressive role has exceeded the proportion of those believing in it . . . Replying to the question as to who today can defend the interests of the ordinary man, only 12 percent of working people mentioned party bodies. Preference was given to the mass media . . . Even Communists—some 40 percent—advocate a multiparty political system.[40]

This collapse of support for the Party accelerated throughout 1989 and 1990, and Gorbachev's eventual turn back to the conservatives would only exacerbate the sense that the country and its leaders were frozen in irretrievable confusion from which only anarchy and violence could result. Indeed, when Gorbachev rejected the so-called 500 Days economic liberalization package in late 1990, Aleksandr Yakovlev would describe it as turning away from "the last chance for a civilized transition," and that "what followed was nothing less than a war."[41]

The Party was caught in a bind of Gorbachev's making. It either had to reclaim, by force if necessary, its monopoly over power and political speech, or enter into direct competition with groups that were essentially acting like opposition parties. In early 1990, Communist Party leaders made a choice that, depending on one's point of view, represented either a courageous acceptance of an inevitable challenge, or a craven inability to find the backbone to use the measures that would save themselves and the Union. In February 1990, the Central Committee voted to repeal Article Six of the Soviet Constitution, thereby ending the constitutional status of the Communist Party as the "leading force" and "nucleus" of Soviet society. This was a quantum leap beyond merely legitimizing the existence of informal groups, and it set the stage not only for the end of the Soviet Communist Party but for the emergence of the Soviet presidency as well. Multipartism and separated powers, of a sort, had arrived in the Soviet Union.

None of this was supposed to happen, of course. The year before the repudiation of Article Six, a popularly elected legislature, the Congress of People's Deputies, had been created, but as David Satter has pointed out, the whole point was to use the institution "to weaken the party's ability to remove [Gorbachev] and to resist reforms, not to surrender moral authority in the country to the democrats."[42] But once again, Gorbachev had set processes in motion that, to his continual surprise, he could not control. Now that a multiparty state had arrived, it could not logically be governed from the Politburo, even if the CPSU had retained any of its former capacity to induce awe or fear or even compliance, which by 1990 it clearly had not. Gorbachev advisor Georgii Shakhnazarov later recalled that the balance of power was shifting from the Party to the state so rapidly that "you could actually see it moving" from the Central Committee offices to the Supreme Soviet. "Power," Shakhnazarov later mused, "is a delicate thing. You can move it in attaché cases."[43]

The Communist Party of the Soviet Union had crumbled and the state was adrift. Here, Gorbachev's personal interest and the growing crisis in society coincided, and in retrospect it is evident why both the leadership and the public might see creating a new presidency as accomplishing several things at once. First, it would provide Gorbachev himself with a firmer claim to national leadership, a mandate that could extend beyond the dwindling numbers of the CPSU. Second, it would answer popular demands for a figure of accountability, for an end to the curtain that protected the members of the collective leadership from responsibility for their disastrous political decisions. Finally, it would provide leverage over a legislature that was increasingly taking itself far more seriously than Gorbachev had ever envisioned, including routinely rejecting the government's nominations of senior ministers. The president, as Yakovlev made clear after Gorbachev's accession, would be a figure of national power and unity, against whom opposition would be not only illegal, but in some sense even immoral:

> Whereas before a nonparty person, say, or a dissident within the party itself could say: That decision by the raikom or the Politburo is to me illegal and therefore not binding on upon me; now the decision of the president, according to the Constitution, is binding upon all . . . Like it or not, this person, if he does not fulfill the decision [of the President], is to a certain extent setting himself against society and against its rights and laws.[44]

"I think," Yakovlev added, "we all have to understand this peculiarity and get used to it."

Debating the Union Presidency

After the desperate winter of 1989–1990, debate began in the Soviet legislature over whether to create a Union presidency. In early March, a joint Soviet-British poll found more than 60 percent of Soviets supporting the establishment of such an office, with over 80 percent favoring direct elections. When asked who should hold the presidency, 72 percent chose Gorbachev, with Yeltsin a distant second at 11 percent.[45] A poll taken solely within the RSFSR a month later showed exactly the same level of support for creating a Russian presidency.[46] Perhaps more important was that the Soviet respondents were not simply choosing to support the most popular or visible leader; a September 1990 poll showed that Yeltsin was a vastly more popular figure Union-wide than Gorbachev.[47] Soviet citizens "fully approved" of Yeltsin's actions by more than a two to one margin over Gorbachev (61 percent to 28 percent), yet supported the creation of a Soviet presidency for Gorbachev anyway, a strong indication that support for the presidency was not merely reflexive support for a strong or popular leader.

Additional anecdotal evidence suggests that popular support for the creation of a presidency was not merely renewed desire for a benevolent dictator. As one factory worker put it, "We don't need the 'great,' 'most wise,' 'father of the peoples' that we once had, unfortunately, and from whom our fathers and grandfathers had to endure so much. We need a chief of state elected at our will."[48] A foundry worker interviewed at the same time agreed, adding this cogent remark in support of a presidency: "Let me add that the current highest authority—the Politburo—is a collegial authority, a general one. You cannot identify a specific party as being to blame for one mistake or another. Afghanistan is an example." Iurii Golik, the head of the Supreme Soviet committee on law and order, also pointedly mentioned Afghanistan in explaining his support for a more accountable executive: "[Not long ago] the Politburo was the de facto president . . . To this day, we cannot figure out who, for example, gave the order to introduce troops into Afghanistan."[49] As the *Izvestiia* commentator Stanislav Kondrashov (a longtime observer of the U.S. political system) put it, a Soviet presidency would not be "a panacea," but rather "an attempt to exit the historical dead-end in which the country was left by the dictatorship of party power. The presidency is not an end in itself."[50]

Despite this relatively strong popular support, there were impediments yet to be overcome. Chief among them was that no one in the Soviet leadership had had any experience with, or had really thought through, a system of separated powers. The Soviet Union in early 1990 was neither a parliamentary nor a presidential republic, but rather a party-state without a party. The administrative and executive institutions of the state had only ever been vehicles for the execution of the Party's will, and left on their own they were becoming increasingly directionless. Sergei Alekseev, chairman of the Supreme Soviet's committee on constitutional compliance and a close Gorbachev ally, pleaded the case for a presidency by asking the Congress of People's Deputies to see what was evident to others abroad:

> I have just come back from France and talked to some of [that] country's most important lawyers and they are saying: Where are you going? Can you really not see that your state system has started to collapse? Isn't our experience of 1958 an object lesson for you?[51]

As it happens, Soviet constitutional engineers were quite candid in their admission that they had taken foreign practices into account, as well as in their doubts about the ability of a single institution to mitigate the growing chaos.[52] Alekseev need not have worried: with few options left to stem growing social conflict, most Soviet legislators were eager to embrace the idea of a presidency.

Discussion on a motion to create a Soviet presidency began almost immediately after the Central Committee repudiated Article Six of the constitution in February 1990, and most prominent Soviet politicians expressed varying levels of support for the idea. The strongest expressions of support focused on the president as figure of national unity, and paid little heed to the details of the post's design. Ironically, some of the most reform-minded legislators expressed deep concerns about creating a what they feared would be a dictatorial presidency for Gorbachev, while hardline elements now rallied behind the idea. Neither side seemed to understand what an elected president could or could not do.[53] Prime Minister Nikolai Ryzhkov was among many who worried that the potential for the new office was being oversold on all sides. "An impression is forming," he said shortly before the vote on the presidential statute, "since things are bad today, give us presidential power, a president will bring order. One power [the party] has become weaker but another has not yet become stronger."[54] In other words, Ryzhkov recognized that the collapse of the Party and the disintegration of Soviet society together meant that there was no way to rule the country either by coercion or by consensus. His own remedy was to return "power to the Soviets," but that slogan had little meaning in the crumbling USSR of 1990.

Particularly strong statements came from leaders in some of the regions that were sliding into open civil conflict. Armenian Communist Party leader Suren Arutyunyan spoke in favor of the motion by emphasizing that "it is the whole of the country that is in crisis, not just those regions which have recently exploded. In this situation we need a supreme power . . . it is not the army that has arrived late, it is power. A president could be a social stabilizer."[55] (Interestingly, Arutyunyan showed a particularly insightful understanding of the capacity of a president when he added that the negative power of the *veto*, rather than the positive force of decrees, might be the most important component of the office.) To this, a Kalmyk deputy added that "it is only the president who can keep peace during moments of conflict," although exactly how this was to happen was left unspoken.[56] One Georgian legal scholar was more succinct: "May the presidency save us."[57]

Some supporters of the motion, including the normally more circumspect Aleksandr Yakovlev, tended to overestimate Gorbachev's capacity to act as a figure of national reconciliation. Yakovlev argued that "a country on the scale of ours . . . requires a certain unity around some idea, some central symbol which personifies this power, this unity," although why he thought Gorbachev could do this while yet remaining CPSU general secretary is unclear.[58] Soviet Minister of Justice V. F. Yakovlev made even more startling claims for the new office:

> In terms of the president's position within the structure of the bodies of power, we should say that it is a very special position . . . In essence, he personifies the unity of the nation and the state, represents society, the people as a whole, guarantees the sovereignty, independence, security and territorial integrity of the given state, and the interaction of these same bodies of legislative authority, executive authority, and even the judicial authority.[59]

The somewhat confused minister then went on to discuss presidentialism in Greece, Italy and Germany, all of which are in fact parliamentary systems. Supreme Soviet leader Anatolii Luk'ianov, who would later betray Gorbachev in the 1991 coup, emphasized that a president must "create conditions for the development of mutual understanding and social dialogue between various social and political movements" and "maintain civil peace and interethnic harmony in the country." He then promised, with no apparent sense of irony, that the new presidency would be both "consistently democratic" and "Soviet" in nature, whatever that was supposed to mean.[60]

Not surprisingly, opponents of the measure seemed less concerned about Gorbachev himself than about the *next* Soviet president, should there be one. "Who among us," asked one delegate, "is confident that after four or nine years, there will not appear someone in the Soviet Union who wants to create socialism of the barracks type?"[61] The mayor of Moscow, Gavriil Popov, along with other liberals, complained (understandably) that the post was being created specifically for Gorbachev and insisted that there "must be a legal and regulatory framework that will protect us against authoritarian temptations, come what may." But Popov's answer was "a strong parliament to counterbalance a strong president," even though he admitted that the nation was "torn by too many splits" even to elect a president, much less a parliament.[62] Academician Dmitrii Likhachev agreed, bluntly warning during the debate that direct elections of any kind for such a post would produce civil war.[63] Even a loyal supporter such as Arbatov sent Gorbachev a letter drawing his "attention to the danger that, at his request, the presidency had been given truly dictatorial powers: 'Many, including myself, consider Gorbachev morally incapable of becoming a despot and a dictator . . . But what if something happens to him or he is deposed?'"[64]

Despite these many reservations, the eventual votes to create the post of president of the USSR and then to fill it were in the end lopsided affairs. On March 13, 1990, the Congress of People's Deputies voted 1,817 to 133 (with 61 abstentions) to create a Soviet presidency; two days later Gorbachev was elected to the post (his name was the only one on the ballot) by a vote of 1,329 to 495, which represented only 59 percent of all deputies, but 71 percent of those actually voting.[65] After the vote, one deputy acknowledged that creating the presidency did not represent the "comple[tion]of the formation of a new political system," but rather only putting in place "the prerequisites for the defense of growing structures from catastrophic collapse, and of society from chaos."[66] Now all that remained was for Mikhail Gorbachev to fulfill his constitutional duty and save the country.

The Soviet Legislature: "Democracy Is Not Anarchy"

While no one was certain that the presidency could save the Union, or even stave off civil war, the failure of Soviet parliamentarism foreclosed any other options short of a return to authoritarian one-party rule. Both the Congress of People's Deputies and the Supreme Soviet had failed not only as forums for the civil expression of political views, but even in their nominal role as legislative bodies. The intense social conflict that characterized Soviet public life was replicated in its legislative chambers, with the added complication of ongoing and personalized political combat among the legislators themselves. Public reaction was setting in against both the Party and the legislature, and it is instructive to note that the Soviet-British study found "a rare unanimity" among the population on the means of electing the president: over 80 percent favored direct election, while 8 percent entrusted election to the Congress. The Supreme Soviet, heavily dominated by communists, was favored to choose the president by only 3 percent.[67]

The combined result of this legislative flight from responsibility and the public reaction against it was to make the Congress and Supreme Soviet independent and besieged actors in the increasingly confrontational public arena, rather than vehicles for the expression of public opinions or interests. As *Izvestiia*'s Kondrashov put it, the Supreme Soviet at this point had devolved to "everyone for himself, everyone only with his own voice."[68] The presidential idea gained currency in no small measure due to the belief that these legislative institutions had become so unstable and confused that they were now irretrievable. By the time the Soviet presidency came into being, Soviet society, the Communist Party, and the national legislature were not only were at war with each other, but were riven by internal conflicts as well.

Under these anarchic conditions, Soviet legislators embraced intensified personal and institutional conflict, as their instinct for self-preservation grew in proportion to the severity of the crises they were supposed to help resolve. This irresponsible behavior set in motion and sustained a circle of cynicism, with public disgust fueling yet more legislative evasiveness and bickering, which in turn deepened the public conviction that the legislative enterprise was worthless. As one analysis later described it:

> Legislators themselves remained ambivalent, and sometimes openly hostile, to the rise of powerful representative institutions in a period of mounting social and economic crisis. And the population, initially entranced by the novelty of open parliamentary debate, seemed to tire of the tortuous and arcane procedures of the legislature.[69]

In fairness to Soviet lawmakers, it is questionable whether any of them could have actually divined the will of their own fragmented and divided electorate by 1990. Except for nebulous and generalized demands to "fix" things—to create a healthy economy, curb crime, and quell the growing chain reaction of separatist movements—it was unclear what exactly legislators were supposed to do or how they were supposed to do it. Under this kind of pressure, and in such uncertain conditions, Soviet legislators sought primarily to assign blame and to protect themselves against the day when the now inevitable reckoning before the public would come.

This created an odd, almost accidental consensus between the public and the legislature on the issue of the presidency. The Soviet citizens wanted a figure who would be accountable, and the legislature wanted to find one to give them. As a *Pravda* commentator noted, "both the democrats and the conservatives understand that at some point the promissory notes of trust will have to be paid. Isn't this why they and others have begun to bustle about the search for a culprit and have been readily prepared to heap their own shortcomings and mistakes on the president's shoulders?"[70] The lawmakers sought a presidency that would mediate between increasingly irreconcilable political and social forces, while thus allowing the parliament to pursue its own confrontational agenda and internal intrigues. In a complaint that would soon be heard again from

President Yeltsin's spokesmen, Gorbachev aide Nikolai Petrakov rightly castigated legislators who "have shown incompetence here and an unwillingness to assume responsibility," in effect beating their breasts about impending dictatorship while gladly offering to delegate their own powers to the president.[71] Unlike Yeltsin, however (who apparently learned from Gorbachev's sad experiences), the Gorbachev team nonetheless continued to walk into the trap of accountability that had been set.

Indeed, Gorbachev's advisors actually played on public fears of the reckless legislature as part of the effort to establish the presidency. Alekseev asserted that "experience shows that a purely parliamentary structure . . . is most of all adapted to dictatorship."[72] Yakovlev promised that "the presidential system could . . . raise an additional barrier to bids to seize power in an unconstitutional way," and that "society should be reliably protected against lawlessness, against the attempts of irresponsible or corrupt forces, representing no one, to usurp power, and should be cured of legal nihilism."[73] (Again, how the president was supposed to do all this without resorting to forceful measures was never clear.) This reassuring message resonated not only with the public but with fearful lawmakers like Supreme Soviet member E. Mal'kova, who said shortly before the vote on the presidency:

> I honestly admit: I am frightened, not just as a deputy, but as a mother as well, by the aggressive spirit pervading the air and the intolerance shown for others' ways of thinking being displayed by other social groupings . . . What I have stated here also defines my attitude toward the question of presidential rule. Democracy is not anarchy [*bezvlastie*]—it is strong authority formed by democratic means . . . The country needs a chief of state, a president who confidently coordinates the activity of the highest organs of authority and direction, and who bears responsibility for his actions and decisions before the people.[74]

Evident in Mal'kova's comments, of course, is that legislators themselves were no longer able to "bear responsibility" before the electorate, since they were too busy trying to protect themselves while seeking to extinguish each other politically. The new Union president, it seemed, would not only have to rescue the country from ruin, but legislators and intolerant "social groupings" from each other as well.

From the point of view of the development of post-Soviet presidentialism in Russia, this ongoing failure of the parliament is even more interesting than the eventual failure of the presidency. Popular support for presidential rule in the last days of the USSR and in the first years of the republic regimes was not so much a product of some irrational attachment to a Soviet or Russian *fuhrerprinzip* as it was a perfectly understandable reaction to the incompetence and venality of the Congresses and the Supreme Soviet. These bodies would provide the first legislators (such that they were) in the new Russian Republic, and in retrospect the conflict between president and parliament in the First Republic now seems almost foreordained when considered in the context of legislative-executive relations in the last days of the Soviet Union.

Soviet Presidential Rule and "Full Social Disintegration"

With Gorbachev's election, the Soviet Union for the first time in its history had foresworn the principle of collective leadership. In retrospect, it is curious that in 1990 even Gorbachev's most faithful followers could have clung to the idea that a president, or any individual leader, could reverse the frightful decay of Soviet society, a process Russian sociologists called nothing less than "full social disintegration."[75] It remains an open question whether even Gorbachev believed he could hold the Union together, but the die was now cast and the responsibility was now his, come what may.

It was clear from the very beginning of Gorbachev's ten-month reign as president of the USSR that he had neither the substantive power nor the moral authority to meet the challenge that had been placed before him. There was little he could do in the area of moral authority (and the shameful use of force in Georgia, Lithuania, and elsewhere rendered that a moot point anyway), but where raw power was concerned, there was the option of asking for more. However, before charges of power-seeking or crypto-authoritarianism are laid against Gorbachev, it is important to point out that he was attempting only to fill the vacuum left by a magnificently incompetent legislature. The Congress of People's Deputies, with 2,250 members, was the largest elected body in the world and would have been incapable of coherent action due to its sheer size, even if its sessions had not been characterized by shouting contests, shoving matches, huffy speeches, and ad hominem attacks. The Supreme Soviet, the standing body of over four hundred members elected from the CPD, was less fractious but also less ambitious and more conservative, and Gorbachev in the end gave up first on the Communist Party as a vehicle of reform, and then on the Soviet legislature.[76]

Although he would eventually seek ever wider powers as the Union collapsed, Gorbachev entered office with what seems to have been a good-faith desire to act as a responsible chief executive. Remarkably, however, Gorbachev began his tenure by accepting his new post with a rambling speech that said much about perestroika—as if that were not, by 1990, a dead letter—but little about the presidency itself. "I consented to stand for president," he told the Congress, "because I am certain of the future of our fatherland, and also because perestroika has become the meaning of my whole life."[77] He promised that he understood he was "especially accountable" and that he did not "wish to evade carrying out his duty to the people."

These were appropriate words, but ones he would come to regret. Barely eight months later he would return to the same hall and plead:

> Listen, we need to act together. The president cannot by himself—just as you cannot solve many questions without his participation and without using his powers. So let us act, come on, let us act. [commotion in hall] Fine, fine, OK. I take it upon myself and am prepared to start acting without waiting for a proposal from the provinces. Is that it? [sounds of approval from hall] Fine![78]

Although this was just so much bluster—the central government by now simply had no ability to stop the fact that many decisions were being made at local and regional levels—it was in its way an admirable attempt by Gorbachev to claim powers that under the law were rightfully his and to shame the parliament into acting on the powers that were rightfully theirs.

The Soviet president had been brought to this point by a deadly political synergy that grew throughout the spring and summer of 1990: as the legislature descended into incoherence, Gorbachev tried to forestall one disaster after another by ruling with decrees that ranged from the grandiose to the ridiculous. In May, he acted against the Baltic declarations of independence, declaring them (as was his duty under existing Soviet law) unconstitutional. But by August, he was reduced to issuing decrees on such crucial matters as "the Responsibility of Functionaries for the Unsatisfactory State of Supplying the Population with Tobacco Products."[79] Robert Sharlet notes that as 1990 wore on,

> Gorbachev's decrees became increasingly arbitrary and controversial [and ignored], resembling more the proclamations of a monarch than the considered executive decisions of a constitutional leader mindful of the division of power within a constitutional system. By early 1991, the Soviet Union had begun to take on the appearance of a system of unchecked presidential power.[80]

Sharlet was not quite accurate in one respect: this Soviet *decretismo* was hardly unchecked power, since Gorbachev seemed unable to get anyone to listen to him. At each step, Gorbachev sought more legal power, and at each step (occasional histrionics aside) the lawmakers were more than happy to provide it, because they realized what Gorbachev apparently did not: delegated power now only meant accountability, but not capability.

The Union, as the Soviet citizen knew it, had practically ceased to exist, buried under an avalanche of declarations of sovereignty from the republics and even the smaller subject territories within the republics. To his credit, Gorbachev seemed to understand even in these desperate circumstances that in the final analysis, chief executives have to *execute;* that is, they have to ensure that laws passed are laws observed. But by the time he asked for the ability to rule under special powers (under which he would have greatly enhanced authority to override both the legislature and regional governments until 1992), too much political momentum had shifted to local and republican leaders who had little reason to attend to decrees from a president who lacked both the instruments and the will to enforce them. And by the time Gorbachev sought a democratic renewal of the Union, it was too late. The Soviet era had passed, in the minds of all but its most dogmatic defenders.

Yeltsin and The Rise of the Presidents

True anarchy is rare. When people lose faith in political arrangements or particular leaders, they almost immediately turn to others. In creating a national presidency, Gorbachev had unwittingly provided the final nail in his own political coffin, by providing for the creation of the alternative institutions and leaders to whom the Soviet public could turn in the last days of the Union. Perhaps nothing could stop growing public attachment to powerful or charismatic local leaders, but even Gorbachev (if only in hindsight) realized that he had helped equip those leaders with the outline of an institution that could both claim popular legitimacy and quell fears of uncontrolled legislative and administrative chaos.

Recalling the debate on the Union presidency, Gorbachev notes that Kazakh leader Nursultan Nazarbaev was among the first to support it, and to press for the replication of the office at the republic level. "Nazarbaev," Gorbachev writes, "an experienced and clever politician, was playing a no-lose game."

> To be frank, the creation of the office of President in the union republics was not part of my plans, as this cut in half the gains we had expected from improving the authority of the central power. While agreeing to give Moscow additional prerogatives, the republics immediately demanded their share. But nothing could be done—any attempt to argue the wisdom of this approach could only arouse passions and produce a situation in which the changes to the Constitution would fail to achieve the required majority.[81]

Gorbachev attributed this to an attempt by the republics "to seize the opportunity to secure themselves" rather than to "yield the independence they had gained." (Gorbachev's lack of reflection on the rather startling admission that the republics were essentially in revolt perhaps says more about his fundamental misapprehension of the events that surrounded him than any of the charges leveled by his critics.) Gorbachev was right: the republican leaders knew exactly what they were doing, and Nazarbaev was among the canniest of those leaders. But even Nazarbaev or Yeltsin could not have pressed for presidential powers had there not been popular support for the idea, and to the extent that Soviet citizens understood the concept of presidentialism, they had Gorbachev to thank.

Fears of presidential dictatorship paled in comparison to fears of chaos, and the idea of republican presidentialism was a fairly easy sell, except in the rather unique case of the Baltic states. In a way, Gorbachev's own eloquence and incompetence had been a perfect combination: he had suggested what a president *could* be, and then shown that even a powerful president could be hamstrung by determined national and local authorities. Even the eventual attempt to depose him redounded to the benefit of arguments in favor of presidentialism. What was the 1991 coup, if not the replacement of the single, legally-elected executive with a committee of charismatically-challenged functionaries that looked nothing so much like a Politburo-in-waiting?

The crowning irony of the whole affair, of course, is that after the putsch had been put down, Gorbachev owed much of his survival to the man he had banished from the Kremlin four years earlier: Boris N. Yeltsin, the first democratically elected president of the Russian Federation.

Yeltsin's Return

The circumstances surrounding the creation of the first Russian presidency are the subject of the next chapter. But some aspects of politics in the RSFSR during this late Soviet period are worth noting here.

Perhaps most important is that the political resurrection of Boris Yeltsin and the strengthening of independent Russian republican institutions were both driven by the kind of social disorder and public disaffection with national politics described in this chapter. In other times, dismissal from the Politburo and relegation to make-work jobs (in Yeltsin's case, the state construction committee) would have spelled the end of a Soviet political career. But when Yeltsin was forced out in disgrace after a speech that was scathingly critical of Gorbachev and the pace of perestroika, his time in the political wilderness was brief, and his return was in fact made possible by the liberalizing policies that Gorbachev had set in motion. By 1989, as John Morrison has put it concisely, there was a growing realization in Moscow that "the Party clearly had no intention of rehabilitating [Yeltsin], but the people might."[82]

The road back from oblivion began in 1988, when Yeltsin successfully sought election to the XIX Party Conference. The Conference itself was an anomaly; it was the first time since 1941 that a Soviet leader had called one, and it was unclear under CPSU rules what could be undertaken at such a meeting. Gorbachev was probably gambling that he could finally take measures to outflank his conservative opponents, and using a *Conference* would spare him the embarrassment of having to call another Party *Congress* so soon, since the next one was not supposed to take place until 1991. Yeltsin also went to the Conference with the intention of outflanking some old foes, and in this he would turn out to be more successful than the general secretary.

At first it was not clear that Yeltsin would be allowed to speak, but Gorbachev relented when Yeltsin walked directly to the rostrum and confronted him personally. When he finally took the podium, he gave a speech that went far beyond the one for which he had initially been sacked. Gorbachev now recalls only that Yeltsin had "supported perestroika in all its specific aspects"; indeed, Yeltsin was so supportive of perestroika that he called for direct elections to all offices, brought his feud with the conservative Ligachev into the open, and called for his own political rehabilitation "while I am still alive" and not 50 years hence.[83] (Ligachev foolishly took the podium to contradict Yeltsin, and his insulting and condescending accusation that "Boris, you are wrong" would later haunt him when protestors would show up at rallies with placards reading "Egor, *you* are wrong!") Gorbachev was for the moment a bystander.

The whole business was televised, a medium in which Yeltsin's personal dynamism was evident. Also evident was the attempt by Party hacks, including Ligachev, to circle the wagons and force Yeltsin back into political exile. (One speaker even accused Yeltsin of driving a local party worker to suicide.)[84] But by the time the Conference ended, growing public support meant that Yeltsin's popular rehabilitation was well underway, and there was nothing that Gorbachev or the conservatives could do about it. Looking back, Gorbachev complains that by late 1988, Yeltsin "had already begun to see himself as the opposition leader."[85] In fact, Yeltsin had indeed come to see himself as exactly that, and for good reason. From man-in-the-street encounters to the hundreds of requests he was receiving to run in the upcoming elections to the Congress of People's Deputies, it was clear that large numbers of Russians were beginning to see Yeltsin as their own spokesman against the government. In a relative sense, they trusted him.

The story of Yeltsin's wily campaign to outfox the apparat and ensure that voters had a chance to send him to the first Congress of People's Deputies is a fascinating one, but will not be recounted in detail here. The important point is that the attempts to keep him from office were transparent to the voters themselves, and this only helped to shift yet more popular sentiment and trust behind Yeltsin personally. In the March 1989 Soviet legislative elections, Yeltsin took nearly 90 percent of the ballots in Moscow's at-large district, defeating his opponent by 5.1 million to 400,000 votes. The Party apparat tried to take small revenge on him by preventing his subsequent election to the Supreme Soviet, and this itself produced an uproar. Lawyer Andrei Kazannik, who had been given the seat, in turn gave it to Yeltsin. Yeltsin went through the formality of protesting, but Kazannik (later to serve as Russian procurator) said, on national television: "Tell me, Boris Nikolaevich, what will I tell my constituents? For they know the six million people of Moscow are behind you. If I remain, they will kill me."[86] Gorbachev ruled that Yeltsin could indeed have the seat—in a very real sense, he had no choice—and Yeltsin then went to meet a triumphal throng of supporters outside the Kremlin. In the space of a year, Boris Yeltsin had gone from "unperson" to superstar.

From his seat in the legislature, Yeltsin would join with others in an ongoing opposition to Gorbachev, a zero-sum struggle that over time seemed to strengthen one at the expense of the other. Within three months of his comeback at the First Congress, Yeltsin would be elected the chairman of the RSFSR Supreme Soviet, making him (in the Soviet tradition) the chief executive in the Russian Republic. His counterpart at the Union level, USSR Supreme Soviet chairman Luk'ianov, called to congratulate him. When asked if Gorbachev had called, Yeltsin cattily replied, "No. Perhaps the president congratulates only fellow-presidents."[87] A year later, Yeltsin would win direct election by a landslide to a new post in the Russian Republic, and provide Gorbachev with opportunity to congratulate a "fellow president."

The popular movement that elevated Yeltsin to the presidency, and the way in which the problem of social trust actually aided Yeltsin in challenging first the Soviet center and then the rebels in his own Russian parliament, are the subject of the next chapter.

Chapter Three

The Rise and Fall of the First Russian Republic, 1991–1993

It's mob rule. And the mob is sitting in the parliamentary chamber.

—A Russian People's Deputy, 1993

In a few hours, I would declare the dissolution of parliament. With that, I was absolutely certain that Soviet power in Russia would be finished forever.

—Boris Yeltsin, 1993

Trust and the Russian First Republic

The ill-fated First Republic is an object lesson in the impact of social trust on politics, and understanding the failure of the First Republic is essential to understanding the relative success of the Second. The legislative and executive institutions that assumed control of the Russian remnant of the USSR on Christmas Day 1991 predated the Soviet collapse, and bore the distinct marks of the mistrustful and divided society that created them. The Russian legislature was, from its inception, incapable of creating stable alliances or parties, keen to delegate hard decisions to the executive branch, and prone to the kind of bickering that had characterized its late and unlamented Soviet national counterpart. The Russian presidency, meanwhile, had been created for goals mostly of denial rather than achievement: it was meant to insulate Russia from the Union, to defend Boris Yeltsin personally from the Communist Party, and to prevent the disintegration of the Russian Republic during the Soviet collapse.

The emergence of a Russian presidency and Boris Yeltsin's ascendancy to it were the result of a steep decline in public confidence in politicians and political movements at both the national and republican levels. This, as we saw in the previous chapter, owed much to the public disorder and political paralysis that followed in the wake of Gorbachev's loss of control over his own reforms. When asked in mid-1990 who was to blame for the Soviet national condition of overall "crisis," over 80 percent of Soviet citizens accused either current or previous Soviet leaders, or the Party itself. "Extremists and nationalists," the groups that were being blamed by the Party leadership for much of the turmoil in Soviet streets, were pointed to by only 6 percent.[1] Throughout 1990, roughly a third of all respondents said that they "do not trust" the national leadership, a figure that would jump to 56 percent by early 1991.[2] Not that the average Russian had much faith in the various alternatives, even within the RSFSR: in 1990, fewer than 1 percent of the adult population of the Russian Republic were members of any Russian political parties, and even the most prominent movements registered only single-digit support.[3] The bright spot in this otherwise gloomy picture was Boris Yeltsin's personal popularity, which grew as faith in the Soviet government fell. Yeltsin had become the personification of the opposition to the old order, and power "flowed in his direction as a wave of political strikes and mass civil actions revealed a central government bereft of substantial popular support and increasingly unable to govern."[4]

The Russian presidency was thus a popular institution that nonetheless sat at the center of a matrix of conflict, serving different purposes at different moments during the brief life of the First Republic. Before the Soviet collapse, it could be seen a symbol of resistance to the central Soviet authorities. During the 1991 coup, it was a rallying point against the Committee of Eight. As the Union came apart, it was the center of a successor state-in-waiting. And after independence, it was the repository of the slim hopes of Russian reformers against an increasingly retrograde parliament. Because it was, in essence, all things to all people, the idea of a Russian presidency was broadly accepted. Virtually all major factions in political life, including Yeltsin's bitter opponents, the Russian Communists, endorsed a proposal to create a separate Russian presidency as early as the spring of 1990.[5]

The parliament in the First Republic, for its part, both reflected the fragmentation of Russian society and contributed to it. Initially, the legislators of the Russian Congress of People's Deputies and the Supreme Soviet were allies in Yeltsin's fight against the Soviet center. Yeltsin, after all, had himself been a legislator and chaired the Supreme Soviet, even choosing (and defending) as his deputy the man he would later haul to prison, Ruslan Khasbulatov. But once the great task of securing independence was over, the legislators of the First Republic realized that they had neither the inclination nor the popular legitimacy to undertake the grinding work of reform. Worse, they lacked the courage to face the voters and seek reconfirmation. Nurturing an agenda that was increasingly divorced from the wishes of their nominal electorate, the activity of the parliament increasingly centered on the twin aims of maintaining the deputies in office while obstructing reform in the name of the recently dispossessed and disheartened.

Out of the chaos of the first year of independence, two large political groupings would emerge in Moscow, replicating in the national government a basic division in Russian society. One would seek a return to the economically less unsure Soviet past (even if it meant the return of repression), while the other wanted to press ahead with reforms (while looking away from the class of plutocrats being made in the meantime). In a society plagued by mistrust and apprehension, this was far more serious than a mere division of opinion. As a group of Russian social scientists wrote in 1994:

> Two alternative variants of socio-economic reform of the nation were laid out. Each of these variants had their own political supporters who proceeded to an irreconcilable clash which split society into two camps on this very basis. For a host of reasons . . . the struggle of political forces, which represented alternative approaches to socio-economic reformation, took the form of a confrontation of two branches of power: legislative and executive.[6]

Thus, the eventual confrontation between president and parliament was not the result of some sort of institutional flaw in the structure of a presidential regime; indeed, it was the existence of the parliament (as it was constituted in 1990) that made this clash worse than it otherwise might have been. The events of October 1993 were not grounded solely in the attempt of one branch of government to gain ascendance over another; rather, they represented social conflict by proxy.

This pattern of legislative-executive relations was the mirror image of what critics of presidential regimes might have expected. The very worst legislators of the First Republic, representative of little but their own narrow interests and revanchist politics, quickly fell into infighting aimed at securing their own positions vis-à-vis both each other and the president. (Reformist legislators, outflanked and outmaneuvered by the parliamentary plurality, stood little chance of successfully moderating the behavior of their colleagues.) The executive branch, by contrast, actually emerged as the institution more capable of social reconciliation; the visibility and fan-fare attached to the post forced Yeltsin and his circle to at least attempt, however incompetently, to govern and, more important, to reconfirm Yeltsin's mandate in society at large after the Soviet collapse. When the final clash between the president and the legislature came in October 1993, what was remarkable in looking back was not that Russian democracy sur-vived an attack on the parliament, but that it had survived over two years of the parliament itself.

The Russian Parliamentary Executive, 1990–1991

The idea of creating an independent Russian president arose almost si-multaneously with the first real steps toward republican autonomy. Until 1990, the Russian Soviet Federated Socialist Republic was ruled by a re-publican government that was "Russian" in name only. The Soviet author-ities had never allowed the RSFSR the same latitude it had granted other republics of the Union, for reasons ranging from a fear that a willful Rus-sia could undermine the USSR itself (as was finally the case) to the prac-tical matter that the Kremlin was the de facto imperial center of the Soviet system and that a "Russian government" was redundant. In 1990, the RSFSR Prime Minister, a Soviet loyalist named Aleksandr Vlasov, candidly admitted on national television that "all of the [republic's] political and economic structures were related to the [Soviet] center," a situation that left the Russian Republic with a "minimum of rights" and himself in a po-sition of relative "impotence."[7] Yeltsin, characteristically, was more blunt. In his memoirs, he describes inspecting his new office after being elected Chairman of the Russian Supreme Soviet and realizing that "the [Russian officials] who earlier sat in this gorgeous office, in this immaculate, brand-new White House, were people on whom practically nothing depended."[8]

The practical demands of the republic's increasing autonomy made it clear that the vestigial nature of the Russian executive had to change. The inexorable erosion of the center, combined with a growing unease among Russian political leaders and ordinary citizens alike about the fractious new Russian legislature, meant that strengthening the executive would rise to the top of the republican agenda.

The RSFSR government, like all republic-level governments, was in 1990 a scale model of the institutions of the Soviet Union itself, a parlia-mentary republic based on the unity rather than separation of powers. The Supreme Soviet was the formal locus of popular sovereignty. In turn, the

Supreme Soviet would elect a small leadership body, the Presidium, whose chairman was the nominal head of the republic. After 1990, power theoretically rested with a Congress of People's Deputies, a huge body that was meant to meet only infrequently while delegating the actual day-to-day task of governing to a Supreme Soviet that was now to be a smaller standing body elected by, and from the ranks of, the Congress. The Soviet Congress was elected in 1989, and Yeltsin was sent with overwhelming support from a Moscow district. The republics followed suit by electing their own congresses in early 1990.

Yeltsin ran for the RSFSR Congress in 1990 (this time from his hometown of Sverdlovsk) fully intending to try to make the jump from mere legislator to the Russian Supreme Soviet, and then to the chairmanship of the parliament itself.[9] This was not going to be an easy body to capture: not only was a large bloc of seats reserved for the Communist Party, but the open voting for the Congress was itself a trial that took several rounds and three months to complete.[10] The result was a divided and politically incoherent Russian Congress, which in turn created a divided Russian Supreme Soviet. Mikhail Gorbachev's supporters, an amalgam of reform communists and hard-liners in favor of holding onto the carcasses both of perestroika and the Union, were almost equally matched against the Yeltsin adherents, an unwieldy grouping of radical reformers and separatist "Russia-firsters."

Through his previous campaigns, Yeltsin had depicted himself as a pugnacious populist, and his base of support among Russian workers was considerable. Now, however, to capture the chairmanship of the Supreme Soviet he needed to join forces with the increasingly powerful and broad-based Russian separatist movement (in which he had had little interest until this point).[11] As John Dunlop noted:

> Yeltsin's meteoric political ascent during the years 1987 through 1989 owed nothing to Russian nationalist sentiment. Social justice and not nationalism was the issue that served to rally industrial workers and, later, intellectuals around his political leadership. By late 1989, however, it had become presumably clear to Yeltsin that his path to supreme power lay not through the structures of the increasingly weakened and unstable USSR but through those of the Russian Republic.[12]

Despite the dismay this compromise caused among his supporters in the Democratic Russia party and other liberal circles, it helped Yeltsin to defeat both former premier Vlasov (who had been Gorbachev's choice) and hard-line RSFSR Communist Party chief Ivan Polozkov for the chairmanship of the Russian Supreme Soviet by a tiny margin of only four votes after three contentious rounds of voting.

However gilded or symbolically exalted the office, the chairmanship of the Supreme Soviet was still a tenuous platform for Yeltsin and his supporters. Although it gave Yeltsin some powers to set the agenda and make internal legislative appointments, the chairmanship had no formal executive authority—that rested with a government confirmed separately by the legislature—and even as a symbolic post it was hostage to a continuing mandate from a deeply divided legislature. This lack of independent standing left Yeltsin dangerously weak should the hard-line forces at the Union level attempt a crackdown, either by using Soviet loyalists to provoke a no-confidence vote in the Russian legislature or even by disbanding the republican legislatures entirely. The speakership, however powerful Yeltsin's personal authority might make it in the short term, would have to give way to a more secure and legitimate institution: a directly elected president.

Here, Yeltsin seems to have learned from Gorbachev's unfortunate experiences with the Soviet Congress and the USSR presidency. Gorbachev, Yeltsin wrote later, created the Union presidency because he "clearly saw the dead end he might find himself in . . . he was insuring himself against the Communists—it would be a lot harder to threaten the President of the USSR."[13] Rather than risk becoming entangled in disputes with a parliament that held power over him, as Gorbachev had, Yeltsin intended to gamble on signs that the Russian people were likely to be impatient with incompetent legislators and would support the establishment of a directly-elected presidency. This was hardly a secret plan: after Yeltsin won the RSFSR chairmanship, a *Komsomol'skaia Pravda* commentator mused, "where does Yeltsin's strength lie?"

> I don't think it's in that four-tenths of a percent margin which enabled him to take charge of the RSFSR Supreme Soviet. He himself feels it lies in the support of the people and, by all accounts, he intends to demonstrate this graphically: Yeltsin has proposed holding direct, secret and general elections for President of the RSFSR. And then not the deputies but the people themselves will nominate the politicians to whom they entrust the republic's fate.[14]

And in fact, from the moment the first Russian Congress convened, public sentiment in favor both of a presidency and an independent Russia would grow. The dilemma for the legislators was that the increasing demand for a president would be driven in no small measure by the public's increasing, and eventually severe, lack of trust in the parliament itself.

In a sense, the formal limitations on Yeltsin's power as chairman worked to his advantage, since, as only one legislator, he could hardly be blamed for the failures of an entire parliament. In the first year of self-rule, faith in the Russian legislature fell steadily, while approval of Yeltsin and the executive leadership grew. In August 1990, after less than three months in office, Yeltsin received an astonishing 85 percent approval rating, despite having done almost nothing of substance. By contrast, when asked in the same poll whether "the elected RSFSR Supreme Soviet is prepared to an adequate degree to conduct professional parliamentary activity" only 20 percent said yes. (A plurality of 42 percent were unsure.)[15]

Although there was little to show in the way of a legislative record, Yeltsin could at least credibly claim to have pacified an angry population from his bully pulpit as chairman. As one Soviet political scientist wrote in the summer of 1990, "Yeltsin's popularity guarantees, at least for a time, stability in the country's main region and staves off the threat of an explosion, and specifically the explosion of strikes."[16] The Supreme Soviet could not claim even that much. "Not one" party or movement, according to Russian legal scholar T.V. Novikova, "managed to create a working [*rabotosposobnuiu*] parliamentary faction," and even a leading organization like Democratic Russia was so large and "amorphous" that it quickly "collapse[d] both as a parliamentary faction and as a movement itself." It is revealing that Novikova does not blame this on provocateurs or poor institutional design; rather, she emphasizes that "the membership of the Supreme Soviet reflected, as a whole, the structure of socio-political and economic orientations of Russian society."[17]

These divisions in Russian society were reflected not just in the incompetence of the legislature, but also in the suspicion felt by the voters toward political parties in particular. The distrust of parties and organized political movements ran deep in society, and this helped spur the emergence of an independent presidency. Yeltsin knew that associating with a particular party would be self-destructive; in accepting the chairmanship of the parliament in May 1990, Yeltsin cannily claimed that the leader of the RSFSR "should not be a member of any party," and at its first meeting the RSFSR Congress approved just such a prohibition on all leading state officers.[18] Yeltsin was reading his audience correctly: 60 percent of Russians agreed with the prohibition (only 20 percent objected, with the rest unsure.)[19] Yeltsin's deputy, Ruslan Khasbulatov, was no less cognizant of this distrust of parties, and he recognized the danger to the parliament from its own partisan behavior. "Seriously working deputies do not have time for rallies," he said in a 1990 rebuke to legislators more interested in politics than policy. "I appeal to my colleagues [in the Supreme Soviet]: get involved in work, because there's a lot of it. The people believe in the Russian parliament and in B. N. Yeltsin. All of the words have already been said, let's get to work on laws."[20] The part about the people's faith in the parliament was more wishful thinking than fact, and it could hardly have helped the image of the parliament to have one of their own leaders essentially pleading with them to make more laws and fewer speeches.

Ironically, the open spectacle of parliamentary debate was a driving force behind the move to create a stronger Russian executive. It did not help that the messy and sometimes embarrassing sessions of the new Russian Congress were televised, and as Jonathan Harris points out, elation among the voters soon turned to anxiety:

> The very first sessions of the huge Congress of People's Deputies revealed it to be an extraordinarily free and open forum for the expression of deputies' opinions and orientations but badly equipped to produce coherent decisions on the RSFSR's problems . . . While citizens were initially clearly encouraged and impressed by the open and direct debate and by the almost complete disappearance of euphemism in the discussion of public policy, they were naturally distressed by the prolonged debate over the agenda, the wrangling over procedural questions, and the failure of these proceedings to provide instant solutions to pressing economic and social problems.[21]

Even *TASS* chided the legislators for "bad-tempered debates" that were hindering even "preparatory" matters, and one exasperated deputy referred to the sessions as "an eastern bazaar."[22] Deputy Nikolai Travkin put it more dryly: "there is no crisis at all; the Congress is in a normal democratic predicament. Each side is doing its best to eliminate the other from the Supreme Soviet list," that is, to ensure that other factions would be excluded from the standing legislature.[23]

Had this behavior been limited to opponents of reform or Soviet restorationists, it would have been disturbing but perhaps less alarming. But this was not the case: the circus-like atmosphere of the Congresses brought out the worst in both reactionaries and reformers. Liberal legislator Anatolii Shabad recalls candidly the tactics of the democrats during the Third Congress of Russian People's Deputies in 1991, shortly before the Soviet coup:

There was an atmosphere of conspiracy and intrigue. So if Khasbulatov was breaking the rules or being rude to some other faction, that was fine if it served our purposes. If it didn't, then we protested. There were very few deputies who opposed such rule-twisting on principle. *The Congress was a reflection of our society at that time.* The structures had broken down, the rules could be broken. (emphasis added)[24]

Russian parliamentary structures, created as miniature versions of the analogous Soviet structures, were replicas that were perhaps too close to the original. Not only did the republic-level congresses mimic the structure of the national congress, they imitated its poor behavior, chaotic organization and confrontational politics as well.

Yeltsin's term as chairman would last almost exactly a year, during which the Supreme Soviet would work, inconclusively, on plans for amending the RSFSR Constitution to accommodate the new office of a presidency. Despite the initial agreement on the need for such an institution, the work was slow going, for as Michael Urban has rightly noted, "in the context of Russia's bitterly divided politics . . . this consensus in principle could not survive the concrete issues of what powers this office would possess, how it would be filled and, perhaps most importantly, who would fill it."[25]

The Making of the Russian President, 1991

It is indicative of the fluidity surrounding the creation of the RSFSR presidency that Yeltsin himself warned the Congress in a televised 1990 interview that as it stood, the deputies "will find that they have invested the president with too many rights, right up to the point where he can dissolve the legislature—in general, so to speak, it is almost a monarchy!"[26] The debate surrounding the Russian presidency was much like the one that had attended the establishment of the Soviet presidency: one side wanted a strong presidency, the other wanted a figurehead, and a small minority wanted no such office at all.

The problem for Yeltsin's opponents was that every indication of public opinion showed overwhelming support for a presidency, and overwhelming support for Yeltsin, and there could be almost no doubt as to who would win in a Russian national contest. (Soviet voters overall, as we saw in Chapter 2, were supportive of Yeltsin overall but still preferred to see Gorbachev as Union president.) But while there was clear public support for a directly elected RSFSR presidency, it is equally true that the Russian public had not spoken with one voice on what *kind* of presidency they wanted, in large part because they had not been asked the question in such detail. Opposition leaders used this as a loophole to hold up the entire process itself, and the Supreme Soviet committee in charge of redrafting the Russian Constitution remained divided and deadlocked over the powers of the presidency. In November 1990, the committee threw in the towel and presented two competing draft proposals for amending the Constitution. As might be expected, there was a Yeltsinite version and an opposition version placed on the table: the former contained provisions for a strong presidency in the American or French tradition, while the latter represented a more European conception of the presidency as a ceremonial head of state.[27] Neither draft was approved, which was just as well, since events were about to overtake the laggardly Supreme Soviet.

In March 1991, the Russian public delivered, via the referendum on the Union, the strongest demand yet for a presidency—whatever its form—and soon after the date was set for the June 12, 1991, election, the first for national leadership in Russian history. Yeltsin's supporters, both liberal and nationalist, were relieved: although the referendum had produced a vote in favor of a Union, it had also delivered a call for the institution—the Russian presidency—that could destroy the Union from within. Better yet, the vote on the Union was hardly the ringing endorsement many had hoped for: what a majority of Soviet citizens actually voted for was to preserve "the USSR as a renewed federation of equal republics in which the rights and freedoms of the person of any nationality must be fully guaranteed."[28] Had this been possible in the first place, of course, the Union might not have been in the state it was by 1991. In any case, the August coup made it clear that this watered-down federation was not one that Soviet hard-liners were willing to accept.

Yeltsin's opponents were accordingly distraught. The message regarding the Union was equivocal (and by late 1991, practically irrelevant), while the vote on the presidency was clear and meant both that the creation of the post and Yeltsin's accession to it were now inevitable. Legislator Svetlana Goryacheva, who would later join the parliamentary opposition to Yeltsin, proclaimed in the wake of the referendum that Yeltsin's push for the presidency represented his "self-unmasking" and that she was "horrified" at the thought of his accession to the post.[29] Goryacheva's horror notwithstanding, events were moving forward. In late spring of 1991, the presidential campaign season was upon Russia.

The 1991 Campaign: Whom Do You Trust?

All presidential elections are, to some extent, a referendum on trust in a particular leader, and the Russian election of 1991 was no different. Russian voters had an array of candidates from which to choose, spanning the ideological spectrum from ultranationalism (professional rabble-rouser Vladimir Zhirinovsky), to neo-Stalinism (General Albert Makashov, an ardent supporter of the 1991 coup), to conservative communist stolidness (former Soviet prime minister Nikolai Ryzhkov), to warmed-over Gorbachevism (former interior minister Vadim Bakatin), to Russian reformism (Yeltsin himself). The details of the campaign will not be recounted here—it took the Supreme Soviet months to agree on the specific rules governing the election, and the actual campaign only lasted all of three weeks—except to point out the important role trust played in Yeltsin's victory.

Yeltsin's campaign differed from the others in two key respects. First, it was run as though Yeltsin (who had been granted special, temporary executive powers in April) was already president. Rather than lower himself to debates (in which he had earlier agreed to take part) or other such activities, Yeltsin hit the road, dividing his time between matters of state and meetings with voters.[30] Second, and related to this Russian "whistle stop" strategy, he emphasized reconciliation rather than fear. He was even careful to address his fellow citizens as *rossiiany,* a term that refers to people living on Russian territory, rather than as *russkie,* a more specifically ethnic designation. This was not a minor point:

> Yeltsin's *rossiiskii* approach contrasted graphically with that of one of his opponents, proto-fascist activist Vladimir Zhirinovsky, who sought to play the "ethnic Russian card" in crude fashion. Asked by *Literaturnaia Gazeta* for a short statement, Yeltsin had begun: "The president must have the trust and broad support of the people." Zhirinovsky, by contrast, had opened his statement by trumpeting: "Today the Russians *(russkie)* are the most humiliated nation in the country."[31]

Although Zhirinovsky was a spirited campaigner and more of a force than anyone realized at that time, he and the other candidates made the mistake of competing to see who could paint the darkest pictures of disaster and civil war. This allowed Yeltsin to maintain a relatively low-key approach that enhanced his image as a statesman and played down his role as an insurrectionist opponent of the old order. He even agreed to negotiate the "nine plus one" (nine republic governments plus one Union government) scheme Gorbachev had devised for reconstituting the Union.

Although this was at first greeted with apprehension among Yeltsin's radical supporters, it reinforced the idea that Yeltsin, and not Gorbachev, was actually controlling events. The intended effect was to show that while other candidates bickered and threatened, Yeltsin governed and led.

Yeltsin even decided to forego a radical running mate, instead selecting Aleksandr Rutskoi, an Afghan war hero and reform communist whose presence on the ticket would siphon off votes from conservatives and military officers who had no love for Yeltsin but might be looking for alternatives to more extreme candidates like Makashov. Rutskoi's politics were less important than the gravitas he brought to the ticket as a military man; Yeltsin needed him to counter Ryzhkov's smart decision to pair up with General Boris Gromov, another Afghan war hero and perhaps the most popular military officer in Russia at the time. Besides, Yeltsin had already wisely chosen to avoid being baited by ideological questions. "When I am asked during my trips," he said during the campaign,

> "Are you for socialism or capitalism?" I say: I am in favor of Russians living better—materially, spiritually, and culturally . . . A healthy society is determined by how people live, how they work, and how they are provided for materially, culturally, and intellectually. As for a name [for that], people will think one up.[32]

It is instructive to note that in the end the Yeltsin team's instincts paid off, as the most serious challenge (relatively speaking) came not from the far left or far right, but from the unsensational Ryzhkov, whose campaign was centered on the simple message that a vote for the former Soviet prime minister was a vote to *zhit' spokoino,* to "live peacefully."[33]

In June, Yeltsin won slightly over 57 percent of the popular vote, with Ryzhkov trailing a distant second at 17.3 percent, and Zhirinovsky, disturbingly, third with nearly 8 percent. Hard-liner Makashov and Bakatin (who had been Gorbachev's personal choice) shared a dead heat for last with 3.8 percent and 3.5 percent, trailing even Kemerovo governor Aman Tuleev, who managed to break just over 6 percent. When the results were final, Yeltsin resigned his chairmanship of the Supreme Soviet, leaving in his place his own nominee and close—for now, at least—associate, Ruslan Khasbulatov. On July 10, Yeltsin placed his hand on the Russian Republic Constitution and took the oath of office as the first directly-elected president in Russian history.

Six weeks later, a group of desperate communist leaders tried to overthrow Mikhail Gorbachev. The events of the August putsch, including

Yeltsin's brave stand against the plotters, have been covered in great detail elsewhere and are no doubt familiar to the reader. During those tense 72 hours, the "Committee of Eight" would discover two things everyone else in Russia already knew: that a great many Russians, and Muscovites in particular, had lost their fear of the coercive power of the Soviet authorities, and that the Soviet soldier had lost his stomach for shooting at his fellow citizens. If this last gasp of Soviet power finished off the Party and made the collapse of the Union a possibility, then it was the creation of regional legislatures and their "presidents," now stepping forth as successor governments in-waiting, that made the collapse thinkable and even feasible.

Once Gorbachev was securely returned to the Kremlin, Yeltsin and the Russian government set about taking control of many Soviet installations and organizations on Russian soil, and dismantling the rest. (Gorbachev had tried, if only for a day, to save the Soviet Communist Party, an act that Yakovlev told him point-blank was akin to "serving tea to a corpse.")[34] The Communist Party was banned on Russian territory and its assets were seized. One by one, Soviet ministries were filled with Russian appointees. In August alone, RSFSR prime minister, Ivan Silaev, became acting Soviet prime minister, Russian internal affairs head Viktor Barannikov took over the Soviet police ministry, and all Soviet KGB communications assets in Russia were seized by the republican government. By October, most of the Soviet infrastructure in Russia was under Russian control, and those ministries not taken over by the RSFSR (nearly 80 in all) were set to be disbanded.

On Christmas Day, 1991, Mikhail Gorbachev acceded to the inevitable by reading a statement of resignation and handing Boris Yeltsin the codes to the Soviet nuclear arsenal. The attempts to keep the Union together in some form throughout the autumn had failed, an effort doomed, depending on one's point of view, by Yeltsin's deviousness and ambition, by Gorbachev's incompetence, by the determination of regional leaders to have nations of their own to rule, or by some combination of these factors.[35] Whatever the reason, most Russians, despite their earlier support for some sort of renewed Union, now apparently agreed with the exit from the USSR and they certainly agreed with the final repudiation of the Communist Party that had once governed it. The First Russian Republic, headed by the first Russian president, was born.

Although the failure of the coup would finish off both the Communist Party and the Soviet Union itself, it would not mean the end of Sovietism in Russian political life. For that, there would have to be another confrontation, in October 1993.

The First Republic and the Failure of Russian Parliamentarism

The political and social conflict that led to the eventual attack on the Russian Supreme Soviet by military and security forces that answered to the president ("loyal" to the president might be too strong a word) is itself a story worth telling at length, but for the purposes of this study the October attack is as interesting in its aftermath as in its proximate causes. The 1993 attack had the support of the general public, as did the elections and the constitutional referendum held in its wake, and it is important to ask now, well after the event, why it did not lead to the paralysis or breakdown of Russian democratic institutions, or even to outright authoritarian rule.

Certainly, from a broadly comparative perspective, Yeltsin's physical destruction of the legislature would seem to confirm the most dire antipresidentialist arguments. Once again a president had suspended a constitution, obliterated his opponents, and justified his own unlimited rule over an uneasy populace. This, unfortunately, is exactly the problem with broadly comparative arguments: from a great enough distance, most things look alike. The Russian case conforms to the model of a presidentialist breakdown at only the most abstract level; that is, it shares with Latin American cases only the most general similarity of a political impasse broken by force by the executive. But even to frame the question in this way—why didn't the presidential attack on the legislature produce dictatorship?—is itself tribute to the ingrained belief that presidents are naturally inclined to authoritarian means, and that legislatures are inherently peaceable bodies, an assumption that does not apply to the Russian case in 1993.

The answer to this question lies in the realization that the real danger to Russian democracy in 1993 emanated from the excesses of the parliament and not from the executive branch. As the liberal daily *Nezavisimaia Gazeta* would charge in the first days after the October attack, whatever the mistakes of the president, it was now clear that "Russian parliamentarism . . . failed the test of history in the past two years and especially in the past two months."[36] A closer look at Russian politics in the 1992–1993 period not only reveals the important role played by the legislature in bringing about the crisis, but also casts doubt on the comparability of the Russian events to other presidential collapses, and thus on the foundations of the brief against presidentialism in general.

Obviously, much of the conflict between the legislative and executive branches was driven not by issues of national policy but by the personalities and ambitions of the various leaders involved. But to explain away the

1992–1993 crisis in Russian politics as merely the result of a head-on confrontation by elite actors seeking final supremacy over each other (and over the material spoils of the Soviet collapse) is to deny the impact of Soviet practices aimed at the atomization of society that later made the formation of stable parties or other coherent political bodies almost impossible. As one Russian observer wrote in 1992, post-Soviet social conditions created an environment in which the practice of national politics was characterized by mistrust and unpredictability:

> What we need is not a search for some ideal model of state structure (a search which, in fact, turns into a skirmish of political ambitions) but confidence in the unshakeability of laws once approved. It is a matter of readiness to play by the already existing rules, and not to change them in the course of the game.[37]

People's Deputy Petr Filippov put it more pessimistically in mid-1993, when he said that Russia's unstable society had resulted in "mob rule [*zakon tolpy*]," and that "the mob is sitting in the parliamentary chamber."[38]

From Victory to Confrontation

Although Yeltsin and Khasbulatov had stood firmly together against the Committee of Eight in August 1991, Khasbulatov had already begun to distance himself from Yeltsin as early as autumn of that year. Political skirmishing between the president and the parliament over the pace and depth of reform had been taking place almost from the moment Yeltsin took office, but for the most part Khasbulatov had stuck by the president in the face of mounting criticism and had even arranged a set of special decree powers to help Yeltsin speed Russia's acquisition of Soviet institutions and agencies. But by early 1992, Khasbulatov was in clear opposition to his former comrade in arms, despite his repeated assurances in the media that he stood firmly behind Russia's first elected chief executive.

The reasons for Khasbulatov's eventual turn against Yeltsin are not entirely clear. It may be that his proreform, anti-Soviet stance was political opportunism, an act that could not be sustained for very long, or, as others suggest, that he was resentful of having been shunted aside as a potential candidate for Russian prime minister during the Soviet transition.[39] Whatever the personal tensions between Yeltsin and Khasbulatov, however, several larger trends were now in motion that were setting parliament and president against each other.

First, the euphoria of independence had been replaced by the pain of reform, and although Russian citizens held the president responsible for that pain, they still held the parliament—much to the chagrin of legislators—in lower regard than the executive branch. Second, the legislators were becoming more distant from their constituents; the parliament had been elected, as many Russians used to say, "in another country," and they had done nothing to reconfirm their mandate after the Soviet collapse. "Such a body is unviable in principle, whatever its composition in terms of personnel," *Izvestiia* charged in early 1992, and therefore was simply "incapable of useful work:"

> Our Congress is patently a remnant of the pre-perestroika Supreme Soviet, which was called upon merely to decorate decisions that were prepared somewhere else entirely. And we have now taken this decoration and are trying to make it fulfill a real function. . . . If the Congress goes on being a superparliament, it is capable of paralyzing any efforts by any government.[40]

This paralysis was in fact setting in quickly. The bewildering and chaotic functioning of parliament was polarizing the deputies, debate was sharp and insulting, and factions were forming and collapsing with alarming speed. Daily life in the parliament was characterized by intense activity but little actual work, in no small measure because, as Lilia Shevtsova noted, "every faction . . . felt compelled to monopolize power" in order to survive, with the predictable result that compromises on passing even routine legislation were rare.[41]

All this led to a severe deterioration of what little prestige the parliament had among the voters, and served only to intensify the public's pre-existing antipathy to parties and political movements. Whatever their anger at Yeltsin's government and its reforms, it was the parliament, and not the president, that was in danger of being voted out of office should the opportunity arise. The opposition's strategy under these conditions was simple and sensible: avoid elections, obstruct further reform, and shift as much blame as possible to the executive branch. The hope, apparently, was that this would not only focus the public's attention on the president's shortcomings, but also allow the legislators to present themselves as the voices of reason and social justice.

Yeltsin's advisors understood this strategy, and while most were deeply hostile to the parliament, they could not get their president to act more decisively against it. Yeltsin bluntly rejected advice by his aides to disband the Soviet-era Congress and call for new elections. Indeed, at a "heated"

March 1992 cabinet meeting, Yeltsin cut short an angry diatribe against the Supreme Soviet by advisor Gennadii Burbulis (perhaps the most avowed opponent of the legislature) by saying "We have to find a way to work with the Supreme Soviet. Above all, we don't need another enemy!"[42] Yeltsin's belief at this point that compromise with the parliament was possible was a sign either of detachment or optimism, but it was unrealistic, especially given the president's own tendency to regard bargaining and negotiating with legislators as somehow beneath him.[43]

Although Khasbulatov was critical of some of Yeltsin's policies in 1991 and early 1992, this was a normal and, given Yeltsin's halting steps, an understandable role to be played by a parliamentary leader. However, his attacks on Yeltsin's policies became steadily more hostile, and in the spring of 1992 the speaker moved to an open break that went far beyond ordinary opposition. At the Sixth Congress of Russian People's Deputies in April 1992, Khasbulatov led a movement to amend the Constitution so as to strip Yeltsin of his powers.[44] It was a daring political attack with much at stake, as a *Radio Liberty* analysis recounted at the time:

> Khasbulatov's main intention was to deprive the president of direct control over the executive, subordinate the government to the parliamentary leadership, and leave Yeltsin as little more than a figurehead without any real powers. He also started to seek personal control over the Russian media. More ominous still was his attempt to gain control over the armed forces and the state security agencies, which he sought to put under the parliament's jurisdiction instead of the president's . . . Many politicians who had not been included in Yeltsin's reformist government supported Khasbulatov.[45]

Or, as *Izvestiia* put it, had Khasbulatov succeeded, "the president elected by all the people would have been transformed into a ceremonial figurehead whereas the man who won the speaker's chair only with great difficulty and thanks to a slim majority of votes would have become the real ruler of Russia."[46] These crude attempts at a power grab, including Khasbulatov's attempt to capture the pesky *Izvestiia* in order to silence it, all failed in open votes.[47] The deputies were not, apparently, inclined to actually take on the burdens of government, nor were they yet willing to hand the reins of power to Khasbulatov.

Indeed, the one significant motion that did pass, a vote of no-confidence in the government, was withdrawn after the cabinet responded by resigning en bloc. Had the vote remained, it would have placed the responsibility for policy in the lap of the Congress. By the end of the Congress, the cabinet had returned, and Yeltsin had won the major battle to keep his powers while agreeing, in principle, that reforms needed to be "amended."[48] But it was too late: Khasbulatov and a plurality of deputies were now in open confrontation with the president. By the end of the year, Vice President Aleksandr Rutskoi (saddled with the thankless job of overseeing the reform of Russian agriculture) would, for reasons of personal ambition and political frustration, join the parliament and go into revolt against his own chief.

Even as the parliament moved into direct confrontation with the president in the name of the "people," the Russian people turned their backs on the legislators. By early 1992, one Russian study found, for example, that only 13 percent of Muscovites had any confidence in the deputies they had elected, while confidence in the Russian Supreme Soviet as an institution stood at a dismal 16 percent. Only 4 percent connected "their hope for Russia's exit from the economic crisis" with political parties or movements.[49] Surveys conducted after the Sixth Congress found that, if elections were held at that moment, only one out of ten voters would return their current deputies to office, while four out of ten indicated that they "entirely distrusted" the Supreme Soviet.[50] One of Yeltsin's advisors, Dmitrii Volkogonov, summed up the mood of the nation in a late 1992 confidential brief for the president: the Russian people, he wrote, were "raised in Soviet society" and therefore could only grasp the concept of sudden or revolutionary change. "It's sad, but it's true: society is governed by an atmosphere of *passive expectation* of changes, and not by efforts to realize those changes." [emphasis original][51] This meant that the public was inclined to view piecemeal or partial legislation as meaningless, and therefore every day that went by without significant results from the parliament eroded popular trust in the legislature itself.

This is not to say that Russians had overwhelming faith in the executive branch. The crisis of power in Moscow had tarred all participants; as the Russian analysts found, there was in late 1992 an "enormous deficit of trust in political leaders and parties."[52] Still, fear of a legislative tyranny was growing, and redounded to the benefit of the president; one 1993 Russian study noted that the Congresses had already shown themselves "professionally unfit" as representative institutions and worried explicitly that the popular will "is capable of expressing itself [only] through a . . . 'dictatorship of the majority.'"[53] A late 1992 poll that asked about trust in various institutions found that although the presidency, at 36 percent, fell far behind the more trusted institutions of the Russian Army and the Orthodox Church, it was still chosen over the parliament by a two to one margin.[54] This was more pronounced in the Moscow area, typically a more liberal electorate. When Muscovites were asked in early 1993 which political leader they trusted, Yeltsin topped the list with 50 percent, "Nobody" ran a strong second with 29 percent, and Rutskoi polled 5 percent. Khasbulatov's support, at 2 percent, was indistinguishable from the poll's margin of error.[55] As the political crisis deepened into early 1993, the Russian public decisively rejected giving the lead role in constitutional reform—that is, in drafting the very rules of the political game—to the parliament, a choice preferred by no more than 15 percent of respondents.[56]

By the time the Sixth Congress adjourned, there was a clear and strengthening migration of popular legitimacy and trust from the parliament to the president. The parliament had became so antagonistic and frighteningly heavy handed (at one point during the Sixth Congress, Khasbulatov referred to the government's ministers as mere "worms," and later managed to constitute a paramilitary "parliamentary guard") that Russians increasingly looked to the presidency as a moderating force.[57] The parliament had managed to deplete whatever small legitimacy it had, and the blame, as one analysis noted at the time, rested largely with a speaker who "has again and again kept the support of an insecure parliament of dubious legitimacy by provoking fierce clashes with Yeltsin and the executive, then saying he really backs Yeltsin, then provoking a new clash."[58] Russians may have been concerned about the impact of reform, but they did not want reform halted; they may have been concerned about the abuses of power and corruption in the presidency, but they did not want the president deposed or stripped of his powers. If the opposition legislators had undertaken these moves in the belief that it was what their constituents wanted (or with the assumption that such actions would not be recognized as a grab for power) they were badly mistaken.

During the summer of 1992, tensions between Yeltsin and the parliament intensified, despite Yeltsin's apparent victory at the Sixth Congress. Believing, correctly, that he had a better sense of the Russian people than his opponents in the parliament, Yeltsin pressed ahead with his agenda, and in June made the daring but provocative move of appointing Egor Gaidar as acting prime minister. (Yeltsin himself had held the post until this point, in part because there was no agreement between the president and parliament on nominees.) By any standard, Gaidar was an extremely liberal reformer, and Yeltsin's choice was sure to provoke a reaction from the parliament already demanding a slowing of the reform process. Parliamentary criticism of the reform process and of Gaidar personally was intense, and by the fall of 1992 legislative-executive tensions had brought reform to a standstill and public support for all national figures to new lows. But whatever the political damage done to Yeltsin over the summer and fall of 1992, the damage to the parliament was worse, and the stage was set for the final months of conflict that would lead to the storming of the White House.

"Well Excuse Me, Maybe You're Not Afraid, but I Am"

By late 1992, the legislators were now less concerned about their constituents back home and more focused on their own viability in Moscow. For people like Khasbulatov and Rutskoi, the battle was no longer about public policy, but about political survival. Yeltsin may not have been as clairvoyant about the intentions of the Russian public as he apparently liked to think, but he was quite right to believe that in any direct political confrontation with the parliament he would, as every poll and editorial indicated, win hands down. To this end, he had previously pushed for the possibility of a referendum to break the political impasses with his opponents in the parliament. Nothing generated more anxiety among opposition legislators than the idea of facing the public, and they went to great lengths to prevent it. To their credit, some legislators grasped the damage that avoiding a referendum was doing; when a deputy in late 1992 warned Khasbulatov that "under no circumstances is it politically acceptable for it to appear that the congress is afraid of referenda all of a sudden," Khasbulatov shot back (in a comment that went out live over Russian radio): "Well excuse me, maybe you're not afraid, but I am, of the kind of referenda that will lead to the ruin of the country. So there you are, I am afraid."[59] Khasbulatov's concern for the "ruin of the country" was a fig leaf: he and his fellow deputies knew that the public had lost what little trust it had in the parliament, and that any referendum on the current deputies or their work would likely be their last.

But the parliamentary opposition had some reason for optimism as well. The Seventh Congress, convened in December 1992, was a feisty gathering at which votes of no-confidence in both the government *and* the legislature were proposed and rejected within the first 90 minutes of the opening session. The president and his team faced the Seventh Congress much fatigued by the struggles of the summer and fall, and the deputies could reasonably believe that the evident failures of reform might yet engulf the presidency and leave the parliament intact, if only they could weather the current political climate. Gaidar had proved an unpopular choice to lead the government (even Yeltsin had criticized him publicly) and the reform process by this point now seemed to be nothing more than an incompetent farrago of proposals by young and inexperienced men that had produced little more than a painful synergy of joblessness, poverty, and hyperinflation. The trick for the legislators was to figure out how to bring down Yeltsin quickly, before the economy swept them all, president and parliament, away in a tide of public anger.

Once again, the weapons of choice at the Congress were constitutional amendments, but this time, Yeltsin did not have the political capital or public support he needed to thwart them outright. Khasbulatov hoped to add a margin of insurance to the voting by making it secret rather than a roll-call (in the belief that legislators would be more willing to act against Yeltsin anonymously), a move that actually provoked a short physical scuffle on the floor of the Congress. When Yeltsin proposed a referendum on national trust from the podium at the Congress and then called on democratic deputies to storm out of the hall with him, only some 150 stunned deputies followed, with the notable exception of Vice President Rutskoi, who took to the podium to support the Congress instead of the president.[60] The Congress then went on to pass resolutions condemning Yeltsin's program, and to debate a series of amendments that, if passed, would have turned Yeltsin into a ceremonial president. The more dangerous of these amendments were narrowly defeated; in fact, Khasbulatov's insistence on secret voting apparently backfired and the deputies again backed away from assuming the responsibilities they would have taken away from the president.

The president was, for the moment, out of danger. Khasbulatov tried to put the best face on the outcome by saying that the Russian government should "draw conclusions from the result of the voting," and warning the executive branch that if "you strive to govern autocratically, this Pyrrhic victory will be your last and final one [sic] and will bring about our country's destruction."[61] Still, Yeltsin paid for this narrow escape. Gaidar and others were removed from the president's inner circle as part of a compromise in which the president appointed Viktor Chernomyrdin, a more moderate figure with strong ties to the industrial community, as prime minister while extracting a promise from the parliament on a popular referendum to be held in the spring.

This so-called December Compromise was supposed to set up a mechanism by which the confrontation between president and parliament was to be resolved permanently, and it was a surprise to almost no one that it began to unravel within a month. The parliament, of course, had no incentive to allow a referendum. Yeltsin, for his part, apparently believed that any sign of compromise from the parliament was merely a delaying tactic, a ploy to buy time to undermine the presidency and seize power. In his recollections of the Seventh Congress he wrote:

> [T]his process of shaking and rattling the constitution couldn't be endless, it had to have some sort of logical limit . . . It was legislative anarchy. When I was able to think calmly about what had happened, I understood: it was collective insanity. Such a body could not run the country. It already smelled like a revolutionary situation. And the smell of revolution is dominated by the smell of blood.[62]

The December Compromise was doomed because Yeltsin and the parliamentary opposition both understood that a referendum would do vastly more political damage to the legislature than to the president. The result was a standoff: parliament was able to prevent the president from governing effectively, but the president could threaten to take his case to the people and thereby undermine the authority of the parliament. "By February [1993]," according to Shevtsova, "all major political actors—the Supreme Soviet, the Constitutional Court, and a majority of republican and regional leaders—had publicly rejected the December Compromise."[63]

"Yes, Yes, No, Yes"

Conflict over the referendum and elections became intense in the first months of 1993, resulting in the convening of an Eighth Congress of People's Deputies in March. Khasbulatov and his supporters openly reneged on the referendum deal, a move that prompted the liberal daily *Moskovskie Novosti* to claim that "Russian parliamentarians have declared war on the president."[64] Even on matters other than the referendum, the legislators were intractable; at one point, Khasbulatov warned the new prime minister that if he did not send the Congress a "normal" budget (that is, one acceptable to him) they would refuse to authorize paying the salaries of the government's employees.[65] Yeltsin finally gave up trying to negotiate with the Congress, and took to the airwaves to declare point-blank that there would be a referendum in April, even if he had to declare a "special regime" to rule until then.

The comment about a "special regime" was ominous, but came to nothing, and it remains unclear whether Yeltsin really intended to impose some sort of direct presidential rule. Still, the escalation of the tension in Moscow led Khasbulatov to convene yet another Congress, the Ninth, within weeks of the Eighth, with the clear intention of impeaching Yeltsin. These efforts again fell short, and all sides sought yet another round of negotiations. Initially, a deal was struck that would have subjected both president and parliament to simultaneous new elections in November 1993. The deal has rightly been described as "political suicide for the deputies" and it was angrily rejected by the legislators, who almost deposed Khasbulatov as speaker for accepting it while demanding that Yeltsin be impeached for proposing it.[66]

With the question of an outright round of new elections deadlocked, submitting the issue to the voters was now the only way out for both president and parliament. Even dedicated opposition deputies understood that Yeltsin had outflanked them by calling for the Russian public to resolve the dispute. Yeltsin foe Vladimir Isakov notes in his memoirs the panic that gripped the legislators:

> The critical situation at the Ninth Congress illustrated the heterogeneity and weakness of the opposition forces. "The question of early reelections of the deputies can't be submitted to a referendum, not under any circumstances!"— a trio of my colleagues had pulled me in a corner—"It's a disaster!" I tried to persuade them: Just how were we going to explain to the people that after including three questions on the president, we weren't going to put in a question about ourselves? They didn't listen, they didn't understand. Their eyes were awash with fear.[67]

But the deputies had one last ace up their sleeve: they could try to control the wording of the referendum. The tables were turned: because Yeltsin had gone on national television and openly dared the parliament to the plebiscite, he could not now deny them this compromise without appearing to be as dictatorial as his opponents were trying to depict him.

The deputies insisted on a minimum turnout of at least half of all registered voters to make the referendum valid, and chose to put four questions to the public on April 25, 1993:

1. Do you trust the president of the Russian Federation?
2. Do you support the socioeconomic policies of the Government?
3. Do you support early presidential elections?
4. Do you support early parliamentary elections?

This was a direct polling of the electorate on the issue of social trust, and Yeltsin asked the voters to send a clear message by adopting his slogan of

"Yes, Yes, No, Yes." Few expected that clarity; indeed, there was a great deal of concern (or hope, in some quarters) that many voters were now so alienated and angry that they would not even show at the polls and thus invalidate any results.

The outcome was a surprise to all sides (as well as to many foreign observers). Yeltsin's support, while always strong in Moscow, apparently extended beyond the capital. Nearly 65 percent of registered voters went to the polls, far more than expected, and they voted as Yeltsin had asked them to: "yes" to trust in the president by 58.1 percent to 39.2 percent, "yes" to support for the government's policies by 53.0 percent to 45.6 percent, "no"—in a very close call—to early presidential elections by 49.5 percent to 47.2 percent, and "yes" to early parliamentary elections by a much larger margin, 67.2 percent to 30.1 percent, a more than two to one margin.[68] It was, by any criteria, a clear victory for Yeltsin. Khasbulatov tried to appear nonchalant by simply shrugging off the results. Although there were no serious claims that the numbers were faked, he made the desperate argument that the 40 million Russians who had not voted constituted a kind of silent constituency opposing the "anticongressional forces."[69] But this was unconvincing, even among the opposition. As Isakov bitterly admitted the day after the vote: "the people have the government they deserve."[70]

In retrospect, the results should hardly have been so shocking, especially if the referendum was viewed not as a referendum on Yeltsin himself, but rather as a choice between Yeltsin or the parliament. Russian pollsters found that while support for the Congress could vacillate a great deal over time (dropping, ominously, during periods of actual meetings when the legislators were actually *visible*) there was a solid plurality of roughly four out of ten Russians who throughout late 1992 and early 1993 consistently felt that the Congress should simply be abolished.[71] When asked in this period if the nation needed a new constitution, Russians answered yes by a five to one margin, although many remained undecided.[72] And in a head-to-head popularity comparison between Yeltsin and Khasbulatov, Yeltsin was chosen 35 percent to 12 percent over the speaker (although once again, "Nobody" ran off with top honors at 53 percent). The most evident sign of danger for Khasbulatov in this latter poll was that his support among pensioners and the unemployed—the groups he and his colleagues were claiming so vociferously to defend—was stuck in miniscule single digits.[73] If the speaker could not find more support among the dispossessed, he could hardly have expected to find it elsewhere.

The April referendum reinvigorated Yeltsin, who regarded the vote as "a second presidential election," and he pressed his advantage aggressively while the voice of the voters was still clearly on his side.[74] (He also took the opportunity to indulge in a bit of pettiness, punishing opponents like Rutskoi and others by stripping them of the perks of their offices.) If the idea of a referendum had scared the deputies, the concept of a new constitution was positively paralyzing, since it was all but certain that in the prevailing political conditions the Congress of People's Deputies and the Supreme Soviet would never survive incorporation into a new basic law for the Russian state. Accordingly, Yeltsin called for a June assembly to draft a new constitution, and even submitted a draft for discussion that would enshrine presidential supremacy in Russia. Conflict in the summer of 1993 moved for a time from the legislature to the meetings of the constitutional assembly that would decide on the rules of the Russian political system for the foreseeable future, but even a new constitution would not be able to stave off the conflict between the newly reconfirmed president and the now completely isolated parliament.

Deadlock

The maneuvering over a new constitution could not have come at a worse time for the members of the Supreme Soviet and the Congress of People's Deputies. Public trust and confidence in legislative institutions had by that point fallen to nearly invisible levels: when asked in June about trust in a variety of public organizations, the armed forces, the church, and the media scored well, while the Supreme Soviet and the Congress far and away led as the *least* trusted institutions in Russian life. Even the security organs and the Russian Cabinet scored higher.[75] And little wonder: the parliament, although now in effect repudiated, continued to pass laws countermanding presidential decrees, thereby repeatedly forcing (or freeing, depending on one's perspective) Russian administrative bodies at all levels to choose which edicts to obey, and inducing a great deal of uncertainty, even chaos, in the execution of even routine administrative matters. There was a growing sense of anarchy among the population and political figures alike: one deputy, a member of the legislature's constitutional commission, wondered if the constitution itself was by now so incomprehensible as to not even be in force. "Is it actually possible," Leonid Volkov wrote in March, "for anyone, for any organ of organization, to do anything *without breaching the Russian Federation Constitution?*" [emphasis original][76]

Many of the deputies knew that the game was up after the April referendum, and that the Supreme Soviet was now less a legislature than a kind of bunker for Khasbulatov, Rutskoi, and their supporters. Shortly after the April results were in, the prominent legislator Nikolai Travkin resigned his seat, and a group of deputies calling themselves the "Independent Civic Initiative" applauded Travkin's example and called on others to do the same:

> In general, the continuation of the game of Soviet parliamentarism and even simply participation in an imaginary representative "power" are tantamount once again to squandering a democratic victory and to causing disappointment among the voters . . . It is necessary to move away, to switch to the side of the majority of voters, to do the right thing, to emphasize before the eyes of the entire population that the era of mendacious Soviet "constitutionalism" has expired . . . Leave, gentlemen, and have no more part in a rotten body, in deceit.[77]

This was easier said by reformist deputies; after all, they had backed the right horse in the referendum and therefore could perhaps resign and return to politics later. But the opposition had received a particularly nasty surprise: several districts represented by some of the most prominent and visible opposition legislators, including well-known figures such as Ivan Rybkin, Svetlana Goryacheva, and even the charismatic Sergei Baburin, all voted both in favor of the president and against the legislature (that is, "yes" to supporting the president's policies and "yes" to early parliamentary elections) by margins that were an average ten points higher than the overall national vote.[78]

Although many of those opposition legislators would in fact manage later to return to politics, during the summer of 1993 it seemed as if they were at a dead end. There were a few half-hearted attempts to reach out to the electorate, including one meeting designed to enlist "mass support" for the parliament, an effort whose irony was apparently lost on the legislators at the conference.[79] The loss in April and the increasing hostility of the public helps to explain why the legislators fought against Yeltsin and in defense of the parliament so tenaciously: in terms of their own survival in national politics, they had no choice but to cling to the institution that was protecting them from their own voters.

Yeltsin's renewed mandate and the now obvious isolation of the parliament produced complete deadlock in Russian politics through the summer and fall of 1993. Work in a recently convened constitutional assembly was slow and tedious, in no small measure because, as one Russian television report put it, "the deputies are very much concerned with their own future. They are dealing with all problems at the sessions, bearing in mind their own problems. The deputies are very nervous during the sessions, to put it mildly."[80] Still, in late July, the constitutional assembly managed to produce a draft, but because it was too strongly presidential, it was rejected by the legislative opposition and the means for ratifying it remained unclear.

Khasbulatov understandably tried to shift attention away from the assembly, arguing that constitutional reform was less important than the economy. To this end the legislature's reckless state budget (which at this point had been vetoed, overridden, and vetoed again) was rammed through and adopted. Meanwhile, the Supreme Soviet busied itself with such mischief as seizing control of billions of dollars in former Soviet assets and trying to muzzle the press. *Izvestiia* described the tense legislative-executive situation in early September:

> Any proposal from the president gets a hostile reception. Regardless of content. Confrontation flares up on any issue. The microphones know only one word—"no" . . . The hyperinflationary budget, which the president vetoed, was adopted by the deputies. All the president's edicts aimed at developing privatization have been suspended, and parliament makes no secret of its intention to bury it them legislatively.

Izvestiia then restated the obvious, making the case that the legislators hated and feared the most: "The parliament, elected in 'another country,' has become in essence a single-party body" that represented only the most extreme social forces, while "the president and his policy have been twice supported by nationwide mandate of confidence."[81] The Supreme Soviet was now, as Volkogonov described it in one of his confidential memos to the president, a "parallel power," an instrument of obstruction whose elite leadership resembled nothing so much as the old Politburo and whose rank and file members were playing the role of the former Central Committee.[82]

Yeltsin felt the same way. Now openly disdainful of the Supreme Soviet, he brought Gaidar and other young reformers back into the government. Anxiety rose among the legislators and their allies, some of it purposely induced by the speaker, who was now openly trying to scare the Russian public. If Yeltsin got his way, Khasbulatov warned, among other things the sovereignty of Russia's smaller republics and regions would be "done and over by sunset," and that millions of pensioners would starve because "you know what our government is like." Khasbulatov called for "a whole bloc" of laws, including "one on the lack of respect for Parliament [and] violation of the relevant procedures by executive power and officials."[83]

These dire predictions had little resonance with the public, but the speaker's charges were indicative of how low the level of public debate had already sunk. Indeed, if Khasbulatov's proposed laws on public disrespect had ever been passed half of Moscow's politicians would have ended up in jail. Even before the rowdy Congresses of 1992 and 1993, one of Rutskoi's own aides felt the need to write a memo admonishing his boss that it was "categorically impermissible" for the vice president of a democratic nation to refer to his opponents using words like "fuckers," "bandits," "fascists," "snivelers," and "punks."[84] In a particularly bizarre moment, hard-line deputy Iona Andronov charged that "conflict in the top echelons of power had been provoked by the U.S. and Israeli special services which are preparing to replace the president, who is unwell. And the famous Israeli secret service agent R. Eitan is playing the main role in this." This managed to embarrass even Khasbulatov, who added feebly that he hoped that Andronov could not possibly mean the same General Eitan who was "a deputy of the Israeli Knesset and a very respected man."[85]

By late summer, the Russian media were thick with predictions of coups, rebellions, conspiracy theories, and warnings of civil war. Yeltsin was certain that "Khasbulatov had given the order to sabotage the constitutional process," and that the speaker had made clear that at the next Congress in September "there would be a new hysteria, yet another battle with the president." The country, in Yeltsin's mind, was now at risk of something bigger than the venomous deadlock between the president and the parliament: "Russia wouldn't put up with our brawls in the Congress much longer," he later wrote, "and this [could] embolden a new Russian Stalin, who could put a stop to all this intellectual fussing over democracy with his little finger. And so I chose my own variant of stabilization."[86]

Yeltsin's "variant" would lead to physical destruction of the White House. When the end came for the First Republic, it was with both a bang and a whimper. The bang came from Yeltsin's tanks; the whimper came from the Russian people, who had not, in the main, rallied against Yeltsin. Even at the last minute, the parliamentarians were shocked to realize that the majority of the Russian people, for whom they claimed to speak and in whose defense they claimed to be acting, had either stood apart in anguished neutrality, or worse, with the president whose soldiers were shelling the Supreme Soviet.

Edict 1400

On September 21, 1993, Yeltsin spoke to the nation about the political crisis, admitting that all semblance of legal order had collapsed. "The existing constitution," he told them, does not "envisage a procedure of adopting a new constitution providing for a dignified exit from the crisis of statehood."[87] Yeltsin's answer was Presidential Edict 1400, which disbanded the parliament, called for new elections, and scheduled a constitutional referendum. Edict 1400 declared that "a political situation has taken place in the Russian Federation that threatens the nation's state and social security" and included particular indictments against the legislature for attempting to usurp executive power and "defying the will of the Russian people."[88] Most of the parliament obeyed Edict 1400 and left the Russian White House.

Now shorn of its moderate members, the Supreme Soviet lived down to its reputation. It impeached Yeltsin, installed Rutskoi as acting president, and named as "defense minister" an outright Stalinist, General Vladislav Achalov. Arms and provisions were brought into the White House, and the remaining legislators and their supporters settled in for a siege and eventual showdown that they believed they would win, once the tide of public support turned against Yeltsin.

Khasbulatov and his colleagues were in fact so sure of victory that early on they made a crucial and irretrievable mistake. They tried to militarize the situation, assuming, incorrectly, that the Russian Army was only waiting for the word to move and depose Yeltsin. To this end they issued a flurry of various orders to the military in the first two days of the crisis, all of which were ignored.[89] Rutskoi—in an ideological about-face, openly lamenting the fall of the USSR—asked his fellow officers to throw off any pretense of political neutrality, and not to stand idle as they had during the Soviet collapse.[90] This was followed by Khasbulatov's call for, in effect, a mutiny: "We must have military units here today. Esteemed deputies, esteemed chairman: bring some military units here . . . What we need here is not just men in military greatcoats, but military units."[91]

One of the "men in military greatcoats," people's deputy and general, Albert Makashov, did little to help the situation with the public when he made clear what those units would do once the Kremlin was taken from Yeltsin. Speaking to a rally at the White House two days after Edict 1400, he promised "to make life impossible for those deputies who disagree, both in Moscow and in the new USSR," adding that he would "lay his hands on the traitors and see to it that they wash in their own blood."[92] Rutskoi, for his part, promised the president's supporters that they would be strung up by their heels.[93] Yeltsin also appealed to the army publicly, addressing the soldiers of the Russian Army as "my sons." He asked them to remain neutral while nonetheless insisting on the legitimacy of his own position

as the chief executive: "Let the people have their weighty say at free democratic elections. As for today, I, the people's elected president, remain
your Supreme Commander in Chief."[94]

Last-ditch negotiations at the end of September, mediated by Patriarch
Aleksei of the Orthodox Church, failed.[95] Tensions finally flared to the
point were violence broke out among crowds in the streets of Moscow
(including an attack on the Moscow City government building and the
Ostankino television station), and on the morning of October 4, 1993,
special military and police teams moved in and took the White House by
force.

The scale of the violence was both great and small. Although it was the
worst bloodshed in the capital since the revolution itself, the events were
limited to a very few areas of the city, and many Russians later reported
that life in other parts of Moscow was by all indications normal while the
drama played out downtown. When the smoke cleared, 149 people had
been killed, and many more wounded. The White House was smoldering
from several direct hits from Yeltsin's tanks. By evening, Rutskoi, Khasbulatov, and several others were in jail, and a curfew was placed on the city.

Aftermath

In the autumn of 1993, it would have been difficult to argue with the critics of presidentialism that the Russian system had not become yet another
of many that had chosen presidentialism and then descended into a spiral
of confrontation that in the end could only be broken by violence.

But to understand the October events as merely the emergence of yet
another dictatorial president is to overlook three important facts about the
attack and its aftermath. First, Yeltsin was acting with the consent and support of a majority of the Russian people. Second, as the previous discussion shows, it was the parliament, and not the president, that was seeking
to seize authoritarian powers for itself; in this case, it was the president defending economic and political reforms, and the parliament opposing
them, the reverse of the situations in Latin America and Africa (with the
notable exception of Peruvian President Alberto Fujimori's famed "auto-
golpe," or self-inflicted coup, of 1992).[96] Finally, the fears that Yeltsin would
use the destruction of parliament to create a presidential dictatorship were
not, as will be seen, borne out.

The destruction of the Russian parliament in 1993 represents a complete reversal of the expectations of the presidentialist critics, one that can

be explained only by reference to the social conditions in Russia at the time and the motives and actions of the president and parliament in those conditions. The attack on the parliament was not a structural conflict between two branches of government that could have been solved through legal or constitutional adjustments; rather, it was the final act of the Soviet tragedy, the result of seven decades of policies that had made normal political association, of the kind on which stable legislative institutions are built, virtually impossible.

"There Are Laws, and There Is Justice"

There can be no question that Edict 1400 was, at best, "extra"-constitutional, in the sense that the Russian Constitution then in force did not make provision for the kind of situation that arose in late 1993. At worst, it was illegal; it would not take a tortured interpretation of that constitution to reach the conclusion that the president could not by fiat abolish all previous institutions and then call for a new political system. The Russian Supreme Court voted nine to four to declare Edict 1400 unconstitutional, but even that was tainted by the fact the chairman of the court, Valerii Zorkin, was clearly a partisan figure whose sympathies were with the Supreme Soviet. It should be no surprise that in a situation where public opinion was against them but legal opinion was with them, Rutskoi and Khasbulatov insisted on strict adherence to the letter of the law, which in turn led to a scathing reproach from *Izvestiia,* who noted the irony of "communist renegades" appealing to the constitution and legalism after "having casually trampled on all legality for the previous 70 years." *Izvestiia,* which had good reason to be disgusted with a parliament that had tried to shut it down, went out of its way to rub salt in the legislators' wounds: "Their Lenin laughs at them. History simply mocks them and says: 'Yeltsin is the Lenin of today.'"[97]

The president's office, wisely, did not even attempt a legal defense of the edict. Yeltsin's legal aide, Iurii Baturin, was blunt: "I am aware that it is not a lawful, legal move, but in the circumstances, it is just. In fact, the president took the well-known view that there are laws and there is justice, laws can be unjust, and we are in a situation where the Constitution, a considerable part of it anyway, has ceased to be legal."[98] Yeltsin's own Justice Ministry added that while Yeltsin "formally exceeded his powers, he employed this violation not to usurp power . . . but to defend the will of the people."[99]

At the time, it was easy to dismiss the president's approach as a rationalization, but in fact Yeltsin did represent the tide of opinion among the

Russian people. But there was more at stake for the political elite than winning the battle for short-term public opinion; the October crisis had, in a way, forced ordinary citizens to take sides in a great contest for Russia's future. It was obvious, after the chaos of the Eighth and Ninth Congresses, that the constitutional order had broken down. Once the Russian people felt that the system was in free fall, they made a pained choice to place the stewardship of the nation in the hands of the president and not the parliament.[100] *Izvestiia's* commentary may have been scathing, but it was largely accurate when it said:

> Of course, this is a step toward authoritarianism. But . . . it is far more important for us to understand: a step toward authoritarianism away from what? From democracy, perhaps? At 20.00 hours yesterday (and the step was taken at 20.00 hours and two minutes) there wasn't any kind of democracy in Russia to be seen anywhere. The country had long been in a state of anarchy, not democracy—an anarchy "established" in part so the soviet-parliamentary structures could keenly dispute first prize with the president.[101]

Indeed, it was hard to imagine Edict 1400 as an overthrow of a constitutional order, because any such order had already vanished. After Edict 1400, a majority of Russians felt not only that the parliament was to blame for the situation, but that Rutskoi and Khasbulatov had actually planned the disorder in Moscow in order to seize power.[102]

Those closest to the events, in Moscow, were also the most supportive of Yeltsin's forceful move against the Supreme Soviet. But even outside the normally more liberal capital, support for Yeltsin, and animosity toward the parliament, grew throughout the autumn and right into the final confrontation on October 4. Shortly before Edict 1400, 70 percent of Muscovites felt Khasbulatov should resign, a finding that was only five points higher than in the nation as a whole. Yeltsin, at 48 percent, was the most popular politician in Russia, followed closely by Chernomyrdin (46 percent) and even Rutskoi (39 percent), which suggests not only that the public had no faith in the speaker but also that the vice president had thrown in his lot with the wrong crowd.[103] Despite Zorkin's decision against Yeltsin, Muscovites by a two to one margin felt the law was on Yeltsin's side, although nearly a third felt that both sides were acting illegally.[104] As events moved toward their violent conclusion, support for Yeltsin grew. A national snap poll just before the attack on October 4 that asked "Whom do you support, the president or the parliament?" found an overwhelming majority behind the president—72 percent to parliament's

9 percent. The same question was asked right after the attack on the same day; the violence cost each side a few points, but the president still led 68 percent to 6 percent, or by more than ten to one.

Was this just the result of emotions running high in the atmosphere of crisis and violence between September 21 and October 4? Possibly, although in the immediate aftermath of the attack, when Russians were asked who they trusted more, the president outpolled the Supreme Soviet 71 percent to 4 percent.[105] More revealing, the use of troops in the capital was approved by a margin of over six to one. It would take a while for real doubts to surface about the October events, but even at the December 1993 elections, exit polls found (at least among active voters) that support for Yeltsin's actions was down, but still approved by a slim majority.[106] But polls taken by the *Mnenie* group in both 1993 and 1994 revealed that support for Yeltsin's actions evaporated within a year. *Mnenie*'s results found a slight majority in favor of the attack in October 1993, but a 46 percent plurality against it a year later. Only the decision to disband parliament managed to keep a small edge in 1994, with a third of respondents approving it, a fifth against it, and nearly half undecided.[107]

The seemingly contradictory results of these polls reflected the fact that Russians saw Yeltsin's actions as disturbing but less frightening than a possible victory by the Supreme Soviet leaders. As time wore on, Russians may have felt that their trust in the president was somewhat misplaced, but they still preferred the presidency, warts and all, to the parliament he had destroyed. Whatever the outcry across the spectrum of Russian politics—the destruction of the parliament did manage to unite for a time former liberal dissidents and hard-line communists in their charge that Yeltsin had seized power for himself—the fact remained that the president had destroyed the parliament and upended the constitution with the people as his willing, if reluctant, accomplices. As Russians made preparations for establishing a new political order in the winter of 1993, there was no movement either among the surviving political elites nor among the public at large to move away from presidentialism, and given their experiences with the Congresses and the Supreme Soviet, which was, at the end, demanding a halt to reform, a Soviet restoration, and a bloodbath for "traitors," it was hard to blame them.

Presidentialism and the Impossible Legislature

The Russian Congress of People's Deputies and the Supreme Soviet it elected were, because of their origins in Soviet society, an impossible legislature. They came from a society that was so divided and anxious (those, that is, who were not simply chosen by fiat of the Communist Party) that it was utopian to hope that it could transformed from a showplace—or more charitably, an experiment—into a legislature capable of undertaking reform in the face of sustained social anguish. Whether the crisis of September and October had to turn violent is another question, but there can be no denying that social conditions in Russia meant that there would be at least one last-ditch attempt by Soviet restorationists and their allies to bring reforms to a halt, perhaps even to reverse them, and that a severe clash of some sort was therefore inevitable. Without a set of presidential institutions that stood apart from, and therefore could not be captured by, the Supreme Soviet, Khasbulatov and Rutskoi might well have succeeded in bringing an end to any kind of Russian democracy, and perhaps the Russian Federation itself.

Perhaps Yeltsin's most serious mistake, and one that helped to ensure that the eventual confrontation would lead to bloodshed, was in underestimating his own support at large. His first and best chance to avoid the conflict lay in abolishing the Congress and calling new elections immediately after the 1991 Soviet collapse. He would have coasted to reelection, while most of the Congress would have been swept from office. Yeltsin realized this later: "I think that the most important missed opportunity of the post-putsch period was, naturally, the possibility of a radical change in the parliamentary system." Still, it may not have solved much, given the underlying problem of trust that even today works against responsible parliamentary behavior in Russia. Yeltsin showed some understanding of this when he defended his decision by admitting that "from time to time, the thought creeps in: was the society really ready to nominate other, 'good' deputies?"[108]

Whether the deputies elected after 1991 would have been any better is less the point than the fact that they could have claimed at least some legitimate foundation in society. Yeltsin knew, as did his opponents, that his was the more popularly legitimate post. The confrontation in late 1993 was, in his view, between "the president, elected by the people," and the various regional and national "soviets, made up from party lists. And not from the lists of the current parties, but from the lists of the single, invincible, mighty CPSU."[109] The First Republic legislature found itself serving a different society than the one that elected it, while facing a president who clearly enjoyed, at least in a relative sense, the trust of the electorate. This turned the White House not into a forum for representative politics but rather a trench from which the enemies of reforms, along with others whose political futures were now in doubt in a post-Soviet world, could carry on the fight to turn back the political clock. After the April referendum the use of force was probably inevitable, especially once the "acting president" and his coterie called on the Russian armed forces to commit mutiny.

The rise of the Russian First Republic owed much to the disintegration of the Soviet state; its fall owed much to the disarray in Soviet society. But even if the reasons for the collapse of parliament and the ascendancy of presidentialism are clear enough, the most vexing question still remains: why didn't the immediate post-1993 reorganization of the Russian state deteriorate into an authoritarian reversion? The answer lies in actions at both the top and bottom of Russian society. At the top, the executive branch showed tremendous restraint, and moved toward reestablishing representative institutions rather than repressing them. At the grassroots, the shock of the violence in Moscow closed once and for all any hope that some groups may have had of turning back the reforms; perhaps more important, the rapid return of elections and civil freedoms reassured ordinary citizens that they need not fear that each political crisis will be the *final* crisis, and suggested that their new democracy might be more robust than they realized.

By any reading of the arguments against presidentialism, this normalization of Russian politics after October 1993 was an unexpected outcome. Understanding this period of stabilization, and the role presidential power played in it, is central to understanding why the Second Republic continues to exist.

Chapter Four

The Unexpected Second Russian Republic

I will state frankly: Some people do not like the smooth working arrangements and the incipient stabilization in economics and politics. Some are inclined toward customary swaggering, rallies, kicking up a racket, and weeping and wailing . . . But for the most part, all this sludge is being submerged by profitable legislative work.

—*Duma Speaker Ivan Rybkin, 1994*

The Unexpected Second Republic

Born in violence, rushed into being during a referendum, populated by a strange and sometimes frightening cast of characters and dominated by a president who had already made plain his willingness to resort to violence, Russia's Second Republic should have been, by any reasonable expectation, an autocracy with a short half-life. The unexpected survival of the Second Republic and the gradual strengthening of the democratic institutions within it were the results of a shock to the Russian political system that ended any romantic notions either of a Soviet restoration or the immediate appearance of a smoothly arranged Western style parliamentary democracy. The realization that foes were not going to be vanquished in hours, that the government could not be captured in a day, and that the country could not be changed completely in a week forced all sides in Russia's political struggles, including the public, to approach the task of rebuilding the system with a more realistic attitude. As David Remnick later described it, after the smoke cleared in October 1993, "the hangover in Moscow was deadening . . . The relatively easy verities of the old political struggle—good versus bad, reformers versus reactionaries, democrats versus communists—dissolved in a bitter soup of uncertainty."[1]

But why, with the literal and figurative wreckage of the First Republic still smoldering, and after seeing the constitution suspended and the Supreme Soviet shelled by the nation's chief executive, would the Russians create an even *stronger* presidential system than existed in the First Republic? The answer lies not with the abuses of presidential power after 1991, but rather with the manifest failure of the parliament. At the moment of ultimate crisis, when the parliament was attempting to revive some of the very worst aspects of Soviet government (and in the very worst way, by calling for a mutiny among the armed forces), it was Russia's presidential institutions, and not its representative chamber, that acted to protect the citizen from some of the most dangerous remnants of the old regime in 1993. Moreover, the October events did not represent the beginning of unlimited presidential rule; the interregnum between the First and Second Republics was less than four months. The collapse of the Supreme Soviet and the failure of this early attempt at Russian parliamentarism ensured that both the public and the political elite would agree to maintain in the new constitution strong presidential safeguards against the unpredictability of Russia's mistrustful politics.

Since the establishment of the Second Republic in the December 1993 constitutional referendum, Russian democracy has been tested by events that would strain even a stronger or more stable state: a vicious civil struggle in Chechnya, the noise and pandemonium of presidential and parliamentary elections, and even by the nearly complete collapse of the Russian economy. Few would have predicted that the system created in 1993 would last a year; hardly anyone would have believed it would survive, as it has, to see the millennium. It is very much an unexpected regime, whose relative longevity can be traced directly to the way in which separated powers and presidential institutions have dampened, rather than inflamed, social conflict and mistrust.

The Constitution of 1993: Democracy by Consensus or Fiat?

Written constitutions, even when carefully drawn, can be ephemeral things; few, save for the American, have remained in force for any appreciable length of time, fewer still without severe changes. If anything of Russian democracy was to be salvaged in the wake of the collapse of the Union and then of the First Republic, establishing a meaningful and effective constitution would have to be first order of business, and this daunting task is still, in truth, unfinished.

By 1993, Russian experiences with constitutionalism were, to say the least, disheartening. The basic law that governed the Russian Soviet Federated Socialist Republic was a communist-era document, like its USSR counterpart more a statement of regime goals and achievements than actual law, and the constitution of the Russian Federation was little more than that same document amended beyond coherence. The 1993 Constitution would have to do better: it could not be a disposable document inflicted on the population by national leaders and their legal specialists, or Russian voters might decide once and for all that constitutionalism was as much a sham as Yeltsin's critics were claiming it to be. Yeltsin's choice—and here he was reflecting public opinion as well as his own preferences—was to hold a national referendum in December 1993 that would create a new basic law for the Russian state and at the same time bring into being a new national legislature that would have the legitimacy and standing to ratify it. The timing of the referendum, less than three months after the destruction of the parliament, would also serve to allay any fears that Yeltsin intended to govern through emergency powers indefinitely.

Unfortunately, this call for a new constitutional order now rang hollow because of the situation in which Yeltsin and his ministers found themselves after October 1993. Edict 1400 had affirmed all laws passed before September 21, 1993, but it had also suspended the Constitutional Court, dissolved lower level soviets, and called for voluntary disbanding of regional soviets, in effect placing the national, regional, and local governments in receivership until Yeltsin figured out what to do with them.[2] Some newspapers were temporarily closed and some extremist parties were banned, although most were allowed to return to politics in short order. With so much power now concentrated in the president's hands, Yeltsin's call for national reconciliation and for a new constitution in late 1993 seemed an almost absurd attempt to institute democracy by fiat.

But Yeltsin's efforts to create a new republic were aided by a paradoxical effect of the October violence. The task of gathering public support to establish a new order should have been hardest after the October attack: after all, the failure of the national government had ended both with violence in the capital and a great deal of disillusionment among ordinary Russians about their leaders. But the attack on the Supreme Soviet apparently lanced a wound in Russian political life by bringing the Soviet era to a decisive close, and public interest in politics actually *increased* after October 1993. To read the Russian media of the period, it would be easy to believe that political participation would hit rock bottom in 1993 and 1994; one Russian report, for example, worried that "political indifference" among Russians was reaching "a critical point."[3] But such reports mistook anecdotal expressions of anger and disgust as evidence of a complete alienation from politics. In time, public support for Yeltsin's October actions would evaporate, but in the immediate circumstances the voters, whatever their disgust with the condition of national politics, were determined to participate in national political life.

Despite these later misgivings about the October attack, many Russians (and, as usual, most urban Russians) in late 1993 thought that Yeltsin had broken the impasse and that the political situation would improve. Not only was there no evidence of smothering cynicism about the upcoming elections, there was actually a dramatic rise among Russians (some 20 percent since the October events) who believed that the elections would be free and fair. Moreover, the steepest increases in confidence about the fairness of the elections came not from Yeltsin's supporters but from his *opponents,* a surprising finding that suggested that even those who had no affinity for Yeltsin personally did not lay the events of 1993 completely at his door. Communist voters, for example, showed an increase of 42 percent over the course of the campaign who agreed that the elections were going to be free and fair, and the call for new elections mitigated at least some of the popular disenchantment about mass political organizations. Just before the elections, 16 percent of Russians (with 34 percent unsure) answered positively when asked if there were any movements or parties with whom they sympathized, a small absolute number but a relatively large increase from the miniscule single digit support registered as recently as 1990.[4] For some Russians, politics now "mattered" again; if nothing else, the October drama proved that there were now distinct and important differences between Russia's competing elites, and Russians were now paying closer attention to those differences.

This is not to say that Russians were being romantic about what was to come; while over 20 percent thought a new parliament would be better than the old one (only 5 percent thought it could be worse), a roughly equal number thought it would be "the same," and a plurality of 40 percent simply did not know what to expect.[5] But the belief that the next parliament would be better than the last one did not translate into a belief that "parliaments" themselves were capable of solving Russia's problems, and Russians continued to look to the presidency for leadership. Most doubted the ability of a parliament to "lead the country out of crisis," and polls taken a month before the elections showed that no more than 10 percent of Russians polled wanted to see the Congress of People's Deputies retained as an institution.[6]

The Congress of People's Deputies and the Supreme Soviet were discarded, of course, but just what *were* the Russians getting in the new Constitution?

Presidential and Parliamentary Institutions
of the Second Republic

The republic that was to be created in the proposed basic law was a feat of political genetic engineering, an amalgam of practices that could be described as a French executive presiding over a bicameral parliament whose upper and lower houses, respectively, consisted of an antique American Senate and a modern German Bundestag, populated in turn by regional Soviet bureaucrats and Israeli parties, and watched over by a uniquely Russian judiciary.

That is, the 1993 constitution envisioned an extraordinarily powerful president who, as in French practice, would appoint a prime minister and thus technically separate the functions of the head of state and the head of government. The lower house of parliament, the Duma, was a close replica of the German system, with half of the Duma's 450 seats reserved for members chosen from party lists (that is, seats doled out based on percentage of the popular vote) with the other half reserved for individual candidates from specific territorial districts. The proportional representation provisions ensured that parties, as in the Israeli system, would be clustered around two main poles, vaguely rightist and leftist, with smaller single-issue groupings able to shift their small pool of votes back and forth. The upper house, the Federation Council, would be much like its nineteenth century American counterpart (it is often referred to colloquially in Russian as a "senate") whose membership would be a symbol of the autonomy of Russia's federal regions. Each federal territory would send two members to the upper house; although these two senators were chosen by the people in 1993 and then indirectly sent after 1995 ex officio as the heads of the elected legislative and executive bodies in the regional governments, in practice they were likely to be members of the former regional Soviet elite or personal appointees of the president. The court system was a unique creation in which three separate national-level courts were comprised, including a Supreme Court specifically designed only to mediate constitutional issues.[7]

The Presidency

The presidency itself underwent little change, although Rutskoi's betrayal in 1993 ensured that there would no longer be a Russian *vice* president. (Presidential succession would now pass to the prime minister, who could ascend to the post as an "acting" president for only 90 days in order to organize a special presidential election.) The president would

serve a four-year term as the directly elected embodiment of the Russian nation itself, the guardian of national security and of the people's
rights. "I swear," the president's oath would now read,

> in fulfilling the full powers of the President of the Russian Federation, to re-
> spect and to protect the rights and freedoms of man and the citizen, to ob-
> serve and to defend the Constitution of the Russian Federation, to defend
> the sovereignty and independence, security and integrity of the state, and to
> serve the people loyally.

This lofty promise to remain subservient to universal human rights and constitutional norms was complimented, however, by Article 80, under which
the president would also be the "guarantor" of the constitution, a nebulous
formulation that unfortunately evoked Yeltsin's decision to break the 1993
political impasse by force. Daily administration of the nation's affairs would
fall not to the Russian president but to his cabinet, led by a prime minister
who would have to seek confirmation by the lower house of parliament.[8]

The chief instrument by which the daily orders of the president would
be carried out (and this was a matter of decree rather than of constitutional
law) would be the president's administration, a bureaucracy whose powers,
in practice, would end up waxing and waning depending on Yeltsin's
wishes at any given time. The head of the administration serves as a kind
of chief of staff, and although the prime minister is constitutionally the
head of the government, Yeltsin would often use his personal staff as a kind
of shadow administrative body. And although the cabinet theoretically has
the upper hand in matters of state, in ensuing years clashes and overlaps between the administration and the government—more severe but nonetheless similar in nature to those often seen between the American president's
White House staff and his cabinet—turned out to be inevitable.

Despite the strengthening of the cabinet, the ability of the president to
rule by decree remained: the president, as before, would be able in effect
to create law with the stroke of a pen. In light of the battles conducted
with presidential decrees that conflicted with parliamentary laws in the
First Republic, the most striking aspect of the 1993 Constitution in this
regard is that these decree powers continued to exist at all. But under the
new constitution, the parliament was given the right to rescind those decrees by vote, or to seek a determination of constitutionality from the
Supreme Court. The creation of a legal means to challenge or overturn
presidential decrees thus deprived the legislative branch of any argument
that its only options were to contravene or ignore such executive actions.

Defeating a presidential decree would now require active, public efforts by the parliament, rather than more indirect or passive options, and in the absence of such active measures, the parliament's silence would become the legal equivalent of assent.

This provision provoked a great deal of anxiety in Russian legislators at the time, and it remains among the most contentious and ambiguous problems in the constitution.[9] At best, the power of decree could be seen as something akin to an American president's ability to issue executive orders.[10] At worst, it is unfettered, nearly monarchical rule. But whatever the nebulous status of decrees, the power to issue them remained explicitly constitutional and there was no serious effort then or now to remove them. As in the short lived Soviet presidential system and then in the First Republic, the legislators and the public both chose to leave decree powers in place so that the president could take—indeed, could be forced to take—the difficult decisions that the parliament would rather avoid or upon which the public cannot reach a coherent consensus. Like the French constitution of 1958, the Russian Constitution of 1993 included "extensive" presidential powers that "serve to break legislative logjams," as part of a complex of legal instruments "designed to meet the needs of a deeply divided society."[11]

The election of the president is discussed in more detail in chapter 5. However, from the point of view of legislative-executive relations, it is important to bear in mind that the constitution made no provision for a "primary" system, but only for choosing the president by direct election. Electoral law, as in France, envisioned a two-stage process in which any number of candidates could fight to reach the two slots of a runoff election, and this in practice has increased the role played by parliamentary elections (and the parliament itself) in bringing presidential candidates and their platforms to public attention.[12]

The Legislature

Legislative powers, in contrast to their executive counterparts, underwent extensive revision, in a conscious effort to prevent the Second Republic from degenerating back into the First. Legislating in the First Republic, even when it was well-intentioned, was hopelessly complex, and the tangled powers of the legal system meant that even those laws that were passed were not necessarily enforced or even enforceable. Because actual legislation (as we saw in the last chapter) was such a difficult process, the executive, and specifically the president's government ministers, simply tried to administer national affairs by informal means ranging from executive decrees to the use of personal influence. Soviet and Russian legislators thus tried to control the political agenda by controlling cabinet formation, based on the reasonable assumption that ministers were more important than bills.[13] The realization that personnel trumped policy in turn led to repeated votes of no-confidence, the blocking of confirmation of senior appointees, efforts to remove one or another minister, and, worst of all, repeated calls to amend the constitution itself.

These efforts rarely succeeded, but they did manage to create severe legislative-executive conflict, constitutional confusion, and general political paralysis. As the pro-Yeltsin daily *Rossiiskie Vesti* would later write, "the supervisory functions of parliaments in world practice are an indispensable condition of steadfast constitutional order. But in Russia, as events from pretty recent history have shown, this condition can easily turn into its own opposite and become a factor destabilizing the situation and an instrument in the struggle for power."[14]

The new constitution accordingly contained provisions clearly aimed at frustrating any attempts by the parliament either to abuse its existing powers or to amend them at will. Articles 111 and 117 of the 1993 constitution cleverly linked legislative obstructionism with a great deal of risk to the legislature itself: two successive votes of no-confidence in the president's government (or three successive rejections of the president's choice of prime minister) in the lower house within 90 days would obligate the president either to sack the government or to disband the Duma. Obviously, the expectation was that the president would almost always choose the latter, and the intent of these articles was explicitly to ensure that no parliament would ever again be able to bring the entire government to a halt without legally endangering itself.[15]

Taken together, these articles were in essence a constitutional self-destruct mechanism, a kind of political booby trap, designed to deter the legislature from paralyzing the government or tampering with its own powers, and thereby to obviate any need for the president to resort to an extraconstitutional act like the hated Edict 1400. They not only helped to tilt the balance of power heavily toward the executive branch, they also indicated that the Russians had learned severe lessons about parliamentary misconduct from the First Republic. As will be seen, this aspect of the constitution did not turn out to be as powerful as Yeltsin or other advocates of a strong executive might have liked, nor did it mean that the government was as untouchable as some might have hoped. But the very existence of these articles meant that the new parliament, whatever its composition, would have to think very hard before seizing on the tactics used by its predecessor.

Aside from this unique constitutional tripwire, legislative process as envisioned in the 1993 constitution was typical of the cumbersome lawmaking found in other separated systems. The lower house would send bills by simple majority to the upper house, which in turn could either amend them and return them to the Duma, reject them outright, or pass them on to the president. A presidential veto would send the bill back down to the lower house, where a two-thirds majority would be required to override. This reflected an explicit understanding of the traditional role of a bicameral legislature in a federal, separated system: the lower house would propose legislation and act relatively quickly, and the upper house would be the more deliberative body, less beholden to popular passions and more protective of federal interests. The executive would have the final say on legislation unless opposed by a supermajority.

When it came to the problem of how actually to elect a legislature, however, Russian political engineers faced a dilemma. Obviously, creating a congress of single-member districts—the first-past-the-post system found in the United States and Britain that hands a seat to anyone who can muster a plurality—would help to squash the smaller and more extreme parties, and reward candidates who broadened their appeal. But if single-member districts are more effective at producing more moderate, consensus candidates, they also magnify the victory of the winner (much like a presidential election) and make it more likely that other interests and opinions go unrepresented. Given the amount of distrust and cynicism still present in Russia, any legislature that did not at least try to represent the spectrum of Russian political beliefs ran the immediate risk of being considered illegitimate by disaffected voters.

However, a proportional representation system, in which seats would be doled out in direct proportion to votes received, carried the potential for disaster. Proportional representation systems make sure that all voices, even the most extreme, are heard, and so tend to be more reflective of the society as a whole. Unfortunately, they also tend (as any Italian or Israeli can attest) to be highly unstable, built on shifting coalitions in which the defection of a few of even the smallest parties can collapse an entire government. Even now many Russians seem to recognize that a proportional system would have been an invitation to chaos. "Imagine a government formed by the State Duma," Vladimir Tumanov of the Constitutional Court would later write, "in which no faction possesses a majority sufficient for the formation of a government . . . it would have been just as unstable as, for example, in Italy and other countries where coalitions fall apart just as quickly as they are created."[16] Only the forces most opposed to Yeltsin hoped for a proportional representation system, out of a calculating recognition that only such a system could concentrate their diffuse national support and translate it into tangible votes in the parliament.[17]

The answer was to split the difference and to adopt the German model, in which half the seats of the lower chamber would go to representatives of single-member territorial districts, and the other half to members of party lists and apportioned according to the percentage of the overall vote gained. To ensure that the smallest parties would not be a disruption in the Duma, subsequent Russian electoral regulations required that any party must reach a threshold of at least 5 percent of the national vote to win a seat in this latter half of the chamber. This division of the chamber not only represented a compromise between efficiency and representativeness, it also raised the possibility that it could deprive some of the extremist parties of candidates. (After all, who wants to run a hard campaign only to be denied a seat when the "5 percent rule" was invoked?) However, it also meant that a large share of the Duma would be politically unaffiliated and therefore somewhat unpredictable, since candidates with strong ties to their home regions would sensibly choose to seek an individual seat and eschew parties entirely. In any case, because of the precarious nature of this experiment in legislative reform, the first post-Soviet Duma would be elected only to a two-year term (and thus would have to leave office before Yeltsin), while later parliaments would sit for four years.

This, then, was the basic system presented to the Russian voter in December 1993. All in all, the 1993 constitution was an impressive, if somewhat verbose, document that made obvious efforts to pick and choose among practices in other stable democracies. Although the document itself is quite large, the basic structure of government envisioned within it was fairly straightforward, and seemed to be understood by most of the voters.

The other nuances of the constitution, however, were lost on most Russians, who were not familiar with its particular details for the simple reason that they had not read it. Polls just before the referendum registered consistent support (52 percent overall, and higher in the cities) for a new constitution, even as other polls showed that no more than perhaps a quarter of the electorate had actually read the draft to be voted on.[18] Still, although the relative confidence in the upcoming elections was a heartening sign that the Russians were not abandoning politics, there were also disturbing aspects of public opinion in this period as well. Perhaps most alarming was that a majority of Russians were in favor of change but seemed to care little about the details, which supports claims made at the time that what Russians wanted above all was order and cared little for how it was created.[19] But a simple craving for order would not explain the increased interest in parties and movements. The voters apparently were turning to the candidates' explanations of their support for, or opposition to, the constitution to get their information about the proposed basic law; they were, in effect, educating themselves via the electoral debate itself.[20] This represented a search for information that transcended merely negative goals of preserving stability.

Even if most Russians had not read every word of the new constitution, they were familiar with its outline. They knew that it would maintain a strong presidency, and it is encouraging to note that their support of a strong executive did not mean unconditional approval of Yeltsin (a plurality of 38 percent objected to extending his term), nor did it undermine a concurrent belief, held by almost half of the electorate, that multipartism was in itself a positive development in national politics.[21] In other words, despite the small number of people who had read the new basic law in detail, Russians were making a thoughtful distinction between institutions and incumbents, and they were rejecting any conception of executive power and legislative representation as mutually exclusive. Thus the new constitution was not merely a ratification of Yeltsin personally, nor did it pick up a "halo effect" from its association with the president.[22] Most Russians, in fact, wanted early presidential elections, and many were explicit that their vote in December for the parliament would not depend on the candidate's orientation toward the president or even previous membership in the disgraced Supreme Soviet.[23]

The voters, wary of each other, disgusted with their leaders, and angry at the ongoing pain of economic transition, were splitting the difference among several options: they wanted to register their protest; they wanted a multitude of parties through which they could express themselves politically; and they wanted a presidential system that would somehow keep order in the middle of it all. As the results of the 1993 elections would show, Russians were capable of strategic voting, choosing both to support Yeltsin's new constitution, thus protecting themselves from the excesses of parliamentarism, while sending some of his worst enemies to the legislature it created, thus keeping an eye on the man in whom they had vested so much power.

The Empire Strikes Back:
The December 1993 Elections and the Last "Soviet" Voters

In December 1993, Russian voters once again surprised political analysts and turned out a majority for elections and a constitutional referendum.

The outcome indicated that the Russians were, in turn, strongly in favor of presidentialism while angry with the current president, and deeply suspicious of parties and parliamentarism while generally supportive of their own individual legislators. It was, in other words, exactly the outcome to be expected in a mistrustful society: a victory both for the institution that could prevent any single party from taking over the government, and for the parties that would be the avowed watchdogs and opponents of that institution.

Yeltsin, in theory, stayed above the partisan fray by refusing to identify with a particular party, but voters understood that Russia's Choice, led by former prime minister Egor Gaidar, was the president's choice (if not, in the end, Russia's). The opposition parties could fairly be said to have included almost anyone who was not part of Russia's Choice: democratic or reformist groups who objected to the sluggishness and corruption of the reform process, centrists who objected to the speed and disarray of the reforms, and the far right and far left who objected to the reforms themselves. From Grigorii Yavlinsky's liberal Yabloko bloc (named, in a pun on the Russian word for "apple," after the initials of three of its founders) to the industrialists of the Civic Union, to the Soviet nostalgists of the Communist Party of the Russian Federation (CPRF), all the way across to the bizarre ultranationalist amalgam that was Vladimir Zhirinovsky's Liberal Democractic Party of Russia (LDPR), all were, to a greater or lesser extent, in opposition to Yeltsin. A total of 13 parties passed muster with the Central Election Commission, and there would have been even more in the "opposition" had nearly two dozen smaller parties not been disqualified because of the inability to harvest enough signatures. (Many candidates from these parties went on to run for individual seats.)

While all parties and candidates had been caught flat-footed by Yeltsin's sudden call for elections, those most poorly organized and most complacent would suffer a surprising setback, while less democratic but more effectively led groups would provide the first serious political shock to the Second Republic.

That shock set in the morning after the election, when it was confirmed that the single largest percentage of the vote, a plurality of 23 percent, had gone to Zhirinovsky's Liberal Democrats, giving him the largest bloc of the party-list seats in the Duma. Considering what the LDPR stood for, it was a disturbing result: the party program was little more than a flatly phrased fascism that reflected the xenophobic and imperial tendencies of the party's founder.[24] Zhirinovsky had run the ugliest of campaigns, laced with racism, threats of violence, and diffuse anger and resentment. And although it was incoherent, it was also, in its way, cunning. Zhirinovsky called for the restoration of the Soviet Union, of the Russian Empire, of the empire within Soviet borders, of the empire beyond its borders (including Alaska), of revenge against traitors in the Kremlin, against intrigues in Washington and Bonn; in short, he lashed out in virtually all directions at various points in his various campaigns.

What was most startling, however, is that Zhirinovsky's votes could not be explained away as the angry voices of the poorest or the dispossessed. Exit polls found that the "backbone of the LDPR electorate consists of the active, able-bodied section of the population," whose "dissatisfaction with the reforms is most likely caused not by the deterioration of its own material base but by the growth of disorder and anarchy."[25] The LDPR had emerged as the new "Soviet" party among middle- and lower-middle class voters:

> LDPR electors stand apart from the others in their irritation and anxiety. Their misgivings primarily relate to Russia's losing its great power status, which was enjoyed by the USSR, and the weakness of state authority in the country . . . [I]dentification with the "Soviet people" is very essential for Zhirinovsky followers. All this suggests that the LDPR is recruiting its allies from among the Soviet working class, in contrast to the Communists, whose [voters] have moved out of the working class by virtue of their age.[26]

In other words, voters who most strongly identified themselves as "Soviets" tended to vote LDPR, while many older and somewhat poorer voters returned to the communists. And in a frightening turn, Russian soldiers—furious at having been caught between the warring factions in Moscow and still stung from the collapse of the USSR—gave most of their votes to the LDPR, with the communists a close second. (It helped that the LDPR fielded the largest single contingent of active-duty military candidates.)[27] The Soviet Empire was gone, but in December 1993, the last of its loyal citizens struck a blow against the men who had brought it down.

A Divided Duma

The December 1993 elections produced a divided Duma, revealing a broad bipolarity in Russian voting. The electorate was roughly divided equally between parties that opposed liberalization and reform and parties that supported more progressive policies, but within those broad groupings there were schisms as well. Russia's Choice, the apparent "party of power" and the one most closely associated with Yeltsin, barely edged out the CPRF (15.5 percent to 12.4 percent) for second place behind the LDPR, although even this small moral victory was diluted by the realization that the Agrarian Party, the closest ally of the communists, had managed to take fourth place with 8 percent, coming in only slightly ahead of Yabloko. This result meant that nearly half the total vote had gone to the groups that were the most opposed to Yeltsin; while it was by no means clear that these groups could forge an effective alliance (except for a shared nostalgia for the USSR and a hatred of Yeltsin, the LDPR and the CPRF were not exactly natural allies) it was also by no means evident that the reformers were going to be able to unite against them, either.

The reform parties could take at least some consolation from the results in the territorial districts, where the moderating influence of the winner-take-all system was evident. Although Russia's Choice was unexpectedly trounced in the national vote, it managed to win 30 districts, more than any other party, and enough to make it, formally, the single largest faction overall in the Duma. The LDPR, by contrast, was able to turn a disparate national protest vote into 59 party-list seats, but when forced to go head-to-head against other candidates for individual district seats could only turn up five victories.[28] These district results suggested that voters were inclined to be more forgiving of local candidates than of Gaidar or the government generally (and also that Zhirinovsky's coattails were fairly short).[29] They also reflected both the personalized nature of these single-seat contests as well as the ongoing distrust of organized parties: when the 1993 Duma was seated, the single largest group of 141 deputies was composed of unaffiliated members from the territorial districts, who (because they came from a single *"mandat"* or electoral district) colloquially came to be known as the *odnomandatniki*.

The overall effect of the distribution of seats in this first post-Soviet Duma was to create something of a standoff, with neither the opposition nor the reformers able to control the parliament outright. Out of 450 seats, the two polar opposite parties, Russia's Choice and the LDPR, controlled a total of 70 and 64, respectively; the communists and their Agrarian Party allies (who together had taken almost as much of the popular vote as the LDPR) ended up with 81. Only four other parties managed to clear the 5 percent threshold: Yabloko and Women of Russia each held 23 seats, former Yeltsin aide Sergei Shakhrai and his Party of Russian Unity and Accord (PRUA) took 19, and Nikolai Travkin's Democratic Party of Russia held 15. Of these, Yabloko was proreform but opposed to Yeltsin personally as an autocrat, while the PRUA and the Democratic Party were generally supportive of the government but oriented to more cautious reform. Women of Russia, however, was a less a party than a hodgepodge of candidates that ran on a variety of women's issues (and these were not necessarily "feminist" in any Western sense), and would prove to be willing to ally with parties of both the right and left at various times. The net effect was that it was nearly impossible to form stable or lasting coalitions, especially when so many legislators had won their seats independent of any party or movement.[30]

Thus, although the 1993 Duma had not resulted in the sort of clear victory for propresidential forces that Yeltsin had hoped for, the initial numbers seemed to guarantee that the major parties of reform would be able to cobble together enough seats to act as a rough plurality, in theory, against any serious threat to the constitution by the parties of conservatism or reaction.[31] This was complimented by the composition of the upper house, the Federation Council. Because it was drawn from representatives of the regions, its main agenda was a practical one of regional autonomy and its members were, if not allied with Yeltsin, certainly more inclined toward cooperation with him than their more fiery colleagues in the lower house. As *Izvestiia* noted with some relief when the legislature opened in January 1994, the Federation Council would be able to "bring the Duma legislators to their senses as necessary."[32] (When the law on electing the council was amended to draw its membership from local executive and legislative leaders, some opposition legislators would come to describe the upper house disparagingly as a "Soviet of Governors" who exist only to do Yeltsin's bidding in blocking the Duma.)[33]

There was also some good news for the constitution itself: it was ratified by over 58 percent of those voting (although that represented slightly less than a third of eligible voters).[34] But the day after what could finally be described as the first elections in the post-Soviet period, Yeltsin and his supporters—like many Western observers—wondered: what went wrong?

Much of the blame had to rest with organizational and personal factors among the reformers. Most of the parties that ran in 1993, whatever their orientation, were ad hoc contraptions, amalgamations of loosely bound interests that would weaken after the 1993 elections and in some cases completely vanish after the 1995 elections. The democrats, always among the least organized factions in Russian political life, failed to unite either into a column of support for the president or a center of radical reformist opposition, instead making the classic mistake of splitting their own vote in the face of a more organized opposition. In part, this was due to an elitist belief held by so many reformers (who tended to be clustered in urban areas) that no Russian could seriously vote for a hideous character like Zhirinovsky or respond to the Soviet nostalgia of the CPRF and that, therefore, the real opponents were not the enemies of reform but the candidates most like themselves. Indeed, in some cases, Russia's Choice candidates were so disorganized and overconfident that they actually ran against *each other.*[35] The lack of a common program or any kind of stable organization among the progressive forces could only play to the advantage of the more disciplined communists or the intensely motivated and driven Zhirinovsky voters.

Also working against the democrats was the fact that the incoherence of parties meant that the elections took on a personal tone. The party system in Russia, such that it was in 1993, tended to be (and to some extent, remains) a "star" system, often pitting individuals rather than platforms against each other. As a commentary in *Komsomol'skaia Pravda* pointed out, this was because for years "it was simpler and safer to rob the State Bank than to set up a party even as a joke." As a result, parties became vehicles for daring or entrepreneurial personalities rather than real political associations: "What is needed to set up a new party? An idea? Like minded people? Anywhere else, but not in our country. Here the chief thing is a popular or influential figure (which are by no means one and the same). The number of figures equals the number of parties."[36] In such an atmosphere, there could be no contest between a fiery and effective public speaker like Zhirinovsky, and the wooden Gaidar, who (in Remnick's apt words) "campaigned as if he were running for head of the math department."[37]

Bad for the Democrats, Good for Democracy?

Although the outcome of the 1993 elections was disheartening in the short term, the elections themselves were a significant step forward in stabilizing Russian politics. Like the presidential elections that would follow them, they were important if only because they took place at all and were accepted as legitimate. This was a feat in itself, as a group of British analysts later noted:

Clearly, acceptance by all sections of the society of the legitimacy of a particular set of "rules of the game" for choosing leaders is an important element in democratic consolidation, and in this respect the elections [of 1993] represent an encouraging development . . . While therefore the elections might not have been good for the "democrats," in many respects they can be seen as having been good for democracy.[38]

The elections were not a defeat for democracy but rather an expression of democracy, whose results "point[ed] not to a defeat of democratic values but to a shift in the public's emphasis: away from exclusive concern with economic revival and toward spiritual and national recuperation."[39] Moreover, the stunning LDPR victory proved, in the most unsettling way possible, that the elections had not been rigged and that the voters were not merely reflexive supporters of the president. If that had been the case, Russia's Choice should have been the clear winner, since it represented, in the words of one group of analysts, "the premier party of power in the 1993 elections," one that "enjoyed every material advantage in that contest," including money, television time, and a lax official attitude toward its tendency to play fast and loose with election rules. None of this prevented Russia's Choice from being "routed nationally by a stronger symbology marshaled by Zhirinovsky."[40]

One thing was indisputable after December 1993: the voters were willing to try to live with the new system, preferring Yeltsin and the new order over the leaders and institutions of the First Republic. In this sense, the elections and the ratification of the constitution represented a victory for presidentialism, if not for the president. While Yeltsin's supporters might have looked on the 1993 elections with concern, public participation in them meant that the Russians had given Yeltsin himself a kind of dispensation for the events that began with the tanks of 1991 and ended with the tanks of 1993. Certainly, Yeltsin had fared better in the public imagination than the former Supreme Soviet, for whom all was decidedly not forgiven. By a large margin, Russians disapproved of the new Duma's decision to declare amnesty and to set free the leaders of the 1993 parliamentary revolt: when given a choice between the Supreme Soviet rebels and the Committee of Eight, a greater number of Russians were in favor of punishing Rutskoi and Khasbulatov (and punishing them more harshly), rather than the 1991 "putschists" no matter what sanction was suggested, even the death penalty.[41] The birth of the Second Republic had been a violent, squalid affair, and in its first days it seemed that it might accomplish little more than its predecessor. But it was, in the eyes of the voters, the best that could be done at the time.

The new constitution had been adopted and a new parliamentary body had been elected. The question remained whether the people and their leaders had chosen wisely, whether the new institutions of the Second Republic would actually work.

Learning by Doing in the Second Republic

The legislature that convened in the winter of 1994 was Russia's first Federal Assembly. The lower house, however, was the "Fifth" Duma, a numbering that spoke of a link to its four ill-fated predecessors in Russian imperial history. But it was, for all intents and purposes, Russia's first truly independent legislature, governing neither under the heavy hand of the Tsar nor the watchful eye of the Soviet Communist Party. It was the first to be able to claim—for better or worse—that it truly represented the views and interests of a free electorate. The 1993 elections themselves were a success if only because they managed to take place fairly and have their results accepted by virtually all participants. But did they produce a government capable of governing?

The answer, as will be seen, is mixed. The president, as before, remained an inconstant and flawed politician, a man better suited, by his own admission, to overcoming crises than to the mundane business of daily governance. And as for the legislature, it is an understatement to say that the behavior of the first modern Duma will not go down in the annals of politics as a model of legislative activity. At the end of the Duma's first year of activity, Speaker Ivan Rybkin would be asked what he thought about one legislator proposing that another be tested for the AIDS virus because "who knows what she might bring back from abroad." Rybkin used a reply that he would come to repeat often during his term presiding over the unruly parliament: "I think what a good thing it is that our deputies are not skilled in the oriental martial arts."[42]

Despite the fireworks and foolishness in the Duma, over time both president and parliament seemed to "learn by doing," and in 1994 and 1995 managed not only to coexist but even to conduct the people's business is a manner that was, by comparison to the First Republic of 1991–1993, relatively orderly. The problems of social trust that plagued Russian politics had not been solved, but they had apparently been mitigated and the damage contained. Six months into Second Republic, two Russian analysts wrote in *Nezavisimaia Gazeta* that "the epoch of political battles has quietly turned to a phase of routine, of work that is often bureaucratic, draft-legislative, and administrative."[43] It was a remarkable testimony to a system that had been put into place even as the detritus of

October, the last shards of glass and chunks of burned concrete, were being cleared from the streets.

Although the new institutions created in 1993 served to help stabilize the situation after 1994, they could not in themselves have imposed order on Russian political life had there been truly dedicated attempts to subvert them, and it is important to note the roads not taken in the first few years of the Second Republic. The restraint showed by all parties concerned is particularly noteworthy given the fact that both the president and the parliament had the means to destabilize the delicate arrangements that followed the constitutional referendum. The president, for example, had set about creating a "Public Chamber," a kind of quasi-official social forum that resembled nothing so much as a parliament in waiting should Yeltsin decide to disband the one elected by the people. The parliament was not without its own weapons; although hamstrung in its ability to dissolve the government, it could push through symbolic votes of no-confidence or even question Yeltsin's right to remain president by impeaching him. As we will see, no-confidence votes and impeachment hearings would eventually take place, but these would not, over the next five years, amount to serious challenges to the structure of the republic or the role of the president or parliament in it.

More to the point, they did not take place as immediate challenges to the outcome of the 1993 referendum. For the moment, both sides accepted the legitimacy of the institutions of the Second Republic, and both stepped away from actions that might be interpreted as threatening or destabilizing. "The fact that with the removal of the Soviets from the political scene [after 1993], Yeltsin did not make threatening gestures toward the representative organs of power," wrote one Russian political observer, "is very important. Yeltsin seems to have stood the test of power this time."[44] The Public Chamber eventually faded into a talking shop rather than a shadow parliament, and finally, in Rybkin's words, "collapsed under its own weight" of over six hundred members.[45] Moreover, Yeltsin seemed more ready to accept the reality that political life would now be characterized by the occasional stinging loss (such as the Duma's amnesty of the Supreme Soviet ringleaders, a move he bitterly opposed).

The Duma deserved a certain amount of credit as well, not least for managing to deprive Zhirinovsky or others like him of any significant role in the leadership. The speakership went to Rybkin, a moderate and relatively cooperative member of the Agrarian Party who would later form his own party and support Yeltsin for president in 1996. The fact of the matter was that the nature of the opposition to Yeltsin changed: there was a recognition among even the most implacable foes of the regime that there was to be no return to the USSR, no creation of a parliamentary system, and no spontaneous popular uprising against Yeltsin or his regime. For many legislators, the time had come to work within the system, however distasteful that might be.[46] No longer would the president's rivals seek to remove him by eviscerating the office of the presidency itself. Instead, they would try, from within the confines of the system, to win the office and thus wrest it away from Yeltsin by fighting him for it in the court of public opinion. In other words, they would continue their struggle by legal, even democratic, means.

Renegotiating the Rules of Combat

The new constitution created incentives for Russian politicians to avoid using the machinery of government to try to vanquish foes from public life, but there was nothing in the structure of the Second Republic that could force the conduct of politics to be more civil or less threatening. For this, Russia's elites would have to come to some kind of new understanding about the acceptable parameters of public conflict. This renegotiation of the rules of political engagement was badly needed in a nation that had been taught by the Soviets for seven decades that political life was little more than warfare with no quarter given or asked. One of the most intriguing developments in this regard, and one that bore directly on the issue of social trust, was the 1994 signing of the Treaty on Social Accord, an act that represented a conscious attempt by Russia's elites to bring some measure of stability and trust back into daily political life. Although the treaty itself faded from Russian political life within a few years (in part, because it was no longer needed), its very signing was a symbol of the agreement among Russia's mistrustful elites that neither they nor the public could any longer afford, as Rybkin would later put it, "to approach elections every time as though they were a major feat, an all-hands-to-the-pumps job, or a 'final and decisive battle.'"[47]

The treaty itself was a simple enough matter. As Yeltsin himself put it at the early 1994 signing ceremony: "In signing the Treaty, we affirm that in Russian politics *only peaceful, only constitutional methods* are allowed. This is the basis of the accord, the basis of the normal work of the state, the basis of a peaceful life for the people."[48] [emphasis original] This was wishful thinking so soon after the violence of the previous October but, remarkably, representatives of most of the major political forces in Russia (even Zhirinovsky) eventually signed the document. In June, Yeltsin decreed the creation of a commission dedicated to the observation and fulfillment of the treaty, headed by his own chief administrator, Sergei Filatov. The commission would, in theory, provide an alternate arena for muting or mediating political conflict, and clarify rules of acceptable political behavior. If Filatov's account is accurate, representatives of the various signatories did, in fact, contact the commission during 1994 and 1995 with exactly such questions.[49]

For most of 1994, the treaty, as two Russian journalists put it, was "a kind of political barometer of the condition of our society. The political actors who have signed the pact have so far more or less met its conditions (or at least have not made any serious complaints against each other)."[50] This was premature, but so were the proclamations by other Russian pundits declaring the treaty dead shortly thereafter. Of course, in the wake of occasional spectacles like the nationally televised brawl in which a deputy ripped the cross from the chest of a priest and Zhirinovsky himself sucker-punched a middle-aged woman on the floor of the Duma, it was hard to argue that it was having a deep or lasting impact on politics.[51] Despite the several obituaries written for the treaty and what it represented, the basic concept of eschewing extremism and resolving disputes through the machinery of government, and especially through elections, seemed to take hold, perhaps if only because Russians and their leaders were simply exhausted. The Duma and the president left each other in place, and a broad public presumption quickly formed that the current Duma would serve out its abbreviated two-year term and that the follow-on elections of 1995 would actually take place. "Our main accomplishment," a Yeltsin aide said in late 1994, "is that civic peace has become a real fact of our life, reflecting a radical change in the general political climate in the country. Even those parties and groups that refused to sign the agreement have been actually adhering to the same rules of the game, forced to do so by the overall political climate."[52]

All in all, despite Zhirinovsky's flying fists or Rybkin's hopes that legislators not learn karate, it seemed that the events of 1994 were cause for optimism. Uncertain days lay ahead: the new Duma, for all the fanfare about its arrival, was a temporary one, and this clearly contributed to some early electioneering and political jockeying. Another Duma would come in 1995, and presidential elections would take place a year after that. And yet, despite a looming cycle of elections so soon after the turbulence of the last months of 1993, Russian sociologists at the end of the first year of the Second Republic found the population of the Federation to be more at ease than anyone might have suspected:

> We have heard so much about the all-out despair, fear, and bitterness that
> has gripped people that we are ready to reduce the public atmosphere to

feelings of violence and fright. The survey results, however, do not present such a picture . . . In 1994 we see a much "calmer" distribution of emotions than one might expect . . . The experience of 1993 apparently looked much more threatening [than it was].

"People do not see their own future through rose-colored glasses," they added "but they do view it in much calmer tones."[53]

Other observers took issue with this interpretation, arguing instead that people had just given up on the system and now sought only a "live and let live" attitude from the government. But even this pessimistic analysis failed to note the stabilizing trend found in its own results: not only did people believe that Russian elites were more inclined to "manage" their political disputes among themselves, but "the [political] orientations which continue to predominate in the mass consciousness are neither the right-ist nor leftist ones, but rather, insufficiently defined centrist ones which are attracting more than 50 percent of Russia's citizens."[54] This movement away from extremists was congruent with a longer term study of Russian social attitudes between 1989 and 1994 that found Russians had become more tolerant of "deviant" groups in society, and more willing than ever before to describe even themselves and others in Russian society with terms like "open," "unpretentious," "hospitable," and "patient."[55]

Russians, it seems, have been learning since 1994 to live with each other, with the twin trends of the normalization of politics and the lessening of social tension reinforcing each other. There was no spectacular collapse of the subsequent 1995 elections—although in truth, people feared an electoral collapse more during the presidential campaign to follow—and the Sixth Duma replaced the Fifth peacefully, an achievement in itself considering that it was dominated even more strongly by some of Yeltsin's worst enemies. The successful execution of this second Duma campaign was perhaps even more important than the first. "The fact that Russian voters were able to participate in a free and fair election in December 1995, to elect a parliament with the workings of which they were roughly familiar," Robert Cottrell rightly noted later, "marked a further entrenchment of democratic methods and democratic institutions in Russian political life."[56]

The Sixth Duma: Coming Up for Air

If the Second Republic itself was an unexpected development after the destruction of the Supreme Soviet, the success of yet another round of elections to the State Duma was in some sense an even bigger surprise. "The

Russians were taught democracy the way that little boys are taught to swim," one Russian daily wrote after the 1995 balloting:

> But it seems that after being thrown into a new element by an authoritarian hand we did come to the surface. The political life of Russia has ceased to remind one of a theater of military operations. Now it is more like an ordinary theater with a great many actors, intrigues, and nearly civilized means of resolving them. . . . The elections themselves will civilize the "wild" multiparty system. [57]

Still, before the election, Yeltsin's critics might well have wondered whether the president would tolerate an election that was so clearly going to damage his own political interests. Everything from the war in Chechnya to rampant crime in the streets had undermined Yeltsin's public standing, and even those who were supportive of the president's policies found themselves mortified by Yeltsin's drunken escapades abroad. More disturbing were signs of internal changes within the broadly bipolar structure of Russian political debate: the balance of power among reformers and the opposition would shift, and although the president would gain new allies to replace those who had fallen away, he would also find himself facing not the clownish Zhirinovsky or his increasingly irrelevant LDPR, but a fit and ready organization Yeltsin had fought before: the Communist Party of the Russian Federation.

The details of the campaign for the Sixth Duma need not detain us long here, but there are three important points to consider before moving on to further discussion of the sources of stability in the post-1993 period. First, it is axiomatic that a second round of elections in a new democracy is in many ways more important than the first, especially if those elections demonstrate that the ruling authorities are willing to accept and to abide by unpleasant or unexpected outcomes. Second, although the basic structure of Russian political antagonisms did not change, the 1995 elections showed that Russian voters still cared about politics; they had watched the behavior of legislators in the 1993–1995 Duma and made judgments about who could best represent their basic beliefs, subsequently rewarding or punishing various movements. Finally, because the elections took place in the shadow of an upcoming presidential elections, they were in a way a reassurance that elections themselves need not be cataclysmic events, and that parties and leaders could replace each other, at least on occasion, to the fanfare of orchestras rather than the clatter of assault rifles.

The most striking characteristic of the Sixth Duma was the collapse of the supposed "party of power," Russia's Choice, and the slashing of support for Zhirinovsky's LDPR. Without party discipline, Russia's Choice and its putative "allies" among the other reform groups could do little more than obstruct, rather than pass, legislation. Without personal discipline on Zhirinovsky's part, it was impossible for the LDPR to shed its image as a vehicle for a party leader who, even in a nation of eccentric politicians, seemed little better than a violent buffoon. These parties, led by relative political amateurs, were displaced by two more forceful and better organized entities, Gennady Zyuganov's Communist Party of the Russian Federation (which had already taken the role of shadow government from the LDPR) and Prime Minister Viktor Chernomyrdin's Our Home Is Russia (or NDR, *nash dom—Rossiia*). This was not surprising: the parliamentary elections foreshadowed the presidential election, in which voters would be forced to choose between two stark alternatives, and so most Russians chose a party representing either the president's supporters or his most credible opponents. As the communists themselves argued, "the chief question" of the 1995 elections would be "whom to believe, whom to trust with your future, your family's future, your nation."[58]

The final results produced a Sixth Duma that, when viewed in terms of general groupings of reform and reaction, looked remarkably like the Fifth. The CPRF increased its share of the vote from 12 percent to 22 percent, while the LDPR dropped from nearly 23 percent in 1993 to barely over 11 percent in 1995.[59] Russia's Choice, which had won 16 percent of the vote in 1993, essentially vanished and was replaced by the more conservative (but still pro-Yeltsin) NDR, which took slightly more than 10 percent of the vote. Yabloko lost about a point of support, dropping to just under 7 percent. Women of Russia, the Party of Russian Unity and Accord, and the Democratic Party of Russia all fell below the 5 percent threshold. Many other parties from the 1993–1995 period just disappeared; the Agrarian Party also fell below the 5 percent bar, but they had plainly (and wisely) thrown their lot in with the CPRF anyway. The communists ended up with 149 seats, more than NDR's 65 and Yabloko's 45 seats combined. The Liberal Democrats held onto 51, and the rest went to the nominally uncommitted *odnomandatniki*. Thus, although the party labels changed, the essential structural tensions between the two poles of Russian politics remained. Although a reformist majority was still out of reach, the propresidential daily *Rossiiskie Vesti* (after lamenting the "amorphousness" and disorganization of the democrats), rightly noted that once again liberal parties could, with minimal cooperation, at least "delay the adoption of the most odious questions" by denying extremist legislation a veto-proof majority.[60]

Between 1993 and 1998, the Second Republic managed not only to defy expectations of collapse but actually to engage in the prosaic business of producing legislation, passing budgets, and making policy. While not an elegant system of government—and the history of this early period will forever be tarred by the disastrous events in Chechnya—it survives and functions, and not merely by decrees and edicts emanating from a supremely powerful Kremlin. An analysis of the 1994–1997 period found:

> Contrary to popular impressions and some academic accounts of "Yeltsin's Constitution," the list of issues for which policy requires a federal or constitutional law is fairly long and includes many important areas related to market and political reform. Consequently, to the degree that he prefers a legislative outcome in these realms to the status quo ante, President Yeltsin has an incentive to compromise with the parliament to get legislation in place.

These incentives produced results: in a system that its critics still deride as so "superpresidential" that Yeltsin supposedly rules as a modern Tsar, "more than 600 laws were enacted through regular parliamentary processes" in this period, "more than enough . . . to conclude that policy has been made by more than presidential decree alone."[61]

How was this stability achieved in a presidential republic, under a chief executive with a record of violence and populated by deeply irreconcilable, even extreme, political parties? The answer lies in the nature of the institutions of the Russian separated system of government.

Institutions and Trust in the Second Republic

In part, the stability of the Second Republic after 1994 can be explained by the unwillingness of either the elites or the average citizen to endure the traumas of the First Republic again, and the efforts of all parties to reassure each other and the public that they would confine political combat to constitutional and civilized means contributed greatly to this end. But the success of the Second Republic also represented the success of a presidential system of government, and as such illustrates the ways that separated systems of power can manage and mitigate social conflict. Two aspects of separated systems in particular bear directly on legislative-executive relations in Russia after 1994: the fixed term of office and the difficulty of legislating. Both of these are normally pointed to by critics of presidentialism as hindrances to democratic consolidation, but in Russia they proved to be essential in staving off the kind of chaos and instability that could have led to authoritarian rule.

Legislating vs. Campaigning:
The Discipline of the Fixed Term

If the Russian Constitution of 1993 made it difficult for the Duma to collapse the government, it made it nearly impossible to impeach the president. Likewise, it deprived the president of the ability to dissolve parliament unless the legislators themselves tripped the provisions in the constitution that allowed him to do so. Despite the existence of formally "semipresidential" arrangements (such as the separate executive power vested in the prime minister), in practice the terms of both president and parliament are for all intents and purposes fixed as strongly as in the United States, France, or other "strong" presidential systems.

This virtual inability to circumvent the fixed term in all but the most extreme circumstances has proved valuable because it thwarts the ability of antisystem parties—groups that reject the basic structures of Russian democracy—to collapse the government and thereby force endless rounds of electoral combat, or even merely to choke the legislative process by constantly invoking the threat of a no-confidence vote. Since the constitution allows neither the automatic formation of a government by the parliamentary majority nor the easy calling of new elections, little can be gained from simple obstruction. "The point," a Yeltsin aide said in 1995, "is to avoid [the tactic of] continual 'voting' [*votirovanie*]—raising [repeatedly] the parliamentary question of confidence in the government, and blocking draft laws submitted by the executive branch."[62]

The inability either to remove the president or to reconstitute the government at will was a specific response to the behavior of the Supreme Soviet in the First Republic, which tried to win battles about policy by attempting to remove various members of the executive branch, including the president and prime minister. As a Russian legal scholar pointed out in 1996, Russia's is an imperfect democracy in which "antidemocratic forces" (ultranationalists and radical communists, for example) can "operate legally (or more precisely, despite an abstract constitutional prohibition); these groups reject the liberal foundations of a constitutional structure and *intentionally use democratic procedures for their destruction.*"[emphasis added][63] Although such factions represent only a minority, it is a dedicated and dangerous minority, and their leaders are doing exactly what their voters want them to do.[64] Russian pollsters have found that the small number of citizens who want to see the "firm hand" of authoritarian rule imposed as the result of "the victory of a party in elections supporting a transition to such a regime" were overwhelmingly likely to be supporters of politicians who have repeatedly called for new elections, no-confidence votes, and even a new constitution, such as Zyuganov, Zhirinovsky, Rutskoi, or conservative, law-and-order proponent General Aleksandr Lebed.[65] Thus in practice the fixed term and the complicated protections against a no-confidence vote deprive antisystem parliamentary groups of the possibility of gaining through a manufactured crisis what they could not attain at the ballot box.

While objections could be raised that the strength of the fixed term places the president and his government beyond parliamentary accountability, Russian legislators themselves seem to see this as an aspect of the constitution that protects them as much as it protects the president or his ministers. For example, Duma member Konstantin Borovoy (leader of a prominent party of entrepreneurs) said in early 1996 that he considered the presidential system to be the only guarantee of the survival of his party and of democracy, despite his vehement personal opposition to many of Boris Yeltsin's policies. There was a recognition among reformist legislators, he said, that many Duma members would, if unrestrained by the separation of powers, "pragmatically" go about the business of "destroying democracy."[66] Given the volatility of Russian society, it is understandable that reformist groups in both branches (who by their nature have to build constituencies for often unpopular and painful measures) would prefer an arrangement in which the antisystem groups could not provoke the collapse of the legislature and call new elections at will.

Perhaps the greatest testimony to the importance of the fixed term in this regard came from the CPRF itself; the communists were for a time explicit in their belief that the existence of the presidency was the single greatest obstacle to their attempts to regain power, and their objections to the establishment of the office led to an early break with some of the more conservative opposition figures who were at one time natural allies in the struggle with the Yeltsin government.[67] The obvious entrenchment of the presidency in the Russian system has since led them to change tactics and to try to capture, rather than to dismantle, the presidency, a positive shift in the communist program from obstruction to participation that is a direct consequence of the existence of presidential institutions.

The question arises, of course, whether this strengthening of the executive's hand was really necessary. Are antisystem parties really out to bring down the government, or are they indulging in scare tactics to alter policy? While most legislators dismiss the idea that there is any danger of a sudden, revolutionary change in the regime, it is clear that the communists and radical nationalists see debate over unpopular (if sensible) legislation, and the consequent threat to collapse the government, as a useful tactic. Were it possible, they might well be tempted to increase their majority in one short-term gain after another, especially if they could change the electoral process in favor of more party-list seats and fewer single-member districts. Russian journalist Gleb Cherkasov believes that only the fear of losing close contests in the single-member districts restrains these groups from provoking a collapse, since "theoretically, an early dissolution of the Duma is quite beneficial to the opposition, insofar as it allows them in parliamentary elections to present themselves as the aggrieved defenders of popular interests."[68]

But even the fight for single-mandate seats is not enough to dissuade the most extreme groups such as the Russian Worker's Party, a communist group which broke with Zyuganov's CPRF. Unable either to break the 5 percent barrier or to win in single-member districts, groups such as the RWP seem more than willing to take their chances on the fear and anxiety of electoral chaos. As one RWP representative said at a St. Petersburg rally in 1995, the only reason to participate in any elections at all is to "destroy the regime from the inside."[69] The Worker's Party is an extreme example, but even the relatively more moderate CPRF is not above such mischief, on occasion introducing legislation in order to provoke a legislative-executive crisis and raise the specter of a no-confidence vote even if there is no intention of seeing one through. A striking example of this kind of destabilizing behavior took place in 1996, when the communists introduced a bill outlawing any illegal "seizure of power" in Russia, a patently redundant bill that makes illegal and declares unconstitutional things that are already illegal and unconstitutional. Observers of the U.S. system would recognize such a bill as, in Capitol Hill parlance, "veto-bait," but there was more to the bill than a simple attempt at eliciting a veto.

The purpose, according to first deputy Duma speaker (and Yeltsin supporter) Aleksandr Shokhin, was to "attract attention and stress that opponents to the Communist majority in the Duma are anxious and eager to overthrow the [government]" if that's what it takes to keep them from power. In other words, the point of the legislation was to press the raw nerve of distrust in society; by creating legislation banning "seizures of power," they hoped to create in the public mind a fear that such a bill was actually necessary. "Now they, the communists, are good boys," Shokhin sneered, "they advocate law and order in the country."

Who will want to go into the substance of the matter? As a result everybody will say that the president has not signed the law because he does not want to cede power. Therefore he will seize and usurp it. Supposing the president returns the law "On the Inadmissibility of the Seizure of Power" to the Duma. What a good propaganda cause to talk about the president's democratic nature! I even think that a number of bills with such ostentatious titles are prepared especially to provoke the president into returning them, giving extra cause for an uproar.[70]

Although the CPRF was behind this particular provocation, Duma deputy Mikhail Iureev believes that the problem is more widespread: "party affiliation has nothing to do with . . . opposition to the president" he said in 1996, but rather is part of the process by which the Duma is carving out its "role in the country's political and social structure as a whole."[71] In other words, depicting the president as a potential dictator and then bravely opposing him is part of the way that some factions of the Duma justify their own existence.

Opposition groups for a time took a new tack, by threatening to introduce legislation to force Yeltsin to step down for health reasons. As of this writing, the most recent, and probably the last, attempt to impeach the president (on a variety of charges, including genocide) did not even manage to get past the Duma. (In passing, it is irresistible to suggest that critics of Russian presidentialism might note that so far the Russian system seems better able to fend off impeachment of the president along partisan lines than its American counterpart.) In any event, threats of a no-confidence vote are a recurring part of the Russian political scene, but all parties have been careful to avoid touching the constitutional third rail of an actual, successful no-confidence vote. So far the efforts to depose Yeltsin legislatively have been desultory and inconclusive. The more important point is that in a parliamentary system, Yeltsin and his government would have been forced out years ago and Russia would now be led by a coalition headed in all probability by the CPRF (who, as the largest single party in the Duma, would get first crack at forming a government).

In addition to the negative or preventive goals it serves, the fixed term also performs an important and positive pedagogical function in Russia, in that it teaches citizens and candidates alike that there is more to governing than just winning an election. The fixed term is a respite from electioneering during which time voters are given the chance to see how their candidates will actually engage in the business of *governing* rather than campaigning. This has been to the benefit of the democrats and reformers, who have shown that the most dire predictions made by their opponents of complete collapse and even civil war were unfounded. Conversely, the radical right and left, forced out of a constant campaign mode, have often succeeded in living down to their reputations, showing only that they are in fact irresponsible when faced with the mundane business of governance.

There is a clear lesson to be drawn in this regard from the steep slide in the popularity of Zhirinovsky's Liberal Democratic Party between 1993 and 1995. The organization of the Russian presidential system meant that Zhirinovsky could not simply take control of, or try to form, a coalition government, as would have been his right to demand in a parliamentary regime. Instead, he had to endure two years as an ordinary (if that word can ever be applied to him) parliamentarian, during which time he showed himself not only to be violent and unstable, but a poor legislator to boot.[72] His extreme rhetoric and physical assaults on other politicians, including the 1995 Duma brawl and a dramatic lunge over a table at then governor Boris Nemtsov on a morning talk show, slashed his popularity and severely damaged the LDPR at the ballot box. While it is true that the structure of the Russian presidential system produced an uneasy cohabitation between the Liberal Democrats and the president from 1993 to 1995, it also enforced a kind of cooling-off period among the electorate that, by the time of the 1995 elections, cut Zhirinovsky's share of the vote nearly in half. While still a vocal presence in Russian politics, Zhirinovsky has since been eclipsed by relatively more responsible politicians; perhaps most important, he has been removed from serious contention for the presidency itself. The fixed term and the constitutional bulwark against no-confidence votes served the dual purpose of exposing a good campaigner as a poor politician, and preventing him and like-minded parliamentarians from taking power or even collapsing the regime during the darkest days of Russia's painful economic transition.

The lessons of Zhirinovsky's downfall were not lost on communist leader Zyuganov, who addressed his followers after the CPRF's victory in the 1995 Duma elections. Zyuganov warned his fellow communists that "whether we like it or not, having won over one-third of the deputies' mandates, the communists are becoming in the eyes of society a new 'power party:'"

> We cannot just sit in the Duma, and in such numbers, and spurn responsibility for what it does. This was not why we were elected. . . . It needs to be clearly recognized that responsibility cannot be avoided, for all that, and that it is entirely a question now of what kind of responsibility the communists

have assumed and for what. There is no need to exhibit false modesty and say for all to hear that we are not "embedded in power." No, we are in actual fact already embedded in it, and the task now is to ensure that our opposition to the policy of the regime becomes opposition within the authorities themselves—opposition between its legislative and executive structures.[73]

While it is disturbing to see Zyuganov hoping to turn a political struggle into an institutional confrontation (evidence that he had learned from Zhirinovsky's mistakes but not from those of Ruslan Khasbulatov) it is nonetheless clear that the fixed term and the consequent realization that the Duma was almost certain to sit for a full four years pressured him into accepting the existing rules of the game rather than trying to collapse the system itself.

Critics of presidential systems would point out that the barriers to impeachment or to sacking the government favor the executive so strongly that the system is therefore "rigid," and more likely to break, so to speak, than to bend.[74] To be sure, Article 117 is a stick Yeltsin appears to be willing to use: during a 1995 confrontation (discussed below) in which the Duma threatened a vote of no-confidence, Yeltsin told Russian journalists that "the Duma can sign its own sentence" and that "if the State Duma does not want to be disbanded, it should not try to disband the government."[75] Advocates of parliamentarism point to this kind of behavior as an example of how the "rigidity" of the fixed term forces presidents and opposition legislators into paralyzing political trench warfare in which the executive has few options but to rule by decree. Short of enduring the traumas of presidential resignation or parliamentary dissolution, neither side can escape the impasse: the presidential term, according to Linz, "breaks the political process into discontinuous, rigidly demarcated periods, leaving no room for the continuous readjustments that events may demand."[76] What this fails to take into account, however, is the possibility that the legislature will, for its own reasons, intentionally seek to destabilize the government, even where there is no indication that "events" may "demand" it.

The Chechen Crisis and the "Rigidity" of the Fixed Term

One instance where the system's putative "rigidity" forced negotiation and compromise rather than collapse and chaos occurred during the crisis associated with the disastrous showing of the Russian military in Chechnya in the spring and summer of 1995. Without its presidential institutions, strong barriers to a no-confidence vote, and the firmly fixed terms of both branches, the Russian government might well have collapsed over the Chechen crisis and plunged the Russian Federation into political disorder or even civil war.

It could also be argued that those same presidential institutions, unaccountable and secretive as they are, got the Russian government into the Chechen mess in the first place. But this misses the point that almost no regime in Moscow, parliamentary or otherwise, was going to let Chechnya and its leader, Dzhokhar Dudaev, simply walk away from the Federation.[77] Indeed, the Chechen crisis now appears to be one that the Russian government would rather have avoided. Despite claims from some of Yeltsin's opponents that the attack on Chechnya was a transparent (and stupid) attempt to gain the support of people such as Zhirinovsky, the president and representatives of the reformist movements paid little attention to the Chechen problem until 1995.[78] Chechens—like just about everybody else in the Soviet Union—declared "independence" in 1991, and while Yeltsin denounced Dudaev's separatist ambitions in early 1994 he seemed little inclined to do much about them. Dudaev's actions, however, created a dilemma for the central government that would have forced any ruling group to face equally painful and unacceptable choices.

Dudaev's rebellion against Moscow had led him to ask for "emergency" powers from the Chechen government in late 1991 that he never rescinded, and in short order he was engaged in a struggle not only with the Federation authorities but against a significant number of his own people who were protesting his dictatorial rule. Chechnya quickly descended into open and often random violence. Moscow, as might be expected, supported the Chechen opposition, but there was as of early 1994, no large-scale commitment to removing Dudaev. Meanwhile, criminal gangs in the region were raiding towns on the Chechen border, engaging in hijackings and other attacks and then sometimes fleeing into Chechnya. In a dual affront to Moscow's authority in late 1994, Dudaev chose to shelter one of these gangs (whose bungled kidnapping attempt had resulted in the death of a Russian military officer) and then threatened to publicly execute several Russian soldiers captured in the fighting in Chechnya proper. Anatol Lieven has argued that these circumstances, and not some grand design, were the catalyst for the Chechen invasion; or as Russian presidential advisors Emil Pain and Arkady Popov put it, Russia's intervention in Chechnya was best understood not as "planned or implemented in a conspiratorial spirit," but rather "in the more prosaic terms of chaos theory."[79]

The deliberations around the decision to invade in force were conducted in secret, and heavily influenced by Defense Minister Pavel Grachev's foolish blustering that Dudaev's forces could be squashed easily. Poor planning and preparation led to military disaster for Russian federal forces, and soon representatives of most political movements, even those who had supported Yeltsin previously, were calling for the president's head. This was, to some extent, hypocrisy: although the war was unpopular, so was allowing Chechnya to secede, and there was no question that the violence would continue one way or another. The public, rather than uniting in opposition to the war, was divided nearly equally between those wanting "decisive actions" to impose "order" and those demanding a complete pullout.[80] The CPRF, likely to field the most viable opponent to the president in the upcoming elections, was critical of the war, but still pressed for a successful conclusion in which Chechnya remained part of the Federation. (Indeed, they could hardly do otherwise, considering that their first act in the Duma had been to call for the restoration of the entire Soviet Union.) Still, even those Duma members who genuinely wanted the fighting to stop knew an opportunity to score points against the president when they saw one, and a no-confidence vote that united the traditional opposition and the liberals duly took place and was carried.

At this point, a parliamentary system would have collapsed. The government's gamble in Chechnya had failed, and the Duma, furious with Yeltsin, could have easily mustered the votes to oust the cabinet. New elections would have had to be called even as Russian boys were fighting in the field. But the first vote set in motion the legal provisions in the Second Republic constitution requiring another vote within 90 days, and this opened a period of intense debate and bargaining.

A second vote was accordingly scheduled for July. Yeltsin was soon to be faced with the dilemma of either dismissing his government, which he clearly did not want to do, or dissolving the Duma, which in all likelihood would have caused massive unrest in Russia's streets. (Article 117 is biased in favor of the president, but it is hardly risk-free.) For their part, the legislators were now in a corner as well. The antisystem parties in theory stood to gain from new elections, but even they could not count on returning to power in such a volatile political atmosphere. As Yabloko deputy Igor Lukashev commented at the time:

> An interesting picture is emerging. The Agrarians, Communists, Zhirinovskyites, and [others] voted for no-confidence in the government . . . Two

days later they refuse to consider the question. Why? Simply because the question of confidence in the government is in fact the question of early elections for the Duma . . . This is why the deputies are evading the question. The majority of the Duma want no early elections are ready to change their stance for that. But they somehow have to save face.[81]

The opposition of the CPRF and the LDPR was in any case a sham; few in Moscow doubted that if given the chance they would attack the Chechens even more forcefully than Yeltsin had, as a way of disposing of the problem while showing the "firm hand" of central power. But the liberals, like those in Yabloko, who were the *actual* opponents of the war also had little reason to believe that they would survive new elections while emotions in the country were running so high.

Both president and parliament were now faced with the implications of the constitutional machinery the voters had put in place the year before. Unlike the arrangements of the First Republic, the provisions of the Second Republic (specifically the 90 day countdown to a second vote) meant that the standoff between the president and parliament could not go on indefinitely. Moreover, neither Yeltsin nor his opponents could evade the formal restrictions on their own behavior; Yeltsin could not ignore the Duma, which had a legal say in the longevity of the president's government, and the Duma could not simply countermand or ignore the actions of the government they themselves had confirmed in power. The incentives to negotiate for both sides were now overwhelming, and after brief but intensive talks, the president agreed to sack three prominent "hawks" in his cabinet in return for the Duma leadership dropping the second no-confidence vote.

The negotiations themselves are less interesting than the fact that neither side attempted to short-circuit Article 117, either by law or amendment (the Duma's options) or by decree or plebiscite (the president's options), and that the standoff ended with an agreement supported by both branches. All this prompted one moderate democratic legislator to marvel: "The word 'compromise' is perhaps not the most popular one in Russia. Yet it looks like for the first time a compromise worked to settle a political crisis in Russia. This is perhaps amazing."[82]

While perhaps not quite amazing, this 1995 compromise suggests that "rigidity" might be just what bickering parliaments need in order to force lawmakers to get on with the business of governing. This seems borne out by the events in the wake of the aborted 1995 no-confidence vote: while the Russian government remained in place, the legislature claimed a small victory in deposing three members of the president's inner circle, and, in time, the military conflict was ended. As of late 1999, Chechnya nominally remains in the Federation (thus satisfying the minimum war aims of the central government) and Russian federal forces have left Chechen territory (thus satisfying at least some of the Chechen demands). Dzhokhar Dudaev was killed in a Russian bombing and a more pragmatic politician, Aslan Maskhadov, replaced him as president in elections certified by the Organization for Security and Cooperation in Europe (OSCE). Negotiations between the Chechen government and Moscow, while tense, continue.

Without the fail-safe of Article 117, the Duma might have boxed itself into having to carry out its own threat, and an understandable confrontation between the executive and legislative branches over a civil insurrection would have ended not in compromise but in the complete collapse of the regime. As liberal Duma member Anatolii Shabad said at the time, "some parties wanted [to use the no-confidence maneuver] to gain political advantage" before the coming parliamentary elections, and as a result got carried away. "But they didn't want the government to fall. They themselves were afraid of the results of the first vote."[83] Other threatened no-confidence votes both before and after this crisis have likewise failed—sometimes with the connivance of the politicians who have called for them—and have more often produced negotiation and debate rather than an actual threat to the government.[84] Indeed, in 1997, the greater degree of cooperation between the president and his opponents would lead communist deputy Anatolii Luk'ianov (one of the conspirators in the 1991 coup) to deride "all talk about an understanding or contract between the government and communists" as "absolute bluff aimed at separating us from the people. Our opposition remains hard-line but responsible and so it will continue working for a balance in society."[85]

The subsequent electoral victory of Yeltsin and other reformers in 1995 and 1996, despite the Chechen crisis, also suggests that the fixed term allows leaders to run on a longer record rather than being forced, on a moment's notice, to fight to survive one electoral test after another in issue-by-issue, socially divisive trench warfare. (The vocal opposition of the media and at least a part of the Russian public to the war did not, in the end, have a significant effect on later parliamentary or presidential elections.) Where it is the parliament that is the source of instability and intemperance, and not the president, this is a valuable contribution to stability and the strengthening of democratic institutions.

The Difficulty of Lawmaking: Trapping "Crazy" Legislation

Not only does the Russian presidential system protect the stability of the government itself, it also serves to snare some of the more irresponsible legislation in what critics might call "gridlock" but others might call safety mechanisms. This is no small benefit when dealing with an institution like the Duma that spawns so much ill-considered legislation (the "seizure of power" ban discussed above is a good example). The reaction of a political reviewer in the daily *Segodniia* to an April 1995 session was a fair reading of the activity of the lower house. "Yesterday's State Duma plenary sitting spawned a fairy-tale mix of decisions," in which legislation could be best classified as "crazy, half-crazy, and non-crazy, that is to say, relatively serious. There [were] only three, however, in the latter group."[86]

Even Vladimir Isakov, one of Yeltsin's most bitter enemies from the struggles during the First Republic (and one of several returned to office in the Second) lamented the Duma's apparent lack of a "filter" that could "screen out superficial, insufficiently worked-out ideas and proposals."

> Any old letter sent to the Duma is quickly treated as a legislative initiative. As a result, parliament has been literally inundated with a vast quantity of "trashy" draft laws which have been "finalized" with the utmost reluctance in various committees and then left to spend months wandering from one agenda to another in the hope of "somehow slipping through."[87]

The virtue of separated systems is that they are more likely to trap "crazy" and even "half-crazy" bills before they can get far enough to be divisive and therefore damaging. The legislative maze of the bicameral legislature and the separate executive may immobilize lawmaking, but this is not in itself, as the Russian experience attests, always a bad outcome.

It is rare that provocative or intemperate legislation (bills that have called for the immediate printing of more money or renationalizing industry, for example) have made it to the Russian president's desk, since many of them are rejected by the upper house and sent back to the Duma, where they then die a quiet death.[88] Legislation is often effectively killed at this level, since bills sent back by the Federation Council need a two-thirds vote in the Duma to bypass the upper house and be sent to the president. The Federation Council, because it meets more infrequently than the Duma, has not proven particularly effective at originating legislation; rather, it has emerged as a kind of "legislative controlling office, to control the process of passing laws" by forcing bills back to the Duma for reconsideration.[89]

In American political debate, the term "gridlock" is a pejorative, referring to the obstinacy of one branch in thwarting the desires of the other. The critics of presidential government argue that separating powers merely invites such gridlock and immobility, and consequently provides a basis for recurrent issue-by-issue crises between the branches. Linz argues that when such a crisis erupts, the fact that president and parliament can claim to speak for separate mandates means that "there is no democratic principle to resolve it."[90] But what this criticism does not take into account is that presidential systems are *designed* to be conflictual, specifically to prevent rapid or intemperate change. "Gridlock" in such a system is the intended outcome rather than an unfortunate side effect.

Indeed, one of the central conclusions of an ongoing study of Russian attitudes, the 1996 New Russian Barometer V (NRBV), was that Russians, suspicious of the motives of both elected branches of government, consciously approve of "gridlock" and engage in electoral behavior to create it. NRBV found that "[a]lthough the 1993 Russian Constitution is 'presidentialist,' Russian public opinion is anti-presidentialist":

> Sixty-nine percent [of Russians polled] think the Duma should have the right to stop the president from making decisions that it considers wrong. Yet 48 percent think there are also circumstances in which the president might be permitted to suspend the Duma and rule by decree if this is considered necessary. The apparent inconsistency shows the tension between the desire for a representative Parliament strong enough to check the president, and a chief executive capable of taking actions that he thinks necessary and effective.[91]

These findings (tantamount, in Richard Rose's words, to "a majority for gridlock") do not support a simplistic view of the Russian electorate as one that reveres the president or completely scorns the parliament, but rather one with a fairly sophisticated understanding of checks and balances. It is especially significant that Russians reported these attitudes after the Chechnya operation, when Boris Yeltsin's popularity had fallen to startlingly low levels, because it shows—and this, from the point of view of strengthening habits of democracy, is heartening—that Russian voters continue to make judgments about the structures of the political system that are independent of the incumbents of those structures. They may not think the president or his opponents in the Duma are worthy of reelection, but their desire that there *be* a president and a parliament remains consistent, despite the various stresses and shocks the system has had to endure since 1993.

These findings also undermine the idea that the irresponsible behavior of the Russia legislative branch is somehow a side effect of its weakness— that is, because Russian legislators are supposedly powerless, Russian voters therefore have no compunctions about sending characters like Zhirinovsky to Moscow. Obviously, the presence of a strong presidency and the executive's ability to issue decrees allows the legislators and parties to duck a certain amount of responsibility, and this in turn hinders their willingness to take political risks. The proportional representation provisions in the constitution mean as well that there will always be opportunities to elect protest candidates. Nonetheless, the amount of legislation actually passed by the Duma, and the importance Russian voters attach to the role of the Duma as a check on the president, should make clear both that the parliament is not as powerless as it often claims to be, and that it is taken seriously as an institution by Russian voters, even if they feel that the parties in it are not often capable of faithfully representing them.

Separated systems may make legislating difficult, but they also benefit by preventing bills from becoming either repeated tests of the regime or incendiary social provocations in their own right. Given the composition of the Fifth and Sixth Dumas, where reformers have managed only to cobble together thin and disorganized pluralities from issue to issue, it is clear that the inability to pass legislation quickly is a virtue and not a vice of the Russian system. The difficulty of lawmaking, like the strongly fixed terms of office, are institutional restraints that mitigate the anxiety of political elites and ordinary citizens alike, and help to explain much about the continued stability of the Second Republic's political institutions.

From the "Primaries" to the Presidential Elections

By late 1995, Russian citizens could feel with some justification that the political system was stable, if not particularly efficient or even civil. Elections to the Duma had taken place without violence or outright fraud, and seemed to produce at least some sense of accountability between the voters and their parliamentary representatives. But in the wake of the 1993 constitutional referendum and the 1995 legislative elections, Yeltsin's critics could now rightly claim that all the leading figures in Russian politics had subjected themselves to the judgment of the Russian people except one: the president himself. The Russian presidency was the first office that had been confirmed by the public, and only a truly contested presidential race could close the circle and confirm that all the offices of the Second Republic were open to meaningful elections.

If the 1995 parliamentary elections served as a kind of primary for the scheduled 1996 presidential elections, then it was difficult to imagine that Yeltsin could possibly prevail and win reelection. Crime, corruption, the economy, and the Chechen war, among other things, had kept the president's approval ratings in 1995 and 1996 at miniscule levels; even though the president was still more trusted by the public to handle their affairs than the legislature, the dissatisfaction with Yeltsin was immense. The question arose in both Russia and the West whether Yeltsin would even allow the elections to continue, or whether he would find a way to cancel or falsify them, thus aborting the Second Republic as a failed experiment rather than risking the election of a communist president.

Certainly, these pessimistic scenarios seemed more likely than what actually occurred: Yeltsin's eventual reelection in a free and fair national presidential contest. But Yeltsin's victory was less important than the fact of the elections themselves. The constitution, the parliament, the courts, indeed all institutions of Russian political life would have been tainted by the failure to place the chief executive before the voters. If the Second Republic was to be built on a foundation of institutions that were meant to allay the fears of a mistrustful and atomized society, then the 1996 presidential elections would have to be the final stone in the edifice—whatever the risks.

Chapter Five

Electing the Russian President, 1996

The most important fact connected with elections of the Russian Federation president was that these elections occurred at all.

—*Roy Medvedev, 1996*

We know Yeltsin and we know what to expect from him. He would not cut Russia off at the knees, burying the reforms. He would not introduce censorship. He would not strangle democracy. And nothing more of a president is required.

—*journalist Leonid Zhukovitskii, 1996*

The 1996 Elections:
A True Test of Russian Democracy?

The 1996 elections for the Russian presidency were not, in the end, a final or comprehensive test of the durability of Russian democracy. That the elections took place at all was important, of course, but they ended in continuity rather than change. The incumbent was returned to office, and so a defining moment in the life of a young democracy—the peaceful transfer of power from the ruling group to its opponents—was put off at least until the 2000 elections and perhaps even beyond. But the elections were a test of something as, if not more, important than electoral procedure: the relationship between the Russian citizen and the democratic process itself. The elections showed that Russians, despite everything they had been put through by their national leaders since 1991, still cared about politics and still believed that participation in the political process mattered.

This was no small achievement, considering the prevailing mood of cynicism that supposedly dominated Russia at the opening of the campaign season. As veteran Russia-watcher (and former U.S. ambassador to the USSR) Jack Matlock later wrote, conventional political wisdom in Moscow in the winter of 1996 "incorporated two convictions: (1) that elections, if held at all, would be a sham; and (2) that, though Yeltsin was unlikely to go quietly, it would not make much difference to the country if he were to lose the election, even to the Communist candidate, Gennady Zyuganov."[1] That summer, the conventional wisdom was defeated, as Russians turned out in large numbers to vote in a free and fair election for candidates among whom there were recognizable differences. Encouragingly, the results were accepted by the winners and losers alike. Less than three years had passed since the destruction of the Supreme Soviet and the collapse of the First Republic, and thus the wide participation and acceptance of the election was itself an encouraging sign that Russians remained, despite evident misgivings, broadly committed to the democratic institutions they had put in place in the new constitution.

But in a society as mistrustful as Russia's, does the mere fact of completing a single presidential election really have any lasting implications for democratic consolidation? Critics of presidential systems argue that presidential elections, even when held successfully, in fact cause more political damage than they prevent. If the only choice, the argument goes, is between two candidates, then the contest is by definition one in which first prize is supreme executive power and second prize is complete political defeat, and this stark, zero-sum struggle can only serve to polarize society. The winner-take-all character of a presidential election should be perceived as especially threatening by social or political minorities; while the electoral process may require some sort of short-term consensus to produce a victory, "the popular election of the president and the concentration of executive power in one person are strong influences in the direction of majoritarianism" that serve to discourage the formation of cohesive parties that might otherwise represent those minority interests.[2]

Such criticisms, however, cannot account for the situation in which Russia found itself after the Soviet collapse. The lack of cohesive parties was not due to the presence of presidential institutions, but was due rather to social conditions created by seven decades of communist rule. Russia's presidential election, by offering voters a clear choice between two broad approaches to government, helped to overcome, rather than to exacerbate, Russian social divisions—a reversal of the expectation of antipresidentialist arguments. As one American political analyst later wrote, "the key factor determining Yeltsin's surprising reelection in 1996 was the consolidation of reformist and centrist voters behind a single candidate," rather than any infusions of money, media exposure, or even a last-minute "great conversion towards Boris Yeltsin." Instead, Yeltsin's win was "directly attributable to the consolidated electoral environment produced by the presidential election itself."[3] The Russian presidential elections of 1996, in short, managed not only to avoid disintegrating into fraud or violence, but to contribute to a growing aggregation in Russian political life around the central question of whether to proceed with reform or return to the recent communist past.

The election, in the end, was not specifically about the economy, or crime, or even a distant civil war in Chechnya. It was not won with money (a popular explanation of Yeltsin's victory in the West, which was itself derived from misconceptions about the effect of money on Western political campaigns), or even due to the president's obviously favorable press. It was, at its core, a referendum on trust, on the question of which candidate should be the steward of the nation's interests, and it is impossible to understand the results without understanding the role played by issues of trust in the campaign itself. Before discussing these aspects of Russian presidentialism in more detail, it would be helpful to recall the basic course and results of the 1996 elections.

1996: The Campaign, the Contenders, and the Results

When the citizens of the Russian Federation went to the polls on June 16, 1996, they had an unusual array of presidential contenders before them, ranging from a famous eye doctor to a former Olympic weightlifter. Among the better known names were perennial candidate Vladimir Zhirinovsky, now forced to compete for opposition voters with new faces like law-and-order proponent General Aleksandr Lebed, liberal Yeltsin critic Grigorii Yavlinsky, and even former Soviet president Mikhail Gorbachev himself. The only name on the ballot that was something of a surprise was that of the incumbent, President Boris Yeltsin, who for most of 1995 and early 1996 hopelessly trailed the heavy favorite, communist challenger Zyuganov, in almost every pre-election poll.

Yeltsin was supposedly damaged beyond all political repair by the war in Chechnya, which in turn was only the worst in a series of spectacular policy failures ranging from privatization to NATO expansion. Even before the complete field of challengers had taken shape, there was plenty of bad news in Yeltsin's poll numbers, particularly where the issue of trust was concerned. In April 1995, only 8 percent of Russians polled said they "fully trusted" Yeltsin; the president could take some small solace that this was twice as many as the 4 percent who "fully trusted" the Duma, but overall it suggested that Yeltsin's personal credibility was gone and that he was finished if a reasonable challenger appeared.[4]

That challenger could only come from the ranks of the communists, for several reasons. First, Yeltsin had no serious "internal" opposition among the liberals. For reasons ranging from a dislikably elitist public persona to poor stump speeches, Yavlinsky had never been able to break out of the single digits as a serious contender; much like Gaidar before him, he was an economist by training and it showed in his campaigning. Gorbachev, for his part, argued that his was the voice of responsibility and moderation, but his message was muted by the fact that he was so widely detested in Russia that he was rapidly becoming more famous for being physically assaulted on the campaign trail than for the substance of his message. Neither he nor the few relatively unknown businessmen who had thrown their hats into the ring had even a remote chance of generating enough money or publicity to displace Yeltsin among reform-minded voters.

If Yeltsin's mandate to carry the banner for the reformers—or at least for those who favored stability and the status quo—was unchallenged, Zyuganov's path to the final round of the two-step election was less clear but generally unobstructed. Although Zyuganov himself was viewed by the voters with a certain amount of skepticism (his poll numbers with regard to "trust" were barely better than Yeltsin's) he appeared early on to be the only reasonable alternative to people like Lebed or Zhirinovsky.[5] Lebed had made his own share of gaffes, including admiring words for General Augusto Pinochet of Chile, and the conservative party he co-founded, the Congress of Russian Communities, had been crushed in the 1995 Duma elections. Although his message of nationalism and discipline had the potential to steal some of the thunder from the communist platform, polls showed him unlikely to gain enough support to overcome the CPRF's name recognition or organizational advantages, especially without a party base to work from in the Duma. Lebed himself was a popular figure, but his glowering demeanor and rumbling voice added an ominous spin to what was already a vaguely threatening platform based on "order" and while Russians seemed to admire his candor and tough talk, they did not seem inclined to place him in the presidency or to entrench his party in the Duma.

Zhirinovsky might have been a more forceful contender to lead the opposition to Yeltsin were it not for the fact that over the previous two years he seemed at times literally to be losing his mind. His violent antics in the Duma had collapsed the credibility of the LDPR as any kind of organized opposition, and his personal behavior had removed him from serious consideration for president. A typical (and by no means the most extreme) example was a February 1996 speech in which he described his opponents as "prostitutes" and the LDPR as a "long-haired, meek-eyed virgin in white." After depicting his party as this fawn-like madonna, he then offered her to his fellow citizens in what has to be one of the most bizarre get-out-the-vote pleas in history: "Let's have group sex on June 16."[6] Apparently, the image of an orgy with the LDPR was a bit hard on the imagination of most Russian voters, who were much more comfortable with Zhirinovsky even when he was talking about blowing radioactive waste into Lithuania or marching Russian soldiers to the Indian Ocean. Zhirinovsky's emergence as the Duma's court jester removed Zyuganov's one serious challenger for the opposition vote, and made Zyuganov the leader of the anti-Yeltsin opposition almost by default.

Perhaps most important in establishing Zyuganov as a credible candidate and a plausible challenger to Yeltsin was that when Zyuganov's CPRF took over the leadership of the Duma after 1995, the sky had not fallen. With the exception of occasional blunders like the bitter, chest-thumping vote deploring the Soviet collapse, communist control of the Duma had turned out to be more moderate than many alarmists had predicted, and this was to Zyuganov's benefit. In any case, people did not know much about Zyuganov beyond his party affiliation—but that meant that they did not know much that was negative about him, either. (Although he was part of the Supreme Soviet resistance to Yeltsin in 1993, he had distanced himself from the rebellion before the shooting started.) By late 1995, it was clear that the choice in the eventual second round was going to come down to Yeltsin or Zyuganov and that the race for the Russian presidency might even be Zyuganov's to lose.[7]

But as Russians began to concentrate on the race as a choice strictly between Zyuganov and Yeltsin (or, in Timothy Colton's words, to "get real" about the election) the distance between them evaporated.[8] Between January and May of 1996, Yeltsin pulled even with Zyuganov in almost every poll, including very specific polls taken about which candidate could do more to end the war in Chechnya, improve the economy, and curb crime. (Zyuganov managed to stay ahead into the spring only on the issue of health care.)[9] The Chechen war, once thought to be the one issue on which Yeltsin could lose the election no matter what the failings of his opponents, fizzled: the war was unpopular, but not as unpopular as letting Chechnya simply secede, and there was in any event little expectation that a communist government would react to a potential Chechen secession any less brutally than Yeltsin had. In a surreal turn, slain Chechen leader Dzhokhar Dudaev's widow actually endorsed Yeltsin toward the end of the campaign, and as Matlock later observed, "Chechnya receded into the background before votes were cast and seems to have had little, if any, effect on the vote."[10]

Of course, this was in part because many in the media had refused to make Chechnya more of an issue, and this reflected the advantages Yeltsin gained from running as the incumbent.[11] Journalists were among many constituencies who naturally felt threatened by communism in principle and therefore aligned behind the president early on. There can be no question that Yeltsin enjoyed disproportionate media exposure as well as the outright bias of journalists, who feared a communist president would mean the end of a free press.[12] Russian journalists were open about their abandonment of objective coverage: an official at Russia's public television station ORT, for example, objected to the term "pro-presidential" as "crude," but admitted that ORT was supporting Yeltsin in the name of "stability."[13] Money, as might be expected, poured into presidential coffers from the business community, who had obvious reasons to fear the return of communism. Yeltsin also had the support of all but one of the Federation's governors, which was to be expected not only because he had given many of them their start in politics after 1993, but also because regional leaders were naturally hostile to the communist program of recentralizing power in a unified, rather than federal, state.[14] These were considerable (but as will be seen, not decisive) advantages that improved Yeltsin's position against all the candidates, and especially against Zyuganov.

On June 16, with nearly 70 percent turnout, Yeltsin and Zyuganov were chosen to go to a July 3 runoff.[15] Yeltsin's showing, despite his privileged position as the incumbent, was a disappointing 35.3 percent, which put him essentially even with Zyuganov, who had taken 32 percent. Still, given Yeltsin's near-death poll experiences the previous winter, his first-place "victory" had to be considered something of a minor miracle. The big surprise of the day, however, was the 14.5 percent garnered by General Lebed, who now could bring nearly 11 million supporters to the table of whichever contender would court him. That Zhirinovsky's stock was falling fast was confirmed by his fifth place showing at 5.7 percent, a figure representing only half as many votes as he got in 1991. Even Yavlinsky did better, edging out Zhirinovsky with just over 7 percent of the vote. "Against all" was the choice of 1.6 percent, which was better than the rest of the field, all of whom came in under one percent (including Gorbachev, who only pulled down an embarrassing 386,000 votes out of more than 74 million cast).

On July 3, turnout remained high, dropping only very slightly to 69 percent. Although nearly 5 percent of the voters rejected both candidates, Yeltsin trounced Zyuganov in what by American standards would have been considered a landslide, 54 percent to 40 percent. Yeltsin's victory this time was undeniable and untainted: he had taken a majority of the vote in an election with a large turnout. But even Zyuganov, despite some grumbling about Yeltsin's unfair financial and media advantages, admitted that the Russian people had spoken: in the best tradition of Western presidential elections, he sent the victor a telegram of congratulations and began his remarks to his own supporters by saying "We respect the will of the citizens of the Russian Federation."[16] It was a stunning political comeback for a president whose support had been in the single digits less than a year earlier, and one that owed far less to Yeltsin's own personality or platform than to the fact that the average Russian simply trusted Yeltsin and his administration more than they trusted the Communist Party of the Russian Federation. Yeltsin's voters were not enthusiastically voting for the president, but rather against risk and uncertainty.

Trust, Risk, and Yeltsin's Victory

The key to understanding the remarkable disparity between Yeltsin's dismal poll numbers and his eventual reelection lies in understanding two important facts about Russian voters in 1996: they focused on the elections very late in the campaign, and they voted strategically. That is, they tended to support candidates early on that reflected a particular message or issue they wanted to emphasize, knowing that their candidate had literally no chance of eventual election. As a French observer noted, the Russian system acted much like its French counterpart by first sorting out voter interests:

> In a two round electoral system, the first round always registers the individual's political preferences most faithfully. It is a manifestation of opinions that does not directly lead to a decision. The elector therefore pleases himself without feeling obliged to vote "usefully," that is to say, to give his vote to one of the best placed candidates in order to keep him on the ballot for a second round.

When faced in the second round with a stark choice between two clear alternatives on election day, however, citizens move from voting positively to voting *against* the most threatening or least preferred candidate, thus consolidating the vote into two broad groupings.[17]

This explains why Yeltsin trailed in the polls all through 1995 and 1996, yet won in the end: the people who voted for other candidates in June *knew* that they would end up voting for Yeltsin in July. Russian pollsters in early 1996 found that even those voters who had sent opposition members to the Duma in 1995 were inclined to come back to Yeltsin in the presidential balloting, indicating that the electorate consciously used the Duma elections and the first round of the presidential election as a kind of primary system in which they could send messages of protest.[18] (Americans are no strangers to this phenomenon: U.S. presidential candidates like Pat Buchanan and Jesse Jackson have received votes from people who had no intention of ever seeing either of them in the White House.) The Russians did not want to remove Yeltsin or risk a drastic change of political course, but they did not want him to coast to reelection without heeding their complaints, either.

It takes no great feat of statistical analysis to establish the strategic nature of Russian voting, if only because Russian voters themselves were so blunt about their intentions. (Indeed, some Russian analysts who looked closely at the polling data could see the outlines of Yeltsin's victory forming early on.)[19] Russians gave votes to such protest candidates as Lebed and Zhirinovsky that they admitted they knew could not win; moreover, many of them had already determined from the start that they would not give those votes to Zyuganov in the second round—in other words, that their first ballot did not reflect their real preferences. Of those who voted for Yavlinsky, Lebed, or Zhirinovsky, only 2, 4 and 9 percent, respectively, thought their man could actually win.[20] Of those who did not vote for either finalist in the first round, all who voted in the second round gave their support to Yeltsin in overwhelming numbers (70 percent of Lebed supporters and 80 percent of Yavlinsky voters turned to Yeltsin), except, predictably enough, the Zhirinovsky voters, 80 percent of whom gave their vote to Zyuganov.[21] Even Zyuganov's voters were not uniformly hoping to see him win: only 34 percent of those who voted for Zyuganov in the first round believed he had any chance of winning at all, and nearly a million Zyuganov voters switched over to Yeltsin later.[22] The voters, it seemed, only wanted to make sure that Yeltsin had gotten the message of general anger, before giving him a second term after having already saddled him with a strong communist presence in the Duma.

Still, why would people return a president whose record was so marred by political turbulence and violence? To some extent, the answer reflected a sense among many voters that their choice was really no choice at all. A commentator in *Literaturnaia Gazeta* put it forcefully in April 1996:

> No matter how long a list of Yeltsin's mistakes and miscalculations we come up with, *this does not give us the right to vote against him.* The reason is simple and well known: The alternative to him is the Communists, whose break-through to power will mean, unequivocally, a national catastrophe for Russia . . . In short, despite formally announced free elections, *we do not have any choice.* [emphasis original][23]

Another Russian political analyst later argued that the 1996 elections showed that there were "clear limits" to the "fickleness and mutability of the electorate's mood" and that in the end, the election came down to the simple fact that "a communist president is not acceptable to voters."[24] But this was not a unanimous opinion: some 30 million Russians felt on July 3 that Zyuganov was indeed acceptable as an alternative to Yeltsin.

But in the end, Zyuganov's campaign was doomed by the fact that the electorate, because of the very structure of a presidential election, could choose only him or Yeltsin, and thus were likely not to vote for the candidate they liked best but against the one they feared most. This was exactly what Yeltsin's handlers intended; knowing that the president could not win on his own record, they made the campaign "yet another referendum on communism," in which voters were asked to choose "between two systems, not two candidates."[25] Zyuganov, rather than trying to use the structure of a presidential election to his advantage by presenting himself as the more sober-minded (in every sense) alternative to Yeltsin, played into Yeltsin's strategy by running a frightening, even alarming campaign, that drove many voters to the incumbent even if their overall appraisal of his policies was poor.[26]

Yeltsin, meanwhile, made the smarter play, by returning to the useful themes of trust that, as we saw in chapter 3, served him so well in the 1991 Russian republican election. Yeltsin made clear moves toward appeasing the voters, including bringing Lebed aboard his administration as head of the security council with carte blanche to fight corruption. (This modus vivendi would last until October 1996, at which time Yeltsin would fire Lebed for, depending on one's view, either being too critical of his boss or simply because the election was over and Yeltsin no longer needed him.) Zyuganov, by contrast, merely demanded allegiance as a matter of obligation from anyone that opposed Yeltsin, even as his campaign veered on occasion to extremism in order to shore up a coalition that included some of the most explosive and aggressive politicians in the country. In short, people may not have liked Yeltsin, but they were downright afraid of Zyuganov—and understandably so.

Zyuganov: "They Will Drink the Wine of the Wrath of God"

For someone who was himself nominally an atheist, Zyuganov did not hesitate to warn that Yeltsin was the Antichrist and that the president's supporters would be consigned to the tortures of hell. "As the Apostle John wrote," he told a rally a week before the elections, "he who bows to the beast or accepts his image will drink the wine of the wrath of God."[27] While resorting to dire warnings from the Book of Revelations might have been an effective means of campaigning for Grand Inquisitor or Ayatollah, it was a foolish platform to adopt in a country already fearful about what a communist president might do once elected, especially in tandem with a communist-dominated parliament.[28] Elsewhere, CPRF spokesmen had resorted to similar brimstone-laden preaching: the official communist declaration demanding a union of patriotic forces referred to the "immoral" nature of Yeltsin's regime, while one communist Duma deputy actually invoked Sodom and Gomorrah in her call to oppose Yeltsin's "policy of cultural genocide of the Russian nation."[29] Russian voters, apparently, had to worry not only about whether the economy would improve, whether the war in Chechnya would ever end, and whether crime in the streets could be curbed, but whether their mortal souls were now in danger as well. More to the point, they had to wonder how they would be governed under a man who was willing to describe his political opponents as servants of the devil.

This kind of fiery rhetoric probably reflected a deeper belief in political strategy than apocalyptic Scripture. It is evident from his speeches that Zyuganov decided early on to secure his own electoral base, rather than to broaden his appeal and reach out to voters who were disaffected with Yeltsin but cautious about supporting a communist. This turned out to be a poor choice, but it was evidently viewed by CPRF strategists as an unavoidable one in order to prevent any splintering of the opposition vote or divisions among the communists themselves. As early as January 1996, *Segodniia* reported, Zyuganov was "trying to avoid a conflict with the radicals."[30] While a more moderate approach might have brought in undecided voters, it also risked opening a breach among the parties, groups, and individuals that together were loosely termed the "national-patriotic opposition." By June, solidarity with the "radicals" and other hard-line opposition groups had been achieved—during his "wrath of God speech" he shared the stage with Aleksandr Rutskoi and the Stalinist head of the Russian Worker's Party, Viktor Anpilov—but at great cost among less extreme Russian voters.

No doubt this was a strategy built around a reasonable assumption that Yeltsin would somehow make it to the second round, and that in the meantime Zyuganov had to consolidate enough of the protest vote (by reaping some of Zhirinovsky's voters, for example) to make it to the second round himself. This is an approach familiar to any observer of American presidential primary elections, in which the candidates play to the more narrow ideological themes of their own party to capture the nomination and then broaden or moderate their programs to win in the general election. If the first round of the Russian election is viewed as such a "primary," it was certainly understandable that Zyuganov would try to ensure that he was on solid ground with his core constituency. As one group of Russian political analysts noted in early 1996, going into the first round "it's already clear that the chief opponent for Yavlinsky will be Yeltsin, and for Zhirinovsky, the communists," and that the initial shakeout of candidates was going to take the form of a fight within the reform and opposition cliques rather than between them.[31] Once the leading candidates had fended off likely opponents of their own general orientation, they would then be free in the second round to concentrate their efforts across, rather than within, larger political coalitions.

Zyuganov's strategy for consolidating his voter base, however, was a costly solution to a nonexistent problem. It remains unclear why the CPRF thought that Zhirinovsky or even Lebed posed any real threat to Zyuganov's near lock on a spot in the runoff. (Yeltsin wisely ran as though he had no serious opponents among the reformers.)[32] Indeed, for a time it seemed the only real question was whether Zyuganov would take first place, or even an outright majority, in the initial ballot and thus obviate the need for a second round of voting. Communist voters were among the most disciplined in Russia; every poll showed that they were certain of their choice of candidate going into the elections and that they were unlikely to defect in great numbers if Zyuganov were forced to a runoff.[33]

Zyuganov, however, ran as though he faced a genuine challenge from both the right and left flanks of his own opposition movement, and tried to appease both with pronouncements that may have placated the likes of Rutskoi or Anpilov but did little else to enhance his appeal. This represented a fundamental misunderstanding not only of the Russian voting public but of even the basics of campaign strategy; Zyuganov spent a great deal of time and energy pandering to a segment of the electorate that, politically speaking, had nowhere else to go, while actively generating hostility and mistrust among undecided voters who might have been inclined to vote for almost anybody except Boris Yeltsin.

If appealing to the loyalists is one way to get past a primary and get to a runoff, the next step is usually to moderate the platform to draw support away from the opponent in the general election or final round. Here, Zyuganov missed an opportunity to compensate for the extremism of the "primary" campaign. According to one account, the CPRF did ask "Anpilov not to run around waving red flags for the time being, and generally to stay out of the limelight," a request Anpilov rejected.[34] But the difficulties Zyuganov may have had with his allies were irrelevant: he himself, after a weak attempt at a more moderate stance, gave into the kind of strident rhetoric that could only alienate the undecided centrist voters who were seeking an alternative to Yeltsin. Zyuganov may have believed that he needed to energize support (or, perhaps, ensure a good turnout) among the CPRF faithful by serving up traditional speeches laden with socialist nostalgia for the cheap sausages, guaranteed paychecks, and the superpower status of the Brezhnev era. Others have argued that disorganization and agitation by the hard-liners within the Zyuganov campaign produced this garbled and troubling rhetoric.[35] But whoever was ultimately responsible, only a fundamental misunderstanding of the mood of the electorate could account for the kind of aggressive attacks and scare tactics that became more sustained as the campaign wore on.

One CPRF attack on the president, for example, cited Yeltsin's brusque rejection of a debate with Zyuganov—"I was a communist for thirty years," Yeltsin said, "and I've heard enough of their demagoguery"—by then going back and quoting from speeches Yeltsin had made as a member of the Central Committee during the Soviet era.[36] Why anyone thought that it would redound to the benefit of the communist candidate to drag skeletons from the closet of the Soviet past and point out that Boris Yeltsin was once a communist himself (something Yeltsin did not deny and of which he was clearly not proud) is a mystery. Was the point to label Yeltsin and other ex-communists as hypocrites, or to imply that Zyuganov had kept the faith by not repudiating his own Soviet past? Or was it to heap guilt on Yeltsin merely by associating him with the Soviet Communist Party? There was no evidence to suggest that the Russian public was particularly inclined to hold CPSU membership against (or for) any of the major candidates, and to raise it in Yeltsin's case was not only odd but pointless, and even a bit unsettling: was the CPRF going to dredge up the pasts of other prominent Russians as well?

This was only one of several bizarre misfires by Zyuganov and his surrogates during the campaign. At one point, for example, Zyuganov tried to hang Zhirinovsky around the president's neck by implying that the LDPR was in league with the Chernomyrdin government. While it was true that the LDPR had voted for many of the government's proposals between 1994 and 1996, Zyuganov's claim that Zhirinovsky had supported Yeltsin and Chernomyrdin on "all questions" had to sound strange even to Russian ears long jaded by campaign hyperbole.[37] (Zhirinovsky would repay the favor by urging his supporters not to vote for Zyuganov in the second round, advice that went ignored.) Nor could Zyuganov resist an old communist standby, the accusation of foreign intrigues and conspiracies against Russia. "It is now no secret to anyone," he told *Sovetskaia Rossiia* in May, "that the crisis which developed in the top leadership [after 1990] as a result of an unprincipled power struggle was skillfully exploited by foreign special services and ideological centers."[38]

There are many Russians (perhaps even a third of the population, according to one 1997 study) who believe that Gorbachev's perestroika and the fall of the USSR were the result of a Western plot.[39] But what Zyuganov did not seem to understand was that these beliefs tended to be found among older, less educated, and more rural voters—in other words, people who were going to vote for him anyway. While Zyuganov's charges played well in the pages of strident, anti-Semitic papers like the neo-Stalinist *Zavtra,* they also raised suspicions that he was not only more sinister than his bland personality suggested, but perhaps even a racist. Once again, Zyuganov had chosen to play to voters who were already safely in his camp at the expense of broadening his appeal to others. When Zyuganov lost, one of his supporters told *Pravda* that although Russians had "voluntarily" chosen Yeltsin, Zyuganov had been right all along: Westerners were clearly in league with Yeltsin to "devastate" Russia: "I now feel, as never before, that the peoples of the West are, with rare exceptions, in essence the soldiers of an army of Russia's enemies. Cruel, merciless, ready for anything."[40]

Had this been the extent of Zyuganov's tactics, much of it might yet have been dismissed as propaganda by voters uneasy with his tone but nonetheless determined to be rid of Yeltsin. But as the campaign wore on, Zyuganov made it clear that he was not merely preaching to the communist choir but rather warning the general public that a vote for Yeltsin was a vote for civil war. Yeltsin's supporters had long claimed that "by natural inclination Communists are revolutionaries," and that "the Communists are always the party of civil war and global confrontation," and Zyuganov and his spokesmen seemed determined to confirm this charge.[41] Their clear message was that anything less than a smashing victory for Zyuganov (that is, one that even Yeltsin, with all his powers, could not falsify) would lead to chaos and strife. If Yeltsin loses, one Zyuganov supporter warned, there would be a civil war

> of which [Yeltsin] himself will be the initiator, just as he was the initiator of the civil confrontation of 21 September 1993 and the gunning down of the democratically elected parliament. It's not hard to suppose that along with the preparations for the elections, the president's forces are carrying out parallel preparations for a new government coup by armed means in the event of a Zyuganov victory.[42]

To be fair, there were grounds for at least some suspicion that Yeltsin would interfere with the election. The head of Yeltsin's personal guard, General Aleksandr Korzhakov, had floated comments about postponing the elections back when Zyuganov was running far ahead, but these statements were quickly disavowed by Yeltsin, who would go on to fire Korzhakov after the first round of voting.[43] But even if it had been true that Yeltsin was seeking to head off the elections, this was a far cry from trying to unleash a civil war, and using this charge to evoke memories of Khasbulatov and Rutskoi on the balcony of the White House calling for a mutiny was probably at least as damaging to Zyuganov as it was to Yeltsin, if not more so.[44]

When the first round results pointed to the probability of a Yeltsin victory on July 3, Zyuganov compounded the errors of the first half of his campaign by stepping up, rather than stepping away from, talk of civil war and conspiracies. Yeltsin, Zyuganov warned, could well be deposed by his own "odious associates"—this, even as Yeltsin was sacking his associates rather than vice versa—and that there was a very real chance that Russia might turn into a huge Yugoslavia. "We once more declare," Zyuganov said on June 20, "we remain decisive opponents of civil war." The rest of his statement implied that such a promise was necessary because the possibility of civil war was so tangible.[45] Zyuganov did make a stab at playing to issues of trust by calling for a "pact of national conciliation" before the July vote, but even here he began his pitch for a government of national unity (albeit one without Yeltsinites of any kind) by invoking the specter of Russia's "self-destruction."[46] For an organization that was so strongly associated with the recent Soviet past, so much talk of violence and revolution was a strategic blunder, and the public debate began to shift from how badly

Yeltsin had governed Russia's democracy to whether there would even *be* a Russian democracy to govern in the wake of a communist victory.

Yeltsin's team didn't hesitate to take advantage of Zyuganov's hard-line rhetoric, running advertisements that prominently featured images of Stalin and the gulag, and warning that a vote for the communists was a vote only for the worst of the Soviet past, for dictatorship without even the small solace of a more stable economic life. As one Russian academic wrote: "Whatever anyone may promise, there will be no return to the 2-ruble-and–20-kopek sausage." Nor did the president's supporters shy away from pointing out that Zyuganov, whatever the tone of his public statements, traveled in the company of extremists.

> The Communists . . . are a leap into the unknown, the unpredictability of a giant political force, which is laying claim to power. And this unpredictability is dangerous for a society in which the mechanisms enclosing any political force within the framework of civilized relationships have yet to be created . . . It is still possible to cooperate with Zyuganov, say, but what kind of common language may be found with [former Soviet general Albert] Makashov or Anpilov? These are people with nothing to lose and with a tremendous reserve of hatred.[47]

This tactic might have backfired on the Yeltsin campaign had Zyuganov been able to repudiate the Soviet past or even been willing to try. But even if Zyuganov had been inclined to depict himself as some sort of social democrat (something he resolutely rejected), consorting with people like Makashov—an unrepentant Stalinist and vicious anti-Semite, the man who had sworn as a member of the 1993 Supreme Soviet rebellion that his enemies would "wash in their own blood"—would still have deprived him of any cover as a possible moderate. The best he could do was claim that the party had gone through a thorough self-examination and admit that, in essence, mistakes had been made. This half-hearted confession was unconvincing, drowned out as it was by the overall tone of stridency that surrounded the communist campaign.

Moreover, the communists were now in a bind. Having chosen to contest the election rather than take to the streets, they had made a commitment to the existing political system. This not only logically prohibited them from calling on their voters to boycott or protest the elections, it also inadvertently dampened some of the atmosphere of anxiety that had brought them to prominence in the first place. As a Russian analysis of the first round results put it:

Support for the new "rules of the game" have led to the lessening of the degree of confrontation in society. Even the communist camp, having consequently rejected the legitimacy of the transformation of the regime that took place after 1993, has had to fight for power according to rules of a liberal democracy that were alien to it.[48]

The problem, of course, was that their harsh rhetoric had raised doubts about whether the communists would remain committed to the existing system if they managed to win. Communist leaders at the outset of the campaign had described the struggle for the presidency as a "final and decisive battle" in which communists "cannot, indeed . . . do not have the right, to lose."[49] This kind of thundering played into the president's hands, and Yeltsin's supporters were quick to use it to make the most simple and devastating argument for voting against the communists: "A vote for Yeltsin means the possibility of the next elections."[50] Or as another journalist put it: "Under a communist president there would be no doubt about the outcome of the next elections"; instead, there would be "the strongest doubts about the *mere fact* of the next elections. Has there ever been an occasion when the Communists, having obtained power, have abandoned it voluntarily?" [emphasis added][51]

In the end, even opposition newspapers like *Sovetskaia Rossiia* blamed the CPRF for running a poor campaign and handing Yeltsin a victory he did not earn, blaming Zyuganov for not expanding his voter base and not taking advantage of the CPRF dominance of the Duma to show that the communists could govern responsibly.[52] The pro-Yeltsin *Rossiiskie Vesti* correctly argued that "the actions of the 'people's patriots' were extraordinary clumsy," and that Zyuganov lost because "the communists and their allies never managed to 'cleanse themselves' of their own aggressive image, of revolutionary symbolism and phraseology, and most importantly of the atmosphere that emanated from them of aggressiveness and violence."[53] This not only allowed Yeltsin to turn attention away from his own record, but to reduce his own campaign down to the simple message that he was not as terrifying a choice for president as Gennady Zyuganov.

Yeltsin: "Do You Really Want to Go Back to the Past?"

The shrillness of the communist campaign was a blessing for a candidate as flawed as Boris Yeltsin. No matter how incompetent the president might be, he could take refuge behind the wall of invective erected by the "national patriots." Yeltsin's defenders were quite open about their candidate's flaws, some in terms that had to make the president wince even as he welcomed their support:

> Yeltsin's shortcomings are obvious—he is not in his first youth, his immediate circle gives rise to questions, he slept through Ireland, he conducted a band, and the war in Chechnya is demonstrating the impotence of the power officials. For this reason a multitude of perfectly decent people intend under no circumstances to vote for the incumbent president. They are asked: So you are for the Communists? They reply: Anyone but Yeltsin.[54]

But even Egor Gaidar—who, given his failures as prime minister and leader of the doomed Russia's Choice party, could hardly be counted among the more astute observers of Russian politics—knew that these criticisms of Yeltsin were more reflexive than thoughtful. "Millions of people are prepared to conduct idle conversations about how great everything used to be and terrible everything is now," he said after the elections. "But when left one-on-one with a ballot, a person was able to ask himself: My friend, do you really want that badly to go back to the past?"[55]

Yeltsin, with Zyuganov's inadvertent help, made this question the central issue of the campaign. Indeed, Zyuganov handed the floundering president a ready-made platform of anticommunism. "Boris Yeltsin," *Izvestiia* wrote in March 1996, "has openly and even with a degree of aggression declared war on communist ideology and on those who are trying to bring it back into our lives."[56] Although his supporters would later claim that Yeltsin's victory showed that "positive values and goals are essential" to winning the Russian presidency, this was an overstatement.[57] Yeltsin's strategy was a defensive one, based on letting Zyuganov and the frightening retinue around him talk themselves into a corner (a "red corner," even) from which they would then have trouble extricating themselves. An early 1996 analysis by a group of Russian political observers concluded that to attain "victory in the [presidential] elections it is sufficient that the current President simply not make any gross mistakes."[58] Yeltsin obviously agreed.

Before the first round in June, Yeltsin generally refused to engage his opponents directly or specifically, and tried to keep his message blandly positive. In keeping with the 1991 strategy of running from the Olympian heights of incumbency, he rarely deigned to attack Zyuganov personally or the CPRF by name, choosing instead to use references like "the past" to indicate the communists. His speeches tended to consist of generalities like a "new Russia," the immutability of reform, and promises, in effect, to do a better job in his next term. While Zyuganov was solemnly vowing to avert civil war and bloodshed in the streets, Yeltsin was promising a "struggle against poverty," the "defense of the family," the "development of culture, education and science," an end to the Chechen war, military reform, and the "strengthening of civil peace in Russia."[59] He even tried to sidestep some of the more pointed and difficult questions that had dogged his first term, including whether he was in fact an alcoholic. ("I do drink," he said in an answer that probably swayed no one. "But I don't abuse it!")[60]

Yeltsin's choice to forego overly sharp criticisms of his lesser opponents showed a better understanding of the two-stage election process than his main challenger. He evidently grasped (as Zyuganov did not) that there was no point in alienating men whose voters he would seek to capture in July. Only Zhirinovsky, whose voters were obviously beyond Yeltsin's reach, was written off as "not a threat" because he was already "exiting the political stage. He has no social base. Our people don't support fascism." Yeltsin's comment on Lebed, however, was more cautious and respectful, but somewhat curt and to the point: "He's too eager to go into battle. No, we don't need 'military actions' right now. Order, but not that way."[61] (Lebed, in the same round of interviews, sniped that Yeltsin was acting only out of "a self-preservation instinct" and that even Gorbachev had more to show for his time in power.)

Meanwhile, Yeltsin refused invitations to public debates, choosing to avoid the risks of head-on clashes with the other candidates in favor of a strategy of making public appearances around the Federation in more easily controllable media events. When he declined to debate Zyuganov specifically (a move that the communists, as discussed above, tried clumsily to exploit) he claimed he was too busy administering affairs of state to be troubled by such silliness: "There are a lot of candidates, but Russia has only one president. If I debate each of them, I simply won't have time to fulfill my immediate presidential duties."[62] Coming from a man who on more than one occasion had reportedly missed appointments with foreign dignitaries while sleeping off drinking binges, this was plainly absurd, but it served a strategic purpose by keeping Zyuganov at bay. Whatever Yeltsin's excuses, it was better to have the communist candidate traveling the country in the company of the 1993 Supreme Soviet extremists than sharing a podium with the president of the Russian Federation.

Yeltsin's calm, generally upbeat reaction to the first round of the elections stood in contrast to the dejection among the communists. Zyuganov practically ceased campaigning, except to appear occasionally to excoriate Yeltsin. The president, for his part, took steps to broaden the anticommunist coalition, turning his attention toward gathering allies rather than engaging in a narrow duel with Zyuganov. The morning after the first round, Yeltsin did not even mention Zyuganov or the CPRF; instead, he described his other opponents as "well-known politicians, respected people," including Lebed and Yavlinsky. Shortly thereafter, he would claim Yavlinsky's voters as his own:

> I consider Grigorii Yavlinsky our own ally. I believe that people who voted for him in the first round will do what Grigorii Alekseevich recommended to them: to go to the elections and to vote against the communists; that is, to vote not so much even for Yeltsin, as much as for themselves, for their children, for a new, free Russia.[63]

The choice now, he continued, was whether to "go back toward revolution and upheavals, or forward to stability and prosperity." Zyuganov, by contrast, thanked his voters for supporting him despite "anti-patriotic hysteria" and called upon the other candidates to rally around him—indeed, he practically demanded it—in the second round as a matter of duty.[64]

The one person Yeltsin could not ignore, however, was Aleksandr Lebed. Those of Yavlinsky's voters who planned to vote on July 3 would almost certainly vote for the president, while Zhirinovsky's angry legions would almost certainly, despite their leader's orders, now move to Zyuganov. But Lebed was a puzzle: he seemed content to cast a pox upon both the government and its opponents. While he made it plain that he had no love for the communists, his nationalist views in theory were more palatable to Zyuganov's allies than to the intellectuals and plutocrats who surrounded Yeltsin. But the president had something to offer Lebed that Zyuganov could not match: power. Yeltsin appointed Lebed to be the head of the presidential security council and gave him a broad mandate to clean house. This move had the dual effect of temporarily neutralizing communist criticisms of weakness and corruption in the regime while increasing the chance that a majority of Lebed's voters would come over to Yeltsin.

By late June, some of the most troubling figures around Yeltsin—including the minister of defense, the head of the intelligence services, several generals, and even Yeltsin's personal bodyguard and old friend Korzhakov—had been evicted from the Kremlin. Predictably, there were accusations that this was the height of political cynicism, and that Yeltsin was in effect trading away political offices for votes. There was some truth to the charge that this was a manipulative attempt to capture Lebed's voters, but Yeltsin responded to this directly by arguing that "mine wasn't the only signature at the bottom of the decree appointing

Aleksandr Lebed. I believe that it is side by side with the signatures of those millions of voters who voted for him on June 16."[65] Although Yeltsin and the troublesome general would part company by autumn, the damage to the communist effort was done: the voters had spoken, and Yeltsin, contrary to what the public had been told by his opponents to expect, had listened.

Yeltsin had isolated Zyuganov as the candidate of social revanchists, and positioned himself as the candidate of broad social conciliation. Even *Pravda* later admitted that Yeltsin "succeeded in impressing on a huge part of the country's population he represented the ideas of progress, democracy and freedom that were the opposite of the undemocratic character of the previous Soviet society."[66] Little wonder that by late June the communists were heavily demoralized; such people as the former Duma speaker Ivan Rybkin, (who spoke for many as a self-described "man of the center-left") had thrown his support behind Yeltsin back in March as the only man "capable of politically consolidating the entire society," and the probable move of Yavlinsky's and Lebed's voters to Yeltsin meant that for Zyuganov victory was now almost certainly out of reach.[67] Even changes in turnout could not save Zyuganov: a major drop in turnout might hurt Yeltsin if the communist voters were the only ones to return faithfully to the polls in the second round, but anything less than massive defection from the balloting would not be enough to turn the tide, and there was simply no evidence that participation was going to take such a huge tumble. By July, all the signs pointed to an inevitable Yeltsin victory.

When Yeltsin buried Zyuganov on July 3, the CPRF candidate had no one to blame but himself. Yeltsin's campaign had not been elegant, but it had been sufficient, and if the communists had emerged as frightening extremists, it was their own fault. They had tried to scare the Russian people, and they had succeeded; instead of running to the communists for security, however, the voters had turned to Yeltsin as the lesser of two evils. The system, rather than dividing Russian society, had produced a consensus, if only on the single question of whether the regime should be placed in the hands of imperfect reformers or volatile communists.

The Role of Presidential Elections in a Divided Society

The Russian presidential elections of 1996 not only produced a broad, reform-oriented coalition that gave Boris Yeltsin his victory, it also illustrated the positive role such elections can play in a divided society. Where social trust and the willingness to associate in parties is low, presidential elections serve two important functions. First, far from undermining the formation of parties, the election process compensates for the weakness of the party system by acting as the vehicle by which people can more confidently vote for a candidate who must spell out a specific platform and ideology. Presidential elections serve to "clarify" Russian politics, by forcing public figures, in effect, to choose sides and to take stands on particular issues and candidates. Normally, choices of party allegiance and other forms of political behavior would serve this purpose, but the entropic nature of parties and other mediating political organizations forecloses this option, at least for the immediate future, in the Russian system.

Second, presidential elections provide accountability. Because Russian parties and leadership are so amorphous and unstable, expectations of Russian legislators and their organizations are low. In this situation, the presidency serves as a useful means of providing at least some sense of accountability before the general public, and voting itself is a means of calling the government to account without destroying it. The chief executive may be beyond the reach of the parliament, but he is not beyond the reach of the voters, and the two-step electoral process ends up serving both as a means of communication between the people and the regime, and as a buffer against the Soviet-era cynicism that the system is somehow immutable. Both of these characteristics are examined in more detail below.

Presidential Elections and the Weakness of Parties

The idea that presidential elections clarify national politics would be rejected by critics who argue that the existence of presidential institutions contributes to, rather than compensates for, the weakness of political parties. This criticism is based on the assumption that there are clear social interests and a basic willingness to associate that could find expression in political parties, but that these processes are undermined by a realization that real national power lies in winning the presidency rather than dallying with parties. But what if society itself is too weak to produce coherent parties in the first place? As Valerie Bunce has described them, Russian parties, like the society that generated them, have "narrow and antagonistic political, social, and economic bases, and they [have] often functioned as, in effect, fickle fan clubs for individual leaders."[68] While it may be reasonable to point to some cases in the developing world, and particularly in Latin America, where parties have been pushed aside by fierce national struggles for executive power, it is also important to realize that these nations were not beginning, as Russia did, from a nearly complete absence of any traditions of free social or economic association.[69]

Of course, half the Duma is selected from party lists, and it would be an overstatement to say that parties are completely meaningless. The Russian parliamentary elections of 1995 did serve as a kind of rough "primary" system in themselves, in which the voters sent basic messages of support or protest to politicians in general and specifically to the presidential contenders.[70] The major parties contested both parliament seats and the presidency, and they all fielded presidential candidates whose platforms were, in effect, taken to be those of their party.[71] (Nominally Our Home Is Russia was led by Chernomyrdin, but it was understood to be, as Russia's Choice was before it, the presidential party or the "party of power.") But in the end, Russian parties are weak vehicles for presidential aspirants—the well-developed infrastructure of the CPRF is an anomaly, another relic of the Soviet period—and in 1996 it turned out that the presidential candidates were forcing platforms on the parties rather than vice versa, by acting in effect as surrogate party leaders. The early presidential campaign was, as Federation Council chairman Egor Stroev put it, exactly the time to sort out everyone's politics, to "separate the yolk from the white."[72]

Although supporting a presidential candidate forces a certain amount of discipline on a party and its legislative cohort, what of the legislators, the *odnomandatniki,* who abjure parties altogether? After all, it might be argued that the legislators elected directly (and whose actions are thereby deprived of the fig leaves of the orders of party leadership or adherence to platforms) would have to be more responsive to their districts and more coherent in their positions. But instead, because many of the *odnomandatniki* are elected based on local issues or even personal appeal, they tend to act as free agents, primarily interested in narrower regional issues.[73] At first glance this might be taken to mean that they are flexible and free to vote their conscience, but in practice it tends instead to mean that they can waffle and waver from issue to issue, allying with any group that serves their own personal or local interests.[74] Presidential elections force these independents to come out for or against basic policies by forcing them to explain to their constituents and to inquisitive journalists why they are for or against particular candidates. Without the clarifying effect of presidential elections, a vote for a party or a particular legislator might not have much meaning; the 1993 and 1995 Duma elections were marked by the kaleidoscopic emergence of groups and parties who fielded candidates but then collapsed, replaced their leaders, or changed political direction even before election day.[75]

Incoherent party organization discipline and legislative "blame avoidance" (to use a term that Gordon Silverstein has applied to the U.S. Congress) is behavior found among the democratic parties as often as it is among antisystem elements such as the LDPR.[76] In 1996, deputy Duma chairman Mikhail Gutseriev, himself a moderate liberal, lamented the fact that legislators of all stripes often seemed to care more about politics than policy:

> In the Duma, a great deal of strength, energy and time went into political confrontation. I saw that there are few deputies in the Duma, half of them at best, who are occupied with lawmaking. Many laws are considered from the point of view of the interests of certain factions, groups or sectors, and not from the point of view of the interests of our country and the broadest strata of its population. There is nothing surprising here, however: the Duma is the direct reflection of our modern society . . . It's a shame that the parliament couldn't consolidate itself.[77]

Russian political scientist Aleksei Kiva has specifically been critical of an overall atmosphere of irresponsibility and scapegoating in the democratic movement at large; the liberals, he charges, "have proved incapable of building a democratic society. [They are] hindered by their resolute reluctance to face realities, their disrespect for the authorities and the law, their desire to have it all now."[78] The only force, it turns out, that could bring the liberals into line and accept that they were involved in a common enterprise was the presidential race and the need to defeat Zyuganov.

The presidential system, then, offers clear choices of platforms around which voters and elites alike can rally, since by their nature presidential candidates do not have the luxury of running by singling out and siphoning off narrowly parochial or ideological votes in a particular district. In other words, presidents have to stand for something besides a seat. They can neither concentrate on local issues (and thereby avoid hot-button national problems), nor can they simply disappear into a thicket of candidates and hope for a plurality when the dust settles. By taking stands, presidential candidates force legislators, even if only every two or three years, to do the same.

This clarifying effect of the elections also undermines the argument that presidential contests are destructively divisive. In the Russian experience, both candidates had to try to broaden their appeal and unify a larger voter base than they originally commanded; Zyuganov, a prisoner of the ideological constraints of his own coalition, paid the price for the inability to capture a wider spectrum of voters. But as important as this effect was on the two main candidates, the impact of the election process on the other candidates should not be overlooked: the lesser contenders, who together represented over 20 million voters, found that they had to make pronouncements on the two finalists, instruct their followers, and make deals with them after the first round of voting (a "realignment of the losers" that would be familiar to observers of the French system). The overall effect was a set of presidential and parliamentary elections that, although characterized by an intense and heated debate, engaged the voting public in a discussion both among themselves and with the elite, and thereby strengthened the electoral process itself.

This runs counter to the expectation of bruising exclusivity that the advocates of parliamentarism claim is inherent in the "winner-take-all" nature of presidential elections. In Russia, the situation (so far, with admittedly few examples) seems to be reversed, in that parliamentary elections are more divisive than the presidential contest. Parliamentary candidates can try to win on narrower or more parochial platforms than the presidential contenders; the *odnomandatniki,* for example, can eschew the idea of being "national" legislators and instead run on promises to do what is best for a particular town or region, or even to run on no platform at all and hope that personal connections or charisma can carry the day. More disturbing is the effect of the races for proportional representation seats; Russia's most strongly oppositionist parties, like extremist parties in other proportional systems, have come to realize that their best chance at gaining seats lies in using extremist rhetoric to galvanize a disparate but deeply angry protest vote. The critics of presidentialism are correct to note that presidential elections are, at least in a structural sense, zero-sum contests. But to argue that presidential elections therefore divide society in some way that parliamentary elections do not is to ignore the reality that presidents must win broad mandates while parliamentarians can settle for narrower ones.[79]

In any case, creation of broad coalitions on both sides of Russia's 1996 presidential election stands in obvious contrast to the divisive tactics employed by many Russian parliamentary candidates in 1993 and 1995, and suggests that in low-trust societies it is the contenders for the presidency who unify society during an electoral cycle—even if only temporarily—and parliamentarians who divide it. Presidential campaigns do not undermine the party system; quite the contrary, the process of electing the president forces a certain amount of coherence and consistency on Russian parties, legislators, and other public figures that they otherwise might lack.

Presidential Elections and Accountability

The Yeltsin presidency will never be held up to later Russian presidents as the model of an efficient administration, but when contrasted with the legislature, the executive branch seems relatively coherent and businesslike. It is therefore unsurprising that Russians at all levels of society overwhelmingly believe that the executive branch really runs the country and therefore should be held disproportionately accountable for conditions in the nation.[80] Moreover, the Russian president, like his counterparts elsewhere, represents at least the semblance of a figure of national unity, an important role in a multiethnic federal state like Russia. None of this is to argue that the Russian president is actually as accountable as democratic theorists might wish, but only to point out that the task of, and accountability for, governing falls in Russia to the executive branch almost by default. Thus, presidential elections in Russia take on exceptional importance as a means by which the public can call the government to account when the legislative branch cannot or will not.

This again reverses the expectations of the critics of presidentialism. Lawmakers in Russia do not act irresponsibly because the president's electoral victories allowed him to seize the important functions of government; rather the president governs with popular consent because the parliament often acts irresponsibly. To be fair to the legislators, it is society, and not the president, that has removed incentives for them to confront difficult decisions. If low levels of social trust mean that voters are fickle and vindictive, then why should any one party in the legislature make a hard or unpopular decision when doing so could lead to defections from its parliamentary ranks and the sudden collapse of its own public support? What logical incentive exists for any one group to do anything but hope to force destabilizing legislation on other groups (or on the executive) in the hopes of taking advantage of shifting coalitions? Even more well-intentioned legislators who might want to act out of conscience no doubt realize that when society is unstable, the price of civic virtue or political courage might be quite high.

Under such circumstances, legislative elections can only impose so much order on political life, especially when proportional representation provisions mean that a representative removed by the voters of a district might still escape electoral punishment by returning to the parliament on a party list. (Likewise, parties cannot discipline members who can freely bolt the party and win election on their own, although this is more difficult to do and usually requires that the candidate have some prior connection to a district.) Only the president unavoidably stands or falls on his own record and statements, and the need to support or oppose presidential candidates smokes out members of weak parties or *odnomandatniki* who might otherwise have managed to lay low and evade their own voters on issues of national importance. Indeed, this means, in practice, that the accountability forced on the Russian president by national elections has a kind of ripple effect of accountability (just as it does in the United States) on members of the legislature.

But is it possible that national presidential elections send too strong a message, and produce a kind of lopsided accountability that presidents can then use to their advantage? Presidential elections, like all single-seat races, magnify the victory of the winner, and critics of presidential systems are right to be concerned by would-be strongmen who might be tempted to use the magnitude of a national mandate to intimidate parliaments. There is always a danger, even in the American system, that the president will seek to take power and responsibility away from the legislature by manipulation of public opinion or executive order. In Russia, the events of 1993 raise the possibility that the functions of the parliament can be suspended by force. But what solution is there to the situation that arises when society cannot produce a parliament willing to accept its own constitutionally mandated duties? To whom can voters turn when legislators (even potentially conscientious ones) simply evade difficult decisions rather than face the political consequences of those decisions?

Here again, presidential elections can sort out crises that in a parliamentary system might otherwise turn into an ongoing cycle of governmental collapse and reconstitution. By handing a clear victory and imposing a clear loss on the major forces in Russian political life, and then forcing both sides (and themselves) to live with that decision for a fixed period, the voters speak with a more united voice than would normally be needed to resolve parliamentary elections. This understandably raises fears among some critics of presidentialism that this is only thinly-veiled majoritarianism, in which the public steps in and circumvents the legislature by directly approving the current government.

But again, such a concern assumes that the parliament is otherwise capable of taking that responsibility on itself. As Giovanni Sartori has pointed out, even in a parliamentary system, gaining legislative support for the government should not be an end itself, and that "to say that governments are supported by a parliament is not saying much":

> [P]arliamentary democracy cannot perform (in any of its varieties) unless it
> is served by *parliamentarily fit* parties, that is to say, parties that have been so-

cialized (by failure, duration, and appropriate incentives) into being relatively cohesive or disciplined, into behaving, in opposition, as responsible opposition, and into playing, to some extent, a rule-guided fair game.[emphasis original][81]

This is especially true where day-to-day legislating is concerned; if the parliament divides its attentions between legislating and conducting internecine warfare, then the president is bound—or perhaps even forced, depending on who is asked—to rule by decree or to go to the presidential bully pulpit and ask the public to support his demands on the legislature, because only he has the power to act when others will not. In Russia, for better or worse, the presidential use of the plebiscite and decree powers, and the accrual of popular accountability for doing so, represents an attempt to fill the gap left by "parliamentarily unfit" parties and legislators.

It is encouraging to note that the need to rule by decree is decreasing, and that both president and parliament seem to understand that plunging the government into crisis at regular intervals will not produce outcomes favorable to either branch—in other words, that there comes a time when legislators must legislate and executives must execute. (Indeed, Russian legislators have been known to twit Westerners, and particularly Americans, that the Duma manages to reach agreements on things like budgets faster than their colleagues in Washington and without having to shut down the entire Russian state in the process.) Still, as Federation Council chairman Stroev complained in 1996, the Duma tends to pass "pinpoint" laws that only "resolve small-scale, short-term questions."[82] The Russian president must step in to fill the void of legislation and mix lawmaking with law enforcement far too often. Although Yeltsin (as *Segodniia* dryly put it) has "decreed punishment for those who don't fulfill his decrees," and legislative performance has improved, the unwillingness of "parliamentarily unfit" parties to share the burdens of government still leaves the president as the sole figure from whom the voters can demand results and explanations at regular intervals.[83]

The problem of legislative "blame avoidance," and the degree to which presidential elections can mitigate it, is especially evident in matters of national security. With regard to Chechnya, for example, Gutseriev noted rather caustically that "the Duma let the war last two years. Now it is criticizing the president because he ended this war."[84] Without a presidential election, the Duma might have had the last word on the Chechen situation, perhaps by scapegoating a prime minister or even collapsing. But in 1996, the voters were able to send a message, through polls and first-round voting, that they wanted someone to answer for the war, and without the elections (whose results brought Lebed into the government and spurred a settlement) the conflict might have dragged on and endangered the stability of the Federation itself.

While concern over the formidable powers of presidents is understandable, the fact that the national elections mean that the Russian president cannot escape popular accountability is an important factor in stabilizing Russian politics. The voters may not know exactly who or what they may get from particular parties—the rather cordial relations that developed after the 1995 election, for example, between the Women of Russia and the CPRF had to come as a surprise to many Women of Russia voters—but they can be relatively certain about the stands of men like Yeltsin, Zyuganov, Yavlinsky, and especially Zhirinovsky or Lebed. While the trend seems, so far, to be toward more mature and responsible legislative behavior in the future, the Russian presidential system in the meantime affords the voter some sense of predictability and accountability from at least one branch of the government, no small achievement in a new, fragile democracy.

Presidentialism Ascendant

Russia's first post-Soviet presidential elections left a great many issues unresolved. Yeltsin was left in office, of course, but as Roy Medvedev noted, this was approval of what Yeltsin stood for only in the broadest sense rather than particular approval of Yeltsin's record: "Anyone who considers Yeltsin's reelection an endorsement of his sociopolitical policies in 1991–1995 is profoundly mistaken."[85] The communist presidential candidate was defeated, but the CPRF remains the dominant party in the Duma and there are strong indications that it will retain that parliamentary dominance through the next election cycle. In the final analysis, Russian voters specifically decided only one question: whether they were willing to press ahead with life as they had come to know it since 1993, or were so disenchanted with "reform" that they were willing to step back to a government run by avowed Marxist-Leninists. Their choice reflected, in one sense, a decision to embrace reform over reaction, but it also represented, at a more basic level, a vote for to maintain their current situation rather than risk an unacceptably frightening alternative.

But the elections of 1996 also affirmed the final ascendancy and entrenchment of presidentialism in Russian political life for the foreseeable future, and this has to be considered a positive development for the further consolidation of Russian democracy. Nobody opted out of the system, or tried to change it. Every major political organization either fielded candidates or took stands with or against the main contenders. Candidates, like their Western counterparts, toured the country, gave interviews, pressed the flesh, and stumped for votes in cities and towns across Russia. (Yeltsin did more traveling within the Federation in six months than he did during the previous three years.) Most important, the voters themselves, by turning out in such large numbers, reiterated their support for the system they had put in place less than five years earlier. They voted the way people in democratic elections typically vote: for candidates they felt represented their interests, or for candidates for whom their support was an act of protest. They did not vote because they were paid, cajoled, forced, or duped into doing so. "[Russian] voting behavior," a Western study later found, "is practical and interest-based in a way that increasingly resembles 'normal' voting behavior in western democracies . . . Russia is becoming a more normal and stable society."[86]

Presidentialism is in Russia to stay. As the 1993 constitution nears its tenth anniversary, it is so far defying expectation by remaining in place as the foundation for further democratic development, rather than being discarded as an outdated stopgap measure. Indeed, neither the Russian people nor the political elite have shown any inclination to dismantle the apparatus of the presidential system. This is especially surprising given the fact that Yeltsin used the Succession provisions of the constitution to hasten the 2000 presidential election, in which Yeltsin's chosen successor won handily. The system remains imperfect, but as will be seen in the next chapter, it is still the preferred alternative among all of Russia's major political forces.

Chapter Six

From Yeltsin to Putin:
The End of the Revolution

Even a few years ago the political stage of the new Russia was empty. By giving a politician the chance to occupy the premier's or the vice premier's seat, I made him instantly famous. I made his actions significant; his personage important. Thus I created an entire cast of political actors for Russia. . . . Sometimes I think that I simply don't know of any other way to bring new people into politics.

—Boris Yeltsin, 2000

Putin now wants to terminate the revolution, not to start a new one.

—Gleb Pavlovsky, 2001

Yeltsin's Last Surprise

Even for Russians used to their president's mercurial moods and sudden changes of political course, Boris Yeltsin's speech on New Year's Eve, 1999, was a shock: in a brief, televised appearance, he abruptly resigned the presidency. "I want to ask your forgiveness," he said. "I want to apologize for not making many of our dreams come true. What had seemed easy turned out to be extremely difficult."[1] Shortly after the speech was aired at noon in Moscow, Yeltsin completed the formalities of retirement, got into a waiting limousine, and went home to take a nap. (Bill Clinton tried to reach Yeltsin during this last drive from the Kremlin; enjoying his first moments out of power, Yeltsin instructed his aide to tell the President of the United States he was tired, and to ask him to call back later.) At midnight, the resignation took formal effect, and the first elected president of Russia became a private citizen.

Yeltsin had always favored the tactic of blindsiding friends and foes alike, and his resignation was the last and most dramatic of the many surprises he had engineered during his life in politics.[2] Unlike previous maneuvers, however, this one was not meant to force a political program, hamstring a parliamentary opposition, or even guarantee the survival of his own government. This time, Yeltsin was clearing the path for his chosen successor, a relatively unknown former KGB agent from St. Petersburg named Vladimir Putin. For three months, Putin would rule as acting president. On March 26, 2000, he easily won the election and became the Russian Federation's second president.

Theories abound for Yeltsin's resignation, ranging from noble to base. In some versions heard at the time in Moscow, Yeltsin was getting out at the best possible moment, leaving behind a functionary who would shield him and his closest associates—the so-called Family—from prosecution for corruption and other misdeeds in office. His departure, in this telling, was little more than a clever tactic that ensured a quiet and comfortable retirement for the decrepit leader of a Russian plutocracy he had helped to create.[3] (The suggestion that Putin was a willing participant in this scheme is difficult to reconcile with accounts that Putin did not want to become acting president, and was as taken by surprise as everyone else in the Kremlin when it was offered to him.)[4] To others, Yeltsin's decision was nearly heroic: it reflected an understanding, even if long overdue, that he was simply in over his head, physically and intellectually, in the increasingly complex job of running a major power. Yeltsin's own explanation in later months was more direct but more self-congratulatory: he felt that his generation of leaders had reached the end of their usefulness, and that it was time for them—beginning with him—to step aside. He also made clear that the strain of the previous years had finally taken their toll on him personally, as when he melodramatically reflected on the moment when he handed over the codes for Russia's strategic arsenal to Putin: "Now I was no longer responsible for the nuclear suitcase and the nuclear button. Maybe I would finally get rid of my insomnia."[5]

Whether Yeltsin resigned out of a sense of civic duty, to escape prosecution, or even due to sheer fatigue is less relevant to the institutional future of the Russian presidency than the fact that there was, in the end, so little immediate consequence to his departure. There was no atmosphere of crisis, no sense of an impending clash between opposing political forces rushing to fill a constitutional void, as there had been in 1991 and 1993. Putin briskly assumed his duties as acting president and began preparations for early elections, both actions mandated by the constitution. (Yeltsin's departure may have been theatrical, but the net effect was only to move the 2000 presidential election ahead of schedule by about three months.) Indeed, Yeltsin's critics could point to the relative calm in Moscow as evidence of how conscientiously the former president had cleared the way for his protégé; by leaving when Putin's popularity was high, Yeltsin placed him in a commanding position to win an election that seemed to be little more than a formality. Even with a victory in March 2000, Putin risked looking less like an elected president than a successor, an heir, chosen not by the Russian people in democratic elections but by Boris Yeltsin in the peace and quiet of his office in the Kremlin.

There is some truth to this last charge, and Yeltsin has not been shy about admitting it. Once he settled on the choice of Putin to succeed him, Yeltsin used the power of his own incumbency to enhance the younger man's image as much as possible. "I deliberately and purposefully began to get the public used to the idea," Yeltsin wrote, "that Putin would be the future president."[6] Although Yeltsin was heavy-handed in his support for Putin, this attempt to position a successor should not seem that unusual to citizens of a presidential democracy, and to Americans in particular.[7] What is different is the scale and relentlessness of Yeltsin's push for Putin, as well as the considerable material and political advantages conferred by the power of the presidency. Whatever Putin himself may have done to bolster his own chances in the eventual election, there can be little question that without Yeltsin's careful nurturing of his career, Vladimir Putin today would still be a Kremlin bureaucrat rather than Russia's chief executive.

Although Yeltsin engineered Putin's initial rise to power, the question remains: What are the actual consequences, positive or negative, of the way in which Putin gained the presidency? Did Yeltsin's blatant attempt to transfer his office to Putin undermine the role of the presidency as an institution capable of mediating conflict in a mistrustful society, or did Yeltsin's exit, and the consequent presidential election, help to stabilize Russian national politics after the ongoing drama of the Yeltsin years? Will Putin's tenure strengthen the presidency as an office more important than its occupant, or will the powers of the executive branch eventually be sapped from the constitution and absorbed by Putin personally?

It will remain difficult even to begin to answer these questions in any detail until at least the election of 2004, when Putin will have to defend a full term's record and run in a full-length presidential election. The elections of 2008, from which Putin will be constitutionally barred from running, will be more telling. In both cases, the effect of Putin's accession to the presidency on the health of the Second Republic will be gauged in no small measure by whether there are credible challenges to Putin, or his chosen successor, that reflect a genuine willingness by the ruling group to risk a loss at the polls. In part, this will be determined not by Putin, but by Russia's opposition groups and their ability both to coalesce as a larger force and, finally, to reject worn candidates like Gennady Zyuganov or Grigorii Yavlinsky. Until then, however, the available record is not inconsiderable, including Putin's short stint as prime minister, his campaign in 2000, and his first year or so in office.

Putin's career so far as president of the Federation gives reason both for pause and for optimism. The 2000 elections that put Putin in office not only took place without incident, but were conducted, according to OSCE observers, "consistent with internationally recognized democratic standards."[8] Although rhetorically committed to maintaining Russia's basic democratic and economic freedoms, Putin is nonetheless known to be irritated with the mass media, particularly those outlets critical of the Kremlin. In the name of bringing more order and coherence to the central government, he has moved to bring recalcitrant regional governors to heel—an action that is either long overdue or a sign of impending authoritarianism, depending on one's vantage point. And while Putin professes to want to maintain good relations with the United States and Europe, he has also moved to renew Russia's contacts with old Soviet friends from Cuba to Vietnam. The "power ministries" have seen their prestige grow, but they have also had to endure Putin breaking tradition and putting a civilian in charge of the military and the police. And even as he proclaimed that Russia's turn toward democracy and a new future is irrevocable, he successfully pushed for the restoration of the old Soviet national anthem (with new lyrics) as the new Russian national anthem.[9]

One clear result, however, of the democratically approved transfer of power—and it is too early to call it much more than that—is that it signals the end of the Yeltsin-led revolution to overturn the remnants of the Soviet order, and the arrival of a more muted and more cooperative style of government. As a Kremlin political advisor said a year after the elections, "Putin has said that now he wants to terminate the revolution, not to start a new one."[10] Putin's victory came on the heels of a successful (and less shrill) Duma election four months earlier, and the period since has been characterized not by the kind of ongoing crises and political warfare seen in the mid-1990s, but rather by more regular processes of negotiation and legislation. As one observer has pointed out, not only have elections "become routinized in Russia, they also reflect the relative institutionalization of political conflict."[11] This is not to say that the president and the parliament do not continue to play hardball politics, and tussles over reform will naturally continue to be the dominant feature of the Russian political landscape under President Putin, as they were under President Yeltsin. But the period that began shortly after noon on December 31, 1999, is noteworthy precisely because it is generally free of the vituperation of the previous decade and may be evidence of the central role the presidency will play in the "post-revolutionary" turn in Russian politics away from confrontation and toward deeper institutionalization of democratic norms.

Yeltsin's Last Term: The Parade of Premiers

To understand the strength of Putin's position at the beginning of his term, it is important to understand the weakness of Yeltsin's position at the end of his. After the 1996 presidential elections, there was some cause for optimism that the Russian political situation was shifting from a series of overlapping crises to a more calm routine. Russian troops had pulled out of Chechnya, Yeltsin's presidency seemed fairly stable (if not as strong, vis-à-vis other Russian political institutions, as it had been before 1996), and younger reformers, including Anatolii Chubais and Boris Nemtsov, were finally given greater rank and more latitude to pursue their agenda.

But when bringing in a new team, Yeltsin had, as usual, acted quickly but not necessarily coherently: despite the evident push for reform, he had left the stolid Viktor Chernomyrdin in place as prime minister. Chernomyrdin was by now an influential and respected figure in his own right, and while Yeltsin's claims that he was not jealous of Chernomyrdin personally may be true, he was probably taken aback by the strength the premiership as an institution seemed to be gaining after 1996. (Journalists in 1997 even referred to the prime minister as one of the "Big Four," the other three being the president, the speaker of the Duma, and the chairman of the Federation Council.)[12] In early 1998, Yeltsin grew impatient with what he saw as a lack of progress, dismissed his entire cabinet, and began a parade of prime ministers that finally ended in the summer of 1999 with Putin's appointment.

If Putin's name was a surprise in 1999, his youth (he was 46 at the time) and background should not have been. In the last two years of his presidency, Yeltsin vacillated between two generations of leaders: the older, Soviet-trained politicians he had known for years, and a younger group of men whose enthusiasm he admired but whose inexperience he distrusted. When he sacked Chernomyrdin, for example, he made the baffling choice of Sergei Kiriyenko, a 35-year-old political newcomer from the energy bureaucracy. Kiriyenko was never on firm footing as prime minister, but when the national economy reeled from the impact of the Asian financial collapse of 1998, Yeltsin turned again to Chernomyrdin, reversing his previous decision and humiliating both himself and Kiriyenko in the process. The Duma, although less inclined to the sort of utterly destructive politics it had practiced in earlier years, knew the president was suffering from a self-inflicted wound and decided to take advantage of a crisis that they, for once, had not precipitated. (Indeed, the Duma could now look at the failure of the young Kiriyenko and claim that they had perhaps been too indulgent of Yeltsin when they approved him as prime minister in the first place.) Yeltsin turned at that point to yet another stalwart of the older generation, Evgenii Primakov.

The appointment of Primakov, previously the foreign minister and chief of the Russian intelligence services, was motivated less by Yeltsin's admiration for him than by the need to find a compromise with the Duma. In a striking example of how the relationship between president and parliament had become more evenly balanced in the late 1990s, the Duma, in the summer of 1998, rejected Chernomyrdin's candidacy for the premiership twice and was now threatening to do so a third time, thereby triggering the constitutional requirement that Yeltsin disband the legislature and call new elections. Opposition legislators had learned much from their struggles with Yeltsin in the previous three years, and they were now seizing their chance during a crisis that Yeltsin called "their lucky lottery ticket."

After the second vote on Chernomyrdin, the Duma announced they would begin impeachment proceedings against Yeltsin if he submitted Chernomyrdin's name again, thus painting the president into a tight legal corner, as Yeltsin himself admitted:

Their maneuvers . . . fit conveniently within the bounds of the law. According to the constitution, if the Duma did not confirm Chernomyrdin on the third try, the Duma had to be disbanded and new elections had to be called. But here was the legal trap: A president who is undergoing an impeachment process does not have the right to disband the Duma. The constitution offered no guidance for this situation. The disbanding of the Duma at a moment of severe social crisis was a risky move in itself. But under these circumstances it threatened to be doubly or triply dangerous. In a country where there is no parliament or legitimate government and the president is hanging onto power by a thread because of the impeachment process, complete political chaos can ensue.[13]

As seen in chapter four, the "fail-safe" provisions in the Russian Constitution that allow the president to disband the legislature are not risk free for either president or parliament, and—like the political equivalent of nuclear weapons, perhaps—they perform their most useful function when their existence is acknowledged but they are not used. Rather than risk the tumult of another round of elections in the middle of a national economic crisis, Yeltsin blinked, a retreat that reflected both recognition of the level of potential disorder (and political defeat) that new elections could bring, as well as a grudging understanding of the limited institutional ability of the young Russian presidency to create a government by simple fiat during times of instability.

The increasing importance of the role of the Duma and the premier made it clear that the next president would have to be capable of fighting what Yeltsin and other partisans of the presidency would see as the institutional erosion of the chief executive's power. One way to strengthen the presidency was to obviate a bruising election if possible, and even before the Chernomyrdin affair Yeltsin had already begun to think about the premiership as a way of creating a successor who would not have to fight tooth and nail for the presidency in the 2000 elections. Reflecting on his appointment of Primakov and the subsequent stabilization of Russian politics after the 1998 financial crisis, he later wrote: "Wittingly or unwittingly, Primakov helped me achieve my main political goal: to quietly lead the country to 2000 and the presidential elections. Then, as I saw it, we would find a young, strong politician and pass the political baton to him. We would give him a place at the starting gates and help him develop his potential. Together, we would help him win the elections."[14]

Yeltsin was convinced that the new president had to come from the ranks of the younger generation. This ruled out Primakov, who had initially made a show of wanting only to retire peacefully in 2000 but was now clearly interested in the presidency. Yeltsin would have none of it because Primakov, despite his relatively successful record as prime minister, was moving (at least in Yeltsin's eyes) to the political left and settling into too comfortable a relationship with the communists, convincing Yeltsin that whatever Primakov's other qualities, he "had too much red in his palette." And Chernomyrdin was too damaged: "his political method of eternal compromise had taken its toll, the hallmark of cautious rule, and people had grown tired of the same old faces in politics." Chernomyrdin, after the defeat at the hands of the Duma in 1998, could hardly be expected to win the presidency nationwide. "Faithful, decent, honest, intelligent Viktor Stepanovich," Yeltsin later wrote. "But not president for the year 2000."[15]

As Yeltsin was combing through the Russian government for a successor, the Duma moved ahead with another impeachment proceeding that had been brewing even before the Chernomyrdin defeat. This time, it was more than an idle threat; the relevant Duma committee actually constructed a case against Yeltsin that was even stronger than perhaps many of the deputies realized. Although five counts were lodged against Yeltsin, two of them, concerning the breakup of the USSR and a vague charge of "genocide" against the Russian people, were little more than rhetorical. But three of them—negligence in allowing the collapse of the army, illegally making war in Chechnya, and criminal misconduct in the events of October 1993—were at least plausible enough to demand further debate.

The Duma, however, was still unwilling to actually govern the country, and this ongoing reluctance to shoulder more responsibility saved Yeltsin's presidency and did much to remove impeachment as a shadow over future administrations. Moreover, the way Yeltsin defanged the impeachment proceedings is a good illustration of how presidents can end up being *given* power by skittish legislators, as opposed to *taking* it. Rather than challenge the Duma head-on in a test of wills, Yeltsin made a daring move that actually threatened to give the Duma a great deal of control over the presidency itself: he promptly fired Primakov.

This came as a surprise to many, since Primakov was well regarded in the Duma and firing him could only further enrage already angry legislators. Yeltsin, however, was banking on the constitutional chain of events that would have to follow Primakov's dismissal. Sacking the government required that Yeltsin choose, and the Duma approve, the next premier. But if Yeltsin were impeached, the new premier would become acting president; thus, the Duma would be approving a prime minister knowing full well that they were in fact choosing Yeltsin's replacement. This was too great a burden for the parliament; they wanted Yeltsin out, but not at the risk of being so closely associated with his successor. (Had Primakov remained in office and therefore in the line of succession, impeachment would have been seen by many in the Duma as far less risky.)

Yeltsin's tactics worked, and the process, as in previous years, fizzled out. The Duma not only backed away from impeachment but effectively ceded control of the staffing of the government back to the president, thus giving up some of the power it had wrested from the presidency during the previous few years. The overall effect has to be considered a calming one on Russian legislative-executive relations: there would likely never be a better chance to impeach a Russian president (unless one of Yeltsin's successors is one day caught red-handed engaging in actual treason), and the failure to remove Yeltsin in 1999 seems to have broken the Duma, for the time being, of the disruptive habit of furthering political arguments with the executive branch by threatening impeachment.

Yeltsin knew that "much depended on the person who would be appointed prime minister after the impeachment vote," since the 2000 presidential race "would kick off at that moment."[16] However, Yeltsin's initial choice—again, if Yeltsin's later account is to be believed—was not his actual choice for president. The president tapped Interior Minister Sergei Stepashin, a candidate likely to be acceptable to the Duma. "Even as I proposed Stepashin's candidacy," he claims, "I knew I would soon be removing him." The point was to protect his real choice, Putin, and to bring him into the public eye more gradually. While Stepashin took on the thankless (and unknown to him, doomed) job of prime minister, Putin remained as head of the Federal Security Service and secretary of the Security Council, posts he had held since August 1998 and March 1999, respectively.

The Chechen situation deteriorated rapidly on Stepashin's watch, finally culminating in a daring raid by Chechen rebels into neighboring Dagestan on August 7, 1999. Three days before the Dagestan invasion, Yeltsin had already decided to dismiss Stepashin and to bring Putin forward. He met with Putin privately, telling him that he would not only become prime minister, but that he would have to shepherd progovernment forces to victory in the upcoming Duma elections. Putin was reluctant, telling Yeltsin: "I don't like election campaigns. I really don't. I don't know how to run them and I don't like them." Yeltsin not only ignored this vacillation, but added that Putin must ready himself for the presidency. "I don't know if I am prepared for that," Putin answered.[17]

Ready or not, on August 9, 1999, Yeltsin proposed Putin as the new leader of the government. His appearance at the Duma went smoothly, with many legislators indicating they were impressed by the fact that Putin was plain-spoken and modest, even to the point of being willing to admit that he couldn't answer many of their questions. Approval followed quickly and without much controversy; the meeting to confirm him, *Moskovskii Komsomolets* reported, "was rather somber and even somewhat boring."[18] Although Putin took office as prime minister in the face of an approaching election season, the contests for the Duma and for the presidency itself were still months away. In the meantime, there were the Chechens to deal with, and it would be his actions in the Caucasus, rather than in Moscow, that would make Putin the man to beat in 2000.

Putin and Chechnya:
"We'll Wipe Them Out"

Boris Yeltsin may have had high hopes for Putin's political future, but Putin himself believed that the Chechen situation spelled the end, rather than the beginning, of his political career. In fact, he assumed that his appointment to the premiership under such adverse conditions sealed his fate in politics, and so he set about fulfilling what he believed to be his "historic mission" of putting paid to the crisis in Chechnya before he was removed from his new job. This was not misplaced cynicism: many in Russian political circles saw Putin's situation as untenable, especially since in contrast to the 1994 conflict, the prime minister and the government would no longer be able to duck full responsibility and push any defeats into the lap of the military.[19] Putin, for his part, was convinced that this was no less a task than saving Russia itself, and that if action weren't taken, there would be a "second Yugoslavia across the entire territory of the Russian Federation" after which "Russia would no longer exist as a state in its present form."[20] It was this conviction that the Chechen situation had to be firmly dealt with, one way or another, coupled with his belief that his career was essentially over, that probably led Putin to use gangster slang in a widely reported comment about his plans for the Chechen rebels: "We'll wipe them out in their crappers."[21]

Although it is tempting to assume that Putin was trying to use the violence in Chechnya as a means of creating a military crisis and rallying popular support behind the government, the truth of the matter is that his policies in the Caucasus followed, rather than led, popular opinion. This is important in that Putin was responding to a perceived need for action, rather than creating one—that is, that he was seen by Russian voters as responding to social chaos rather than instigating it. It is a persistent misconception in the West that Russians have not supported the use of force in Chechnya; what they do not support is the indecisive use of force that will do little more than create casualties among Russian troops. There is little reluctance among ordinary Russians about using the harshest measures to suppress the Chechen rebellion; indeed, a year after Putin's move against the rebels, a common criticism of his policy among a majority of Russians would be that the government's military response hadn't been severe *enough*.[22] This was especially true by late 1999, after a series of bombings—widely and probably correctly attributed to the Chechens—ripped through residential areas in Moscow and other Russian cities, killing hundreds and leading to demands that something be done.

Putin's response was to let loose a storm of military violence that borrowed much from the Western practice of using air power to inflict massive damage against targets on the ground with relatively little risk to the attacking forces. In the previous Chechen war in 1994–1996, Russian forces under then - Minister of Defense Pavel Grachev and his subordinates used operational concepts and tactics that might have been effective in World War II but that in the Chechen context can only be described as ridiculous, and Russian soldiers paid dearly for the incompetence of their commanders. This time, instead of sending in green troops in some sort of replay of the taking of Berlin in 1945 (which allowed Chechen squads and snipers to turn downtown Grozny into a shooting gallery), Russian forces flattened suspected rebel enclaves, heedless of civilian casualties—at least among those civilians who had not by now fled the tiny republic—which rose into the tens of thousands.[23] By early 2000, Russian federal forces occupied Grozny, and have since changed their tactics to conduct ongoing search-and-destroy missions in the region. Although there was some criticism of the savageness of the campaign in the press—"yes, we need victory," *Izvestiia* warned, "but not at any price"—Putin's reputation and approval ratings soared.[24]

Insofar as the twin goals were to keep Chechnya under the Russian Federation's flag and to put a stop to the audacious raids of the rebel groups, the campaign was a military success. But more to the point, Putin's actions were widely approved by Russians, who quickly came to see in the new prime minister a potential president. Yeltsin's insistent cheerleading didn't hurt, but even among the normally more liberal media, there was a lack of the kind of opposition seen in 1995 to the Chechen events, which had taken on less the character of a police action and more the drama of a patriotic war.[25] Russians, in the main, were plainly fed up and more than willing to support a government (and a prime minister) that seemed as angry and frustrated with the Chechens as they were.

When he entered office in 1999, Putin barely registered in the summer's polls of the upcoming presidential election. The heavy favorites at the time—and of course, in Russian presidential politics, this means anyone who can break out of single digits early on—were the CPRF's Gennady Zyuganov, and farther back, Primakov, while Putin garnered a barely noticeable 2 percent. By December, Putin had broken from the pack; at year's end he led the polls at 40 percent, a rise almost entirely attributable to his handling of the war.[26] Every major party in Russia, even the CPRF, supported Putin's approach to Chechnya, with the unsurprising exception of Yavlinsky's Yabloko. (Voters did not share Yabloko's aversion to a violent solution in Chechnya and would punish Yabloko in the legislative elections, thereby eradicating any possibility of a serious Yavlinsky presidential challenge.)

In the space of a few months, Putin had gone from an unknown to the presumptive choice for president in the March elections. But even though he was ahead, there was still a campaign to run, however shortened it might have been due to Yeltsin's resignation.

The Sprint to the Presidency, 2000

Putin's electoral strategy was in many ways a close copy of Yeltsin's in 1996: he ran as though he were already elected, keeping himself above any kind of ideological fray and declining to get into personal scraps with his opponents. Still, three major differences were evident between 1996 and 2000, and all of them played to Putin's advantage.

First, in contrast to Yeltsin's flamboyance, Putin had handled the challenges of his short stint as acting president with aplomb, and even a certain degree of conspicuous humility. The record of success in Chechnya combined with a reluctance to boast struck many Russians as a sign of competence and level-headedness, thereby allowing Putin to turn his relative lack of charisma to his advantage. This aided Putin in maintaining allies in the press; even the media that had treated Yeltsin harshly were now treading a bit more lightly around a man who was clearly enjoying the favor of a normally irritable electorate. It is a safe bet to say that the major Russian media are always going to tilt heavily toward noncommunist presidential candidates, but public approval of the war in Chechnya meant that even by the biased standards of Russian journalism Putin was treated well by the media.

A second difference between 1996 and 2000 concerned political parties, and specifically the question of a "pro-presidential" party. Yeltsin had always run outside of parties, even if he had blessed Russia's Choice or Our Home is Russia (NDR) as the "party of power" that represented the Kremlin's views and interests. But in 2000, Duma elections were going to take place within months of the presidential contest, thus increasing the importance of the parliamentary elections in the eyes of both the candidates and the voters as a kind of presidential primary.[27]

In late 1999, it was not yet clear which party would be carrying Putin's banner, especially since Chernomyrdin's NDR had failed to solidify as a centrist umbrella group. Initially, there was dissension in the Putin camp about supporting any particular party, but Putin was faced with a new problem that effectively closed off Yeltsin's earlier tactic of steering clear of parties. The jilted former premier, Primakov, along with Moscow mayor Yuri Luzhkov and others, had joined forces to create the "Fatherland-All Russia" party (*Otechestvo-Vsia Rossiia,* or OVR), a loose affiliation of Moscow insiders that was formed as an anti-Yeltsin (but not antisystem) organization. With NDR and Chernomyrdin in decline, reformers like Kiriyenko, Nemtsov, and Gaidar formed the so-called Union of Rightist Forces (*Soiuz Pravykh Sil,* or SPS), but like similar, earlier groupings, SPS could barely agree on a direction, insisting that it was not NDR's replacement as the nominal "party of power" but rather an opposition movement.[28] This left OVR in a commanding position not only to win a respectable slice of the Duma in 1999, but also to give Primakov a solid boost going into the presidential elections in March.

The response to this threat to the pro-Yeltsin group inside the Kremlin came from a wealthy Russian industrialist, one of the so-called oligarchs, Boris Berezovsky. Berezovksy initially tried to cobble together a group of governors who could fight OVR in the regions, a reasonable move considering the natural tendency of the regions to resist any group interested in strengthening central federal control. This umbrella organization was called the "Interregional Movement of Unity," or "Unity" (or "Medved," meaning "bear," drawn as an acronym from the group's full name). This putative regional group "quickly morphed into a Moscow-based organization guided by Kremlin insiders and campaign consultants and funded by friends of the government."[29] Putin, perhaps understanding the importance of a primary "win" in the Duma, extended explicit approval to Unity; his endorsement, as two observers later wrote, gave Russians "cues that a vote for Unity would be a vote of confidence in him, a signal that the Unity publicity machine drove home relentlessly in the closing weeks of the campaign."[30]

Putin's support of Unity (and Unity's support of Putin) was not based on any explicit ideological formulations, and in this the Putin campaign most closely emulated Yeltsin's earlier playbook. Unity candidates "conveyed an attitude rather than a concrete program," and "placed no faith in abstract concepts such as socialism and capitalism," choosing instead to represent something called the "center" in the name of stability.[31] This was much the same strategy Yeltsin used so deftly in 1991 and 1996, and it not only played to a generalized aversion to the ideologically militant communists but also gathered voters in the name of a comforting commitment to order and calm. Putin, in effect, created a broadened base of voter support by reducing his campaign to a minimalist (and therefore widely acceptable) platform. As one analysis of the election later put it: "After a decade of more-or-less free elections, Russian voters had coalesced into two fairly stable blocs of democrats and communists, with about 20 percent and 30 percent support, respectively. There was a large group of floating voters in the middle who were skeptical of both ideologies and preferred strong, pragmatic leaders at the national and regional levels. This was the group of voters that Putin targeted."[32]

Finally, perhaps the most important change was that all of Putin's possible opponents were so weak. To a great extent, this was their own fault. The 1996 election should have taught the Russian opposition that it was time to move past the usual roster of candidates; only dedicated (and deluded) loyalists, for example, could believe that men like Zhirinovsky or Yavlinsky were now capable of winning the Russian presidency. Less well known candidates, as Peter Rutland has aptly put it, were probably only running for the "vicarious thrill of participation."[33] Only the communists had the recognition, support, and discipline needed to challenge Putin, but that very discipline led yet again to Gennady Zyuganov's claiming the right to go up against Yeltsin's chosen successor. This was a serious error, if for no other reason than that Putin was a new face, relatively free of baggage, while Zyuganov was already a spent force in presidential politics. American politicians might have told Zyuganov that second acts for losing presidential candidates are rare; victories in the wake of earlier national losses, like those of Richard Nixon or Grover Cleveland, are far more unusual than the repeated defeats of perennial candidates like Adlai Stevenson.[34]

In the end, Zyuganov tried to run against Putin as though Putin were Yeltsin, confirming the CPRF's tendency (noted in the previous chapter) to cater to its own base of voters at the expense of a broader message. In particular, "Zyuganov stuck to his patriotic rhetoric and did not play up leftist economic discontent," a strategy that "had not worked against Yeltsin in 1996 and was even more ill-advised against Putin, who was obviously attractive to patriotic voters."[35] To judge from Zyuganov's earlier campaign, this should not have come as a surprise; even when Yeltsin was pulling ahead in 1996, the CPRF was loath to change tactics and fight him on more suitable ground, a mistake they repeated in the race with Putin. The Chechen war was the defining issue of the campaign, not least because Putin and the Russian media made sure to make it so, and on this there was hardly any difference to be seen between Putin or Zyuganov. (Eighty-seven percent of Putin's voters "strongly" or "somewhat" approved of the government's policy in Chechnya, but so did 82 percent of Zyuganov's voters and even 69 percent of Yavlinsky's voters.)[36] Had Zyuganov chosen to shift attention to economic anxieties, he might have done somewhat better, but the shallow communist learning curve—combined with Putin's formidable media and financial advantages as the incumbent—ensured that Zyuganov would not be able to climb much beyond the 30 to 35 percent of the vote that constituted his base. Because it was soon evident that Zyuganov would never manage to get within the same striking distance of Putin he had once covered with Yeltsin, the only real tension in the election was whether Putin could win outright on the first ballot and avoid being forced into a taxing runoff with his communist challenger.

On March 25, Russian voters produced a 69 percent turnout, a figure all the more impressive considering that the pre-election polls made clear that the outcome was hardly in doubt. Putin managed both to trounce Zyuganov (by a lopsided 52.9 percent to 29.2 percent, representing a ten-point decline for Zyuganov since 1996) and to edge past the requirement for a second ballot. Yavlinsky and Zhirinovsky continued to see their popularity slide, polling only 5.8 and 2.7 percent respectively. The rest of the field all drew less than 3 percent.[37]

Unlike the fairly responsible concession that Zyuganov gave to Yeltsin in 1996, his speech in the wake of Putin's victory was considerably less gracious, calling electoral fraud "a tradition for Russia's party of power."[38] International observers could not substantiate Zyuganov's charges, but whatever their possible merit, Russians did not in any case seem particularly inclined to look into allegations of fraud from a candidate who, in their minds, never had a chance of winning in the first place. Despite his grumbling, Zyuganov had managed to hold on to most of his base of support; the real damage was done among the squabbling democratic forces, who once again campaigned as if they were running against each other rather than against the communists. This unseemly lack of coordination among the democrats made it that much easier for voters who wanted to protest the disorderliness of the Yeltsin era (but who didn't want to vote for Zyuganov) to vote for Putin. This led one Russian pundit to suggest that while the CPRF could hardly claim the election as a victory like "Austerlitz," for Yavlinsky and the others in the democratic opposition, it was very much a "Waterloo."[39]

Putin's popularity at the time of his election was undeniable; not only had he followed in Yeltsin's footsteps by vanquishing a communist challenger, he had done so by presenting himself as a relatively positive alternative rather than the lesser of two evils.[40] Shortly after his appointment as prime minister in the summer of 1999, his job-approval rating climbed to 66 percent, hit a high of nearly 80 percent, and never dipped lower than 64 percent right up until the presidential elections, a year of numbers that would be the envy of any American or European political figure.[41] The 2000 election, although brief, was encouraging if only because it was the first in which many Russians did not feel that they were voting in self-defense.

But there was a disturbing aspect to Putin's victory as well: like Unity's candidates in their successful run at the Duma three months earlier, Putin campaigned on an image of stability and competence rather than on any kind of detailed platform. Critics of presidential government are right to argue that this kind of vagueness is to some extent unavoidable in presidential elections, since by their nature they require that a single candidate present himself broadly as the embodiment of the nation. In recent years, for example, American presidential candidates have long ignored the party platforms crafted by partisan activists, often choosing instead to emphasize personal qualities over intricate policy positions. Russians knew little about Putin except that he had put the Chechens in their place, and that he seemed to be a reasonable, businesslike—and, for a change, healthy—politician committed to admirable if unremarkable virtues like stability. (Although no one campaigned with a message of instability or panic, the intemperate rhetoric of Zyuganov and his supporters created the opportunity for Putin, like Yeltsin before him, to appear statesmanlike.) But the fact remains that neither Putin's time as acting president nor his campaign could really answer the question of what kind of president he would be once elected in his own right, with Yeltsin truly gone from the picture.

The Putin Presidency—So Far

Putin's candidacy and his first days in office have been a kind of inkblot test for Russians, many of whom see in him what they wish (or fear), even though Putin himself has done little either to gratify his supporters or to inflame his critics. "Western-oriented liberals," a recent report noted, "vehemently and openly castigate him, as participants at an 'emergency' human rights conference did [in early 2001], when they alleged that 'a creeping constitutional coup' was taking place and condemned Putin's 'distinct tendency to authoritarianism.'"[42] Meanwhile, the ultranationalist *Zavtra* warned Russians before the election: "Don't believe Putin. He's only wearing the mask of a patriot so that he can better prepare Russia's capitulation before the Western nations." (After the election, *Zavtra* made its feelings clear by announcing Putin's victory in an edition featuring a reproduction of a Bosch painting of Hell on its cover.)[43]

Russian citizens overall are more measured and more hopeful about Putin than either the right or left: while a slight plurality of 31 percent in September 2000 saw political developments after Putin's election as tending toward a "continuation of the Yeltsin system," 28 percent felt Russia was headed toward more democratic development, and only 9 percent feared an approaching dictatorship. Not surprisingly, 24 percent simply couldn't answer where they thought the country was headed.[44]

This last response probably reflects the nature of the current administration in Russia. So far, hesitancy and caution seem to be Putin's watchwords, a surprising outcome given his record in Chechnya and his carefully cultivated image of decisiveness and competence. After a year in office, little has been done one way or another, leading former deputy prime minister (and leading SPS member) Boris Nemtsov to complain: "Our main task is to push the government to do something concrete and useful. Unfortunately, nothing has happened in this area."[45] Some of this inertia can be attributed to the kind of disorder that necessarily surrounds a new president; even more, however, can be attributed to the fact that Russian voters continue to prefer slow, cumbersome government and are voting in ways that ensure they get it. When asked if the president should continue to have the right to suspend the parliament and rule by decree, 67 percent of Russians in 2000 agreed. (Only during the low points of Yeltsin's first term in 1995 and 1996 did the positive response to that question dip below a majority.) However, nearly as many people—62 percent—also agreed that the Duma should have the power to stop presidential actions to which it objects.[46] Gridlock is still the preferred method of government among Russians.

In practice, this means that despite the impatience of reformers like Nemtsov, Russians are not inclined to blame the president for the relative lack of legislative activity. When asked in early 2001 if their hopes in Putin and the new Duma were justified, 44 percent said "definitely" or "probably" yes regarding Putin, as opposed to only 26 percent for the Duma. (Only 5 percent of respondents thought either the Duma or the Federation Council were actually getting anything done.)[47] Of the "Big Four" institutions, Putin by 2001 was still more popular than the Duma, the Federation Council, and his own prime minister, Mikhail Kasianov. He is also the most trusted leader in Russia, with 40 percent naming him as someone who inspires confidence, as opposed to 17 percent for Zyuganov and just 7 percent for Primakov. In an especially encouraging change, the president finally managed to best "no one," a response that still manages to garner roughly 20 to 25 percent.

If Putin is so popular, and apparently covered in political Teflon, why has he been so reluctant to expend his political capital? One answer might be that Putin's popularity is steady precisely because he has done so little, a "rose garden" strategy based on sitting back and reaping credit, merited or otherwise, for the improving condition of the Russian economy in 2001. A year after his election, Putin's approval rating hovers between 70 and 80 percent; if the presidential election were held again in April 2001, polls indicate Putin would beat Zyuganov by a 5 to 1 margin. Moreover, economic indicators have been moving in the right direction: since Putin's election, GDP rose by almost 8 percent, industrial output by 10 percent, and capital investment by almost 20 percent, making 2000 one of the best years yet for Russia's battered economy.[48] High popularity and good economic news are not usually incentives for politicians anywhere to undertake complicated or risky initiatives, and certainly not in Russia, where legislating is so complicated a business.

And in any event, why ram through an ambitious agenda either by decree or legislation in a system that is designed to thwart such dramatic changes? While there are things Putin could conceivably accomplish from his bully pulpit in the Kremlin, it is possible that he has learned the lesson so well known to his Western counterparts: the quickest way to erode popularity is to spend it on unpopular or difficult programs. With only a year in office under his belt, Putin may be trying to protect the store of good feeling that brought him into the presidency, even if it means forgoing opportunities to advance an agenda. It is important to remember that Putin, for all that is said about his competence or personally admirable characteristics, is a neophyte in politics, and even leaders with far more experience would find the challenges of helming the Russian state in the twenty-first century to be daunting.

The desire to insulate an early advantage in popularity, while hardly admirable, is all the more understandable given the severity of Putin's earliest lesson in how quickly the popular mood can sour. In the summer of 2000, the Russian submarine *Kursk* sank with all hands during an exercise in the Pacific, probably due to the explosion of a mishandled weapon on board. Putin's government attempted to seal the incident in secrecy while suggesting, in a throwback to Cold War conspiracy mongering, that the *Kursk* might have collided with an American or British submarine in the area. This explanation satisfied no one—especially since it was rejected in private by many Russian military officers and publicly by at least one retired Russian submarine commander—and a group of military mothers promptly threatened to sue the president and the government. Putin, for some reason, stayed on vacation during the early days of the crisis, while Russian divers struggled to get to the stricken submarine and the Russian Navy stubbornly refused to ask nearby Western naval vessels for help. The result was a public-relations disaster, a nightly televised parade of infuriated and terrified families castigating the government, that culminated with the thuggish incident (captured on video) in which a hysterical woman was involuntarily sedated at a public meeting.

Putin moved to shore up the damage, flying to meet the families, making a show of mourning, and personally accepting blame for the disaster. But the tragedy, and the government's mishandling of it, cost him; comments quickly surfaced in the Russian media that his honeymoon with the public was over. His approval rating, although it would later recover, dipped to a low of some 30 percent by summer's end. Despite the passing of the public outcry over the *Kursk,* the lesson was hard to miss: the Russian public is fickle, tense, and easily angered. While the *Kursk* incident would have been considered a national disaster anywhere, in Russia it took on added significance because it directly raised the issue of how much the executive branch could be trusted with the lives of Russian citizens. Although Putin's image has since recovered (in part due to his ongoing effort to retain a strong association with stability in the minds of voters), some Russian observers believe that the public reaction to the *Kursk* disaster has led Putin to indulge an already strong tendency toward cautiousness.[49]

Still, this slower, more deliberate approach to governing has had some undeniably salutary effects on Russian politics. In particular, Putin has sought to tone down executive-legislative tensions, and even to shore up relations with the CPRF. Again, this seems to be indicative of his desire to end the "revolutionary" phase of post-Soviet politics and to govern through carefully managed coalitions rather than brute political force or dramatic decrees. (When asked about the difference between "strong" [*sil'naia*] governmental power and dictatorship, Putin answered: "I prefer another formulation—not strong but effective [*effektivnaia*] power."[50]) Rather than castigating the communists, his comments seem almost like advice designed to help them shed what he calls "ideological cockroaches" infesting an otherwise acceptable party of the left: "Listen, there is always going to be cooperation with the communists in our Duma. Not a single law has been passed without the support of the communists. . . . They have every chance of becoming a modern parliamentary party in the European sense of the term."[51] Although Putin has been skittish about forcing legislation on the Duma, the legislators have generally reciprocated this deference by avoiding the type of hyperventilating rhetoric and obstructionism they deployed against Yeltsin.

In early 2001, this new comity was tested in an episode of political tension that seems to have done little harm to Putin but relatively more to Unity. During Putin's first year in power, the CPRF was relatively cooperative as a legislative faction, due as much to the fact that communists were given senior leadership posts in the Duma as it was to the cold realization that Putin and forces sympathetic to him held the upper hand in public opinion. Dissent among the more radical communist elements, however, grew over the year; as the 1996 election showed, Zyuganov and his party are continually obligated to contend with forces to their left that either do not comprehend or do not care how they are regarded by the Russian electorate. In what was probably an attempt to placate the radical wing of his own movement, Zyuganov led a shaky move in February toward a no-confidence vote, the first such institutional showdown between the parliament and the president in Putin's term. [52]

Unity then surprised just about everyone, and announced it would join the no-confidence vote. This was a case not only of being too clever by half, but of stunning arrogance; what Unity was saying, in effect, was that it was willing to help collapse the government so that Putin could then call for new elections and reconstitute the Duma. While this might have seemed like a good idea in the heat of the moment, many of Unity's rank and file, as well as those of other parties, realized that when the parliament is disbanded, *everyone* has to run for re-election, and there is no guarantee that any particular legislator would have been able to win his or her seat again. After first boasting that it would support the motion, Unity then backpedaled quickly and reiterated its support for the president's government.

But Unity members need not have worried; there was dissent as well, even within the CPRF. Duma speaker Gennadii Seleznev declined to support Zyuganov in the final vote, a defection that probably meant Seleznev valued his position as speaker more than his loyalty to the communists. The whole fiasco quickly collapsed under its own weight—after all, if it took the Asian debt crisis to bring the government to the brink in 1998, it was foolish to think chances would be improved during better times—and Putin's government remained untouched. The primary victims in the whole scheme were the democratic parties and especially Unity, whose amateurish power play left many observers puzzled, and to a lesser extent the communists, who had jeopardized their positions in the Duma leadership.[53] What role Putin had in directing Unity remains so far unclear, but the outcome of the attempted vote has served only to strengthen his position vis-à-vis the legislature, in yet another illustration of how power and legitimacy can flow toward the executive due to legislative missteps rather than presidential overreach.

There have been only two areas, aside from the Chechen war, in which Putin has shown an early willingness to fight. These two issues are not only related, but similar, and involve curtailing the power of two of the most powerful groups in post-Soviet politics: the "oligarchs," and Russia's regional politicians.

The story of the rise of Russia's oligarchs—men who profited immensely during the early free-for-all of the redistribution of state assets after the Soviet collapse—and their influence on politics and economic life in Russia is too long to recount here.[54] Suffice it to note that the interplay of money, media control, and access to the halls of power made men like Berezovsky and media magnate Vladimir Gusinsky political forces to be reckoned with in their own right. Yeltsin's administration, out of necessity or greed (or both), made arrangements with such figures that worked as these arrangements always do: staggering sums of money and biased press coverage flowed to the political patrons, while access, special consideration, and insider deals were returned to the businessmen. At its best, this is the overly cozy relationship too often found between business and government in any democracy; at its worst, it is outright corruption of the most brazen kind.

Whatever it was, Putin has had enough of it, for now. When asked what they liked least about Yeltsin, most Russians mentioned their sense that he was "surrounded by corruption, bribery, [and] abuses," and some observers believe that Putin knows that much of his image rests on distancing himself as far as possible from the risk of being tainted even by the whiff of corruption.[55] But Putin also seems genuinely to dislike the idea that his administration is beholden to holdovers from Yeltsin's days in office, and his initial moves against the oligarchs—including the highly controversial move of jailing Gusinsky briefly—were meant as much to distance himself personally from them as they were to make plain that their influence in the Kremlin was at an end.[56] It should also be remembered that attacking the oligarchs is, in a political sense, cost-free. The Russian public has always resented the oligarchs, and any move against them was bound to be popular. But more important, Putin no longer needs them the way Yeltsin did; at this point, the president has a reserve of popularity and support that even Berezovsky's money or media coverage cannot buy. (It is conceivable that any media outlet that turns against Putin at this point risks a "shoot the messenger" public backlash against itself rather than against the president, at least until Putin endures his first major stumble or policy defeat.)

Finally, it may be that this "divorce," as *Izvestiia* called it, was simply over-due, and that only the weakest Russian president would have failed to dis-tance himself from men so closely associated with Boris Yeltsin. The oligarchs were the result of a particular period in the post-Soviet transition, perhaps even an unavoidable one under the circumstances. Although Putin ran on only the thinnest gauze of a platform, the Russian electorate, as in previous elections, demanded at the least that the president be a figure of accountability. As long as the oligarchs remained an unaccountable and nearly untouchable class, no Russian president could fully respond to that demand. As of this writing, Putin has since sat down to a meeting with the remaining oligarchs (at least three are now in severe legal trouble) and a kind of truce has taken hold. How long it will last depends not only on what steps the oligarchs take to transform themselves into more responsible corporate citizens, but also on whether Putin foregoes strong-arm measures against them or their holdings that could precipitate a more severe struggle between Russia's wealthiest businessmen and its most powerful politician.[57]

Efforts since 2000 to increase federal power relative to the regional gov-ernments have, like the attack on the oligarchs, raised fears that Putin is trying to create an authoritarian center in Moscow. But for all of the con-cern about resurgent "authoritarianism" or the creation of a dictatorial ap-paratus in the Kremlin, it is hard to imagine that any Russian president could allow the arrangements made between the center and the regions in the 1990s to continue much longer. Yeltsin's deals with the regions con-sisted of a series of bilateral arrangements in which Moscow granted a great deal of political and fiscal autonomy in return for public commit-ments to maintaining the Federation. (What these treaties actually say in detail is unclear, since few of them were published and many of them are probably of "dubious" constitutional standing.)[58] While the Kremlin's at-tention was focused on struggles in Moscow, the regions went about gov-erning themselves, often in contravention of federal law, and by 2000 Russian federalism was not so much a constitutional construction as it was a set of informal arrangements that regional politicians observed as they saw fit. As with the oligarchs, it would be difficult for a Russian president to present himself as a champion of order or accountability while ignor-ing the frayed condition of the federal state.

In his offensive against the oligarchs, Putin relied on the enforcement of existing laws; against the regions, he sought the creation of new laws and structures. Critics of Russian federalism have suggested that with 89 re-gions, the sheer number of federal subjects is unmanageable, and to this end Putin pushed for the creation of a supra-regional structure, overlaid on top of the existing 89 regions. Each of these seven new "super-regions" is overseen by a presidential appointee (the *polpred,* or presidential plenipotentiary), who in theory is responsible for the implementation of federal laws and policies, and who reports directly to Putin. The fact that these new federal districts correspond to the nation's military districts initially caused some anxiety, since logically they are well placed to coordinate a coercive move against the individual regional governments. So far, however, the *polpredy* have not emerged as prominent players—an October 2000 poll showed that Russians in six out of the seven new districts couldn't even name their presidential representative—and in any case the governors have more pressing threats to worry about.[59]

The most immediate of those threats is Putin's new ability to remove them. Putin asked for, and the Duma overwhelmingly approved, the right to remove governors and other regional officials who were under investigation for violations of federal law. (The law also gave the president, subject to Duma approval, the ability to disband a regional legislature.) This in theory meant that almost any accusation of misconduct could expose a governor to dismissal by the president, and the Federation Council swiftly rejected it, only to be easily overridden by the Duma. Putin has since been reluctant to use this power, probably recognizing that the capricious dismissal of regional officials could lead to the kind of fratricidal economic and social warfare between the center and the regions that Yeltsin was trying to avoid during his terms in office. So far, only one governor, Evgenii Nazdratenko of the Primorskii region, has been forced out, but even that episode was more about Nazdratenko's rank arrogance and incompetence during an energy and heating crisis in Primorskii than it was any kind of power play from Moscow. (Technically, Nazdratenko "resigned," and Putin's *polpred* in the area has since begun to clean house in the Primorskii bureaucracy.)[60] However, there is as yet no evidence that Nazdratenko's removal is the start of a pattern, and it may turn out that Putin will hold his ability to dismiss governors in reserve as a means of leveraging resignations rather than inflicting dismissals.

Two other legal changes will have important effects on regional political leaders in the longer term. The most dramatic change is that the current practice of sending the top legislative and executive figure from each region ex officio to the Federation Council is to end in 2002, when the current group of Russian senators must by law leave office. After that, each region's two seats on the Federation Council will be filled by one senator appointed by the regional governor (subject to a two-thirds veto by the regional legislature), while the second will be elected by the regional legislature itself.

Like the law on dismissing governors, this was passed in the summer of 2000 over the severe (and hardly unexpected) objections of the current Federation Council.

What this will mean after 2002 is an open question, but if it works as Putin and his team seem to hope it will, the restructuring of the Federation Council should accomplish two things: first, it will undermine the power of the governors by forcing them to stay in their regions and govern, rather than allowing them to come to Moscow, where they can pass laws that directly affect their political and personal interests back home. Second, diffusing the power of appointment to the Federation Council should, hypothetically, dilute the influence of Federation Council members who not only would no longer hold the immunities of federal office, but also would now be answerable to the local legislature. If this change, along with other pending bills reducing the power of the Federation Council, has its intended effect, it will dramatically alter the relationship not only between Moscow and the regions in favor of Moscow, but will also strengthen the power of the presidency and the Duma at the expense of the upper house. While this may undermine the governors and their freelancing ways, it should also raise the question of whether the Federation Council will still be able to block intemperate legislation from the Duma—assuming, that is, that there are no changes to the structure of the Duma in the next few years.

The second change Putin has undertaken as part of the ongoing attempt to bring the regions in line with Moscow is the creation of what might be thought of as a kind of "backup" or "reserve" upper house, called the State Council. This is reminiscent of the move Yeltsin made in 1994 when he created the "Public Chamber" as an alternative to the Duma (see chapter four). Putin created the State Council in September 2000 by decree, describing it as "an executive body" composed of regional governors and other heads of the republics that form the Russian Federation. It is supposed to convene every three months in a "consultative role," but what it can do (or is even supposed to do) beyond that is unclear. What the State Council promises, for now, is access to the president, and Russia's top politicians seem fairly eager to participate in it—which in turn offers Putin another avenue for influencing leaders who up until now have been beyond the reach of the federal presidency. In fact, some regional leaders, including current Federation Council President Egor Stroev and Tatarstan President Mintimer Shamiev, quickly suggested strengthening the power of the State Council, perhaps anticipating the progressive weakening of the Federation Council; Putin showed no interest in such a move, probably since it would undermine the whole point of creating the State Council in the first place, and the members of the State Council for the time being seem to accept that it is little more than a decorative body.

A postscript: Despite this description of Putin as deeply cautious, in early 2001, he seemed to be making preparations for attacking the nearly intractable issue of military reform, a move that might suggest the end of his post-*Kursk* hesitancy. In March 2001, Putin "civilianized" two of the power ministries, placing trusted colleagues Boris Gryzlov at Interior and Sergei Ivanov at Defense, moves that Putin called "a step toward the de-militarization of Russian society."[61] This may signal a readiness to begin Russia's long-awaited military drawdown and restructuring, although in the short-term, it seems at the very least an attempt to clear out yet more Yeltsin-era officials and to place Putin's stamp on the new Russian gov-ernment.

(Tentative) Conclusions

There are scenarios under which Vladimir Putin's ascension to the Russ-ian presidency, and all of the steps he has taken since, could be cast in a most threatening light. Instead of a messy succession that has since led to an attempt to sort out some of the chaos of the initial decade of Russian democracy, the events of 1999–2001 could perhaps be interpreted differ-ently: a cabal of Yeltsin's wealthy cronies pressures the old man to retire, handing power to a former KGB agent who goes on to win a sham elec-tion; after "legally" taking the presidency, the new leader systematically dis-mantles what few democratic institutions are left from the revolt against the Soviet system, turns on his former benefactors, grips the media by the financial throat, and places former intelligence service colleagues in charge of the police and the military, as well as in positions of new authority that coincidentally correspond to the outlines of national military districts. From there, any threat to the new president's power can be swiftly crushed through intimidation, economic pressure, or even the outright threat of military force. In 2004, "elections" are held as a formality, but Vladimir Putin wins them—as he will continue to win them for as long as he cares to remain Russia's president.

No doubt, there are people in both Russia and the West who foresee this kind of outcome or something similar to it. (However, Russians seem far more optimistic about their political future than most of the American academic specialists who study Russia.) But Putin's actions after a year in office suggest not only that he is not inclined to this kind of dash for power, but also that he would find it almost impossible to pull off even if he were. The transition in 1999 and the subsequent election in 2000 show that Russians have gotten accustomed to speaking their minds, to communicating freely with each other, to voting, and even to the idea that Russia is, and will remain, a capitalist state. As Egor Gaidar, speaking for many Russians, put it in early 2001: "Russian society and Russian elites accept the market and private property. It is not a matter disputed anymore. No serious political party would run with a slogan for dismantling markets and building socialism." Gaidar is less sanguine about Russia's democratic institutions and basic freedoms, which he believes "are not as well established and accepted," but neither he nor most Russians feel that political or economic liberties are in danger.[62]

Still, there can be no question that Putin is trying to impose "order," of some sort, on the fractious Federation and to restore a sense of pride in the nation among ordinary Russians. Americans in particular may find this worrisome, but it is important to ask what else one might expect from any of Yeltsin's successors. The Russian state is a battered ship, in need of serious maintenance now that it has weathered the storm of its first decade. To expect that Putin or any Russian president in the twenty-first century would allow the republics to continue to amass power at the expense of the central government, or the oligarchs to continue to monopolize large chunks of the media and other crucial assets, or even to allow Russia to continue adrift in foreign affairs as it was in Yeltsin's last years, would be unreasonable and would only reflect a lack of confidence or competence in the Kremlin.

From the point of view of institutional development, Putin's first year is important because it confirms that the presidency, as an office, can actually survive Yeltsin's departure and function much as it was intended to. Putin, whatever his ulterior motives (if any), cannot change the government overnight, in secret, or alone. Even actions like the changes to the composition of the Federation Council have been debated, voted on, amended, voted on again, vetoed, overridden, compromised on, and eventually passed in the light of day. The moves against the oligarchs, which many in Russia feared were an attack on free speech and the mass media, have been discussed, opposed, and debated in detail, in the mass media. Elections are not only commonplace, but expected, and perhaps even taken for granted. Without a presidential system, it is hard to imagine how Putin—or anyone—could have cobbled together a parliamentary majority that could instill the same level of confidence the Russian public has in the presidency. Perhaps even more important, the obstacles and safeguards in the Russian presidential system seem to be creating more responsible legislative behavior as well, as legislators finally come to understand that political participation is a process, not a one-time grab for ultimate victory. As Russia enters its second decade of democracy under its second president, this growth in responsible behavior in both the legislature and the executive is a hopeful sign.

No discussion of Vladimir Putin, however, would be complete without acknowledging the most disturbing social repercussion of his presidency: the emergence, however small, of a "cult of personality." If nothing else, Boris Yeltsin did his country a great service by being such a flawed human being that Russians easily grasped that the "president" and the "presidency" were not the same thing. The October 1993 standoff forced many Russians to hold their noses and support a man they did not particularly like, because he was the responsible steward of an office they trusted to protect them. Yeltsin never had a "cult"; inside the Kremlin, he may have been treated by his staff and other political insiders as a kind of aging mafia don whose word was law, but he was never able to govern his fellow citizens without taking his case to them and asking for their support, like any other elected politician.

Putin's popularity among some Russians, by contrast, is out of proportion to anything he has done in office. In February 2001, a privately funded exhibition called *Nash Putin* (Our Putin) was held in Moscow, where statues and portraits of the new president by various artists were on display. Some Russians reacted to it with disdain, while others made it clear that they looked up to Putin as a hero. Artist Fedor Dubrovin told a reporter that "People are trying to be like him. He's a role model," which might seem a reasonable sentiment, except that being "like Putin" even extends to having Putin's hairdo, which barbers are offering men.[63] Before being too critical of the Russians, Americans might remember the adulation that has followed modern U.S. presidents like John F. Kennedy (whose own hairstyle, among other things, was emulated by Americans), Ronald Reagan (whose popularity led to the coinage of the term "Teflon president"), Bill Clinton (who was sometimes referred to by Democratic and Republican pundits alike as "Elvis" because of his indestructible charisma), and even Jimmy Carter, who was once immortalized in a 1976 poster that placed a beard, halo, and robes on the then-Georgia governor over a caption that said "J.C. Can Save America!"

But American institutions are neither new nor untested, and American society, by its individualistic nature, is less inclined to place too much faith or trust in a particular leader. (And public adulation, even when it reaches beyond 90 percent approval levels, is no guarantee of anything, as George H. W. Bush can attest.) Whether this burgeoning adoration of Putin is merely transitory—and Russians can hardly be blamed for having a young, tough president in whom they can finally show some pride—or whether it will corrode their understanding of the Kremlin as separate from its occupant has yet to be seen. For his part, Putin reacted to the exhibition in his usual understated manner: "I would like to thank them," he said, "but ask them not to do this." Russians, however pleased they are with Putin at the moment, would do well to heed their new president's advice.

Chapter Seven

The Future of Russian Presidential Democracy

We will develop political processes in the sense of the word that is traditional—and I wish to stress this—traditional for Western democracy. But this does not mean that anarchy and total permissiveness must flourish in Russia.

—*Vladimir Putin, 2001*

A Russian "Institutional Presidency?"

The Second Republic is nearing the end of its first decade. While this might otherwise be cause for optimism, the relative longevity of Russian presidential democracy has not reassured those who doubt that Russia is a democracy or those who believe it is unlikely to become or remain one. Even in Russia, there is still talk of Yeltsin's time as a tsar, an "elected monarch," the puppet (or master) of a cabal of powerful interests, and any other number of images that describe him as everything except what he was: an elected chief executive. Now that the office has passed to Vladimir Putin, some of these concerns—many of which were more a commentary on Yeltsin's flamboyance than his actual power—have been revised, and center now on Putin as a shadowy autocrat who is quietly dismantling those few democratic institutions "Tsar Boris" once allowed.

But the evolution of the Russian presidency since Yeltsin's 1996 reelection suggests that the institution is becoming more prominent than the incumbent, and that the presidency itself is more important to the eventual deeping of democratic culture than any one president. It is as true of Russia as it is of America that "what the presidency is at any particular moment depends in important measure on who is President," but in neither

Russia nor America is the office itself so malleable that any one personality can appropriate it completely.[1] By the time Yeltsin left office in 1999, his presidency had been battered by crises and opponents beyond his control, leaving the presidency weaker, not stronger, than it was before 1996. (An *Izvestiia* commentary suggested that Putin's appointment was a last-ditch effort on Yeltsin's part to recover some of his influence over the national agenda: "Never," it wrote in the summer of 1999, "has Boris Yeltsin's presidential power been as weak as it is now.")[2] Yeltsin's smashing defeat of Zyuganov did not vest him with the glow of unfettered populist power; rather, the trials he suffered during the winter and spring of 1996 seemed to have diminished him and his office by proving, if nothing else, that anyone who wants to lead the Russian Federation has to work for it by stumping the country and actually winning votes. (An "elected monarch" would not have had to touch the hands of the common folk or shuffle his ministers in order to keep his throne.) His actions after his reelection were not those of a satiated prince, but rather of a politician who narrowly escaped defeat. Moreover, other institutions have grown into their roles and begun to shoulder more responsibilities, and more is now expected of legislators, judges, and cabinet members than even five or ten years ago. As the power of the political leaders and bureaucrats around Yeltsin grew and the president was cut down to size, it is little wonder that many Russians began to ask, as one Moscow construction worker did in 1998: "Does it matter what Yeltsin does?"[3]

Yeltsin's growing irrelevance in Russian politics actually had a healthy effect on Russian democracy, in that it helped to weaken the idea that a single person controlled the destiny of a state the size of the Russian Federation. It also helped to disabuse Russians of any sense that one branch of government could by decree solve problems in the others; thus, when Yeltsin left office, there was no panic or disorder, not least because people realized that other parts of the government could perform their duties normally during a transition of executive power. Yeltsin resigned, Putin was sworn in, the sky did not fall, the daily institutions of Russian political and economic life continued to function, and Russia's major political figures set about preparing for the next rounds of elections in a relatively businesslike way. The presidency is the center of constitutional gravity in Russia, to be sure, but the lesson of Yeltsin's shortened second term is that the president is not the sole arbiter of Russian political life.

Critics of presidential systems would be hard-pressed to explain both the 1996 elections and subsequent events. Not only did the presidential elections fail to divide Russian society into a triumphant majority and a desperate minority, they served to chasten rather than strengthen the president himself. This should lay to rest the idea that Russia is a European variant on the Latin American "delegative democracies," in which "whoever wins election to the presidency is thereby entitled to govern as he or she sees fit, constrained only by the hard facts of existing power relations and by a constitutionally limited term of office."[4] (Some critics of presidentialism have actually argued that these and other disturbing elements of "delegative democracy" are actually inherent "pathologies" of presidential systems.)[5] Nor is the Russian president (not even one as popular as Putin) some sort of "monarch": two eminent Russian political scientists who have tried to make this argument have found themselves forced to admit that their "elective monarch" actually has insufficient power to enforce his will—thus rendering the whole concept contradictory.[6]

The Russian president, then, is neither a dictator nor a king. Events in 1993 and again after the elections of 1996 and 2000 point strongly to another possibility: that the presidency in the Russian Federation is becoming, to borrow a term from Edward Corwin's study of the American executive, an "institutional" presidency, in which "the President becomes merged with—albeit not submerged in—a cluster of institutions designed to base government in the national area on conference and consensus."[7] In looking back over the history of American presidents, Corwin accepted that many of them, including Abraham Lincoln, Franklin D. Roosevelt, and Ronald Reagan, had placed the stamp of their own strong personalities on the office. (It is instructive to note that the Russians were not the first to worry about electing tyrants. Senator Henry Clay lamented that America under Andrew Jackson was "in the midst of a revolution, hitherto bloodless, but tending rapidly towards a total change of the pure republican character of the Government, and to the concentration of all power in the hands of one man.")[8] Corwin argued that Americans found a solution to the problem of the excessive personalization of power by creating this "institutional" presidency, and strengthening other parts of the regime that would both share and limit the president's power and decrease the influence of any one man in the Oval Office.

To argue that this is happening in Moscow might seem overly optimistic, but it appears to be the most likely outcome of the past decade of Russian political development. Perhaps most important is that neither the judiciary nor the legislature have become pawns of the presidency; the Russian Constitutional Court's blunt rejection of any possibility of a third term for Yeltsin should be proof enough that Russia's justices do not answer to the president, and the composition and activity of the Duma speaks for itself. Other politicians have gained stature and forced the executive into negotiation not by force of will or charisma, but by their own institutional standing. In 1997, for example, when the Duma was threatening yet another vote of no-confidence in the president's government, a meeting was held by the "Big Four": the president, the speaker of the Duma, the chairman of the Federation Council, and the prime minister. At this particular meeting Yeltsin, according to one account, "decided to abandon the customary method of talking to the Duma in the language of ultimatums and vetoes in favor of a . . . dialogue at the level of top officials behind tightly closed doors." This kind of more cooperative approach was described by Russian journalists as "Chernomyrdinite," since they associated it with the former prime minister's quiet manner; however, the idea of the president as one *of* four, rather than one *over* three, has outlived Chernomyrdin and Yeltsin, and a style of political negotiation that once provoked comment has now, under Putin, become routine.[9]

Obviously, the idea of a growing institutionalization of Russian political life and of the presidency specifically is a conclusion that has to remain tentative, for now. But a comparison of the current presidency with its predecessors reveals the distance the Russian Federation has covered since 1993.

Mikhail Gorbachev's presidency of 1990–1991 was an act of desperation, an attempt to hold together a crumbling Union with a symbol of national unity. The Soviet situation was so unstable that Gorbachev did not risk allowing himself to be elected directly. His choice to seek election from the Congress of People's Deputies ensured that the office was one specifically created for him; there was no serious competition for the post (not least because no one else really wanted the job) and the legislators knew it. Of course, this personalized presidency was exactly what the Soviet parliament wanted, because it created a national executive who would in theory hold nearly supreme power but in practice would suffer from the ultimate accountability that the legislators wanted to abdicate. The Soviet presidency was created at the expense of other institutions around it, and when Gorbachev's own authority as a leader collapsed, the USSR presidency collapsed with it.

Boris Yeltsin's own Russian republican presidency was an improvement over the Soviet presidency, if only because it had its roots in a national plebiscite and was accompanied by a Russian republican parliament that was less eager to delegate its own powers to the executive. But the office Yeltsin won in 1991 was his for the asking; there was no other Russian leader whose stature remotely approached Yeltsin's and he won the office with so crushing a mandate that it was almost impossible to separate the man from the title. To be fair, the Russians (like the other Soviet republics) were not thinking carefully about ways to institutionalize a presidency, they were looking for a leader of national reputation who could guide them from the disintegrating USSR, with the messy details of democratic government put off until another day in the haste to exit the Union.

The presidency in the First Republic did not, like its Soviet predecessor, become a black hole into which the accountability and functions of all other institutions were drawn. Neither, however, did it become a stable institution with clear and limited powers. Rather, it became the rallying point for a final assault on the last elements of Sovietism in the parliament. The April 1993 referendum was a major step toward institutionalizing the power of the presidency rather than the president, since it represented a genuflection toward public opinion: Yeltsin asked for legitimization from the public instead of choosing to rationalize presidential actions by relying on his personal authority. Still, the referendum asked Russians to choose, in effect, between personalities, and the voters went on to make something of an unholy pact with the presidency in which the chief executive would save them from the terrors of the past, and they would turn a blind eye to the sins of the present. The October 1993 conflict between two belief systems was played out as a conflict between two branches of government, but in the end it could just as easily have been described as two presidents—one elected, one the self-appointed "acting" president—warring for the future of Russia.

The turning point for the Russian presidency came in the first days after the destruction of the Supreme Soviet in 1993. Yeltsin could have either ruled by decree indefinitely, keeping his opponents in prison and rewriting the constitution at his leisure, or he could present the voters with a new constitution and a parliamentary body that would actually have the power to ratify it. Yeltsin's decision to hold a constitutional referendum so quickly after the fall of the First Republic has been criticized as naked opportunism, a bold move to ram through a new political system while he was at the height of his popularity. But one can only imagine the criticisms that would have been made had he continued to rule in the absence of a constitution, a parliament, effective local government, or a functioning national court system. The 1993 referendum and the 1996 elections were decisive turns toward entrenching not only the Russian presidency but other Russian political institutions as well through constitutional means rather than by personal fiat.

Although the abbreviated election of 2000 made gaining the presidency relatively easy for Vladimir Putin, his cautious first year in office is testimony not only to the growing power of other Russian political institutions, but also of the sensitivity of the presidency to public opinion. Putin, from his first days during the Chechen campaign, through the *Kursk* tragedy, and even in his battles with the oligarchs, has shown a recognition that raw executive power cannot accomplish alone what a president supported by public opinion and buoyed by parliamentary support can achieve. Putin, in other words, seems to accept what Yeltsin eventually learned as well: presidents in a system of separated powers cannot simply "rule," they must actually "govern"; that is, they must play their part in a larger network of institutions that must also be allowed to play theirs.

Still, without a successful series of presidential elections in which power clearly shifts from the ruling group to the loyal opposition, it is too early to say that Russia is out of danger and that a return to authoritarianism, perhaps in some more mundane, bureaucratic form, is impossible. A central problem is that the only serious organized opposition in Russia is still the Communist Party, and the current governing elite in Moscow might well do almost anything to prevent the transfer of power to the communists. This is a test no one in Russia will probably ever have to face, since the communists cannot win a national mandate; still, the longer the communists displace more responsible opposition, the more the whole situation raises the question about what would constitute a "loyal opposition" and whether Putin or his successors would be willing to risk being swept from power in future elections.

What would a failure of presidentialism look like in Russia? Dire scenarios ranging from a second Russian civil war to a "nuclear Yugoslavia" have appeared from time to time since the Soviet collapse, but Russians need look no farther than neighboring Belarus to try to imagine life under a presidential regime that has collapsed into autocracy.

A Warning from Minsk

This book has argued that presidential arrangements have served Russians and their young democracy well, but the great drama of Russian democracy has overshadowed cases of presidential failure in the former Soviet Union, including the emergence of president-for-life schemes in Central Asia that are better described as failures of state-building than of particular political arrangements. The European states left by the Soviet imperial collapse have done better, some with parliamentary regimes (as in the Baltic states) and others such as Ukraine and Poland with more mixed systems (that is, systems that are essentially parliamentary but nonetheless have presidents with significant powers). If the relative success of the Russian Federation as a democracy is a case that opponents of presidential systems cannot explain, the failure of democracy in Belarus is a cautionary tale that fulfills all the most pessimistic expectations of presidentialism. Events in Minsk since 1991 stand in sharp contrast to those in Moscow since 1993 and make plain that the Russian system is not one of presidential authoritarianism. But they are also a warning that presidentialism is not without its risks.

Like its Soviet and Russian counterparts, the Belarusian parliament fell into internal warfare for the first two years after independence. The man who had joined with Boris Yeltsin and then Ukrainian republican leader Leonid Kravchuk to dissolve the Soviet Union, Stanislav Shushkevich, was ousted as Supreme Soviet chairman by his own prime minister, Viacheslav Kebich. Belarus was declared a presidential republic in 1994, and Kebich ran for president with every expectation of winning. Also in the race, however, was Aleksandr Lukasheko—a sort of Belarusian version of Vladimir Zhirinovsky, right down to his mercurial nature and open nostalgia for the Soviet period. Kebich may have won the struggle in parliament, but Lukashenko won the struggle for the people, and in 1994 he took his place as the first elected president of Belarus.

Lukashenko ran on a platform that promised discipline, order, and an attack on corruption. He made good on all those promises, clamping down on political freedoms, smothering the media, arresting and beating members of disorderly groups (particularly pesky student protesters), and displacing many corrupt officials with corrupt appointees of his own. When finally confronted by serious legislative opposition and growing unrest in the streets of Minsk, he took his case to the people, telling them that they had a choice between "parliamentary chaos" or "presidential discipline" and calling for a referendum on his own powers, after which all arguments with parliament would "vanish."[10]

In November 1996, Lukashenko presented a draft constitution for public approval that included extending his own term to 2001, eviscerating the powers of the legislature, and subordinating anything of relevance to the president's authority. Lukashenko claims that his draft constitution received over 70 percent of the vote, but how Belarusians actually voted remains a mystery, as there were wide accusations of fraud from the Belarusian opposition (such as there was), as well as from the European Union and the United States. In any case, the Belarusian Supreme Court had already tried to take a stand by ruling that the referendum was a nonbinding one; Lukashenko promptly showed his lack of respect for the Belarusian judiciary by announcing he would ignore it, signing all the referendum's provisions into law and reconstituting the legislature by handpicking its members and stuffing it with cronies.

Democracy in Belarus, barely breathing in 1994, was dead by 1996 and remains so today. A 1997 investigation by the Organization for Security and Cooperation in Europe found that "the authorities are constructing a system of totalitarian government" under presidential rule.[11] The presidential referendum was the last serious attempt at a public ballot in Belarus and will probably remain so until Lukashenko is ousted. (In his forties, he is still a young man and does not seem inclined to retire. Legally, he can only run for one more five-year term but there is nothing preventing him from simply amending the constitution again.) Local elections originally scheduled for 1999, if they are ever held, will be a sham: all opposition parties have refused to participate and the electoral rules are so obviously rigged that the OSCE and the EU have refused even to send observers.[12] Belarus has, in a matter of a few years, made great strides in returning to the Soviet past its president so openly reveres.

To some extent, comparisons between Russia and Belarus are flawed, if only because of the size and international importance of each country. A figure like Lukashenko might never have been able to tame a huge federal nation like Russia, since that would entail having to run roughshod over scores of governors and mayors. It is also doubtful that he could have survived (or, more to the point, rigged) an election and then a referendum in so large and diverse a country as Russia.

There is nonetheless one important similarity, as well as one crucial difference, between these two cases. First and foremost, it is important to note that it was only a failure of parliamentarism in the first place that made each president's reign possible. Whatever criticisms may be made of presidentialism in Belarus, the fact remains that presidentialism, as in Russia, was the result, and not the cause, of social disorder and parliamentary failure. The difference comes in what happened after each man triumphed over his parliamentary opponents: Yeltsin used the 1993 referendum both to ratify a constitution and to elect a parliament under international supervision; Lukashenko imposed a constitution that allowed him to choose a parliament. In one case, the president protected democracy from a renegade parliament; in the other, the president seized power from a corrupt parliament and has since ruled as poorly as the legislators he ousted.

The current arrangement in Belarus will almost certainly not last once Lukashenko is gone, but his speedy capture of the entire Belarusian political system is a frightening lesson in what can happen when an office like the presidency is handed to a would-be dictator by an exasperated electorate. The Russians, to their credit, have resisted this temptation at least twice, first when they rejected Zhirinovsky and again when they turned away from Zyuganov. It remains a pressing question whether Belarus would have done better, or will do better in the future, under any other kind of regime. Indeed, would either nation have fared better under a parliamentary regime? Probably not; presidentialism was a popular choice in Belarus if only because the parliament—which was not without a few would-be dictators of its own—was incapable of governing. But since Lukashenko's original term has been extended, Belarusians will have to wait until at least 2006 to find out. The Russians by that point will have gone through another cycle of parliamentary and presidential elections, and will have more opportunities sooner rather than later to tinker with the structure of their system of government.

The Second Republic might eventually be discarded, not as the result of violence or upheaval, but rather of evolution and change. It may turn out that the institutions of the Second Republic will one day be looked upon as having served Russia well over ten or twenty years of transition, and that once Russian society has healed from the wounds inflicted by the Soviet experience, Russia might be ready to move on to other arrangements. What might those look like?

A Third Republic? Some Possibilities for the Russian Future

The question of whether there will be a Third Republic (or a Second Empire, or a Soviet Restoration) is complicated by the fact that so many Russians and Westerners thought the Second Republic would be gone by now and that any new Russian government should already be in place. New arrangements were supposed to emerge after the Chechen war, the 1995 communist sweep in the Duma, the 1996 near miss with a communist president, the 1997 government shakeup, the 1998 Asian debt crisis, and any of a number of times when Boris Yeltsin seemed about to die. In each case, the wide expectation seemed to be a sudden concentration of emergency powers in the executive branch and the suspension of parliament, or, in the nightmare scenario, the collapse of central Russian power and the breakup of the Federation into its individual regional components. The only scenario that fell out of consideration early on was that of a military coup, probably because Russians themselves understood that the military has been so demoralized that it would not want the burden of governing even if it were offered.[13]

The ability of the institutions of the Second Republic to endure under this succession of crises, and to remain intact during the first major transfer of power, suggests that they will remain a part of Russian political life for the foreseeable future. Many Russian intellectuals (particularly those allied with parties like Yabloko that get trounced regularly in elections) have called for a change to a completely parliamentary system with a ceremonial president, but this idea has found no purchase with the Russian public for two reasons. First, many Russians believe that abolishing the presidency would result, in Boris Nemtsov's words, in "federal disintegration"; strong governors would step in and fill the void of authority left by parliamentary bickering or paralysis, and simply ignore the central government. Given the delicate relationship between Moscow and Russia's regions, the presidency is likely to stay, if only to maintain the stability of Russian federalism.

Second, the process of rebuilding trust takes a long time—generations perhaps—and Russian social conditions are simply not stable enough to create meaningful political parties that would in turn be able to constitute or sustain a new parliamentary regime. One response to this, of course, is that no party will ever learn to govern as long as power resides in the executive branch, and that presidentialism will, by virtue of its existence, undermine the potential for a transition to parliamentarism. This is a variation on a criticism discussed in chapter four, that the relative meaninglessness of the parliament frees the voters to elect extremists; here, the idea is that the impotence of the Duma frees legislators to act irresponsibly and that arguments in support of continued presidentialism are actually self-fulfilling prophecies.

There is simply no evidence, however, to suggest that instituting a parliamentary system in Russia would do much more than place a prime minister in the same kind of no-win situation in which Yeltsin often found himself—that is, saddled with the need to implement unpopular measures that have been left untouched by the legislature. Even in the West, as some American analysts have pointed out, legislators generally "are not in the business of creating effective, accountable government. They are in the business of making themselves popular and their jobs secure."[14] This may be a bit harsh (legislators have consciences, too), but it seems especially applicable to the Russian case, in which parliamentarians are often preoccupied more with such issues as their own immunities and privileges than with actual law-making.[15] A parliamentary system in Russia, especially if designed with any provisions for proportional representation, would likely result only in the creation of a body paralyzed by a plethora of parties that would in turn keep collapsing until some canny prime minister was able to wrangle emergency powers and rule for a set period as, in effect, a president. Although some Russians have argued that the "Italian variant" would be less disruptive than people fear, neither the Russian public nor the political elite seems inclined to test the effect of rotating governments in a series of parliamentary crises and it is difficult to imagine the abolishment of the presidency in the near future.

If there is a Third Republic, it is likely to look much like the Second, but with considerably expanded parliamentary and judicial powers and more substantial limitations on the presidency. One obvious possibility, for example, is that Russian constitutional experts will finally try to resolve the problem of decree powers and create a presidency that has some power of executive order (like its American counterpart), but without the ability to create law at will. This would have a dramatic effect on governance in a Third Republic, because it would in one stroke decrease the power of the presidency while forcing responsibility on the legislature. Without the power of decree, the Russian president's most potent weapon would be the negative power of the veto rather than the positive power of the *ukaz*.[16] This would in turn deprive parliament of political cover on difficult issues, because they could no longer count on the executive to step in and act if they chose to avoid taking action themselves. If this resulted in more policies that were the result of legislation originating in the parliament, it would mean the rectification of an important constitutional imbalance in Russian politics.

The Second Republic, with its provisions for legislative and judicial vetoes of presidential decrees, has already taken steps in this direction. As trust grows between the public, parties, and parliament, the Russian constitution could be amended to take this dangerous power from the hands of the executive and vest it in the legislature where it logically ought to reside, which in itself would go far toward helping Russian parties and legislators learn to govern responsibly. However, for the parties to create a more stable legislature, the parties themselves will have to become more stable. One important step to this end would be to reduce the number of parties overall, so that each electoral cycle will not create a sudden and confusing blossoming of small, narrow, and short-lived parties. Discussion has already begun on this issue, with Putin on record as seeking to reduce the number of parties to three or four, at most, by raising the number of members it would take to register a party.[17] So far, the harshest critics of this plan have not been the communists (who can easily muster enough voters to re-register legitimately) but the smaller democratic parties, such as Yabloko, who would have to compromise with each other to form a larger organization—exactly the kind of social aggregation proponents of Russian party reform would argue is needed.[18]

Other alternatives in a future Russian republic might include reestablishing direct election of the upper house (a move that might help to tame some of the more heavy-handed local and regional authorities in the Federation's territories), changes in the number of proportional or single-district seats (lessening the number of list seats could effectively extinguish some of the extremist parties and would probably break the back of the CPRF), and consolidation of the federal courts from three benches into one (which would establish the principle that the civil, criminal, and constitutional codes are all part of a single body of Russian law). The current reorganization of the Federation Council is a step in this direction; while the upper house is not yet formed by direct election, after 2002 it can no longer be derided as a powerful "Soviet of Governors."

While these changes can be accomplished even now by legislation or constitutional amendment, the wholesale creation of a new republic may not be necessary to adjust the relationships among the branches of the Russian government over the next decade. Indeed, the future Russian political system may not emerge in the proclamation of a Third Republic but in the gradual mutation of the Second over time to the point at which Russian constitutional scholars may look back and realize that the regime put into place in 1993 has been supplanted by a more efficient and rational system of separated powers. Democratic politics is as much as matter of tradition as it is of law, and over time a tradition of greater comity between the legislative and executive branches, with both pledged to respect the independence of the judiciary, could do more to stabilize the parliament and to strip the Russian executive of some of its more dangerous powers than could any written law. If Vladimir Putin commits to maintaining a Russian presidency that is a symbol of federal unity and acts to ensure—as chief executives ought—that national laws are being observed throughout the territory of the Federation, then the presidency itself, as the institution that sheltered Russian democracy when it was most threatened, would be Boris Yeltsin's most valuable legacy, one that would overshadow even his worst personal and political failings during his terms in office.

In looking back at the American experience, Harvey Mansfield describes a paradox that captures the essence of the modern Russian situation as well:

> Executive power, expanding when needed, kept the rule of law from being, in effect, the rule of ambitious legislators and contrary judges. The beauty of

executive power, then, is to be both subordinate and not subordinate, both weak and strong. It can reach where law cannot, and thus supply the defect of law, yet remain subordinate to law. This ambivalence in the modern executive permits its strength to be useful to republics, without endangering them.[19]

Critics of presidential systems would be less charitable, calling this expansion "ruling at the edge of the constitution." Perhaps it is; but there are times when the pursuit of parliamentary democracy as an abstract ideal is nothing less than suicidal. Presidential power is not an undemocratic alternative to which such mistrustful societies must relegate themselves out of frustration. Rather, the establishment of a presidential republic may be the means by which a new democracy can weather the social storms that must inevitably pass before civic life reemerges and parties and other institutions can reassert themselves and take their rightful place in the business of government.

The Russian people seem to have defied the odds (and the best guesses of many in the West) by choosing an arrangement that has served to stabilize what in 1992 seemed to be an almost unrecoverably chaotic situation. The Americans, the French, and now the Russians seem to have found something of value in presidentialism; perhaps Western social scientists should consider if they might be able to do the same. Russia in the early twenty-first century may find that the arrangements derided by Westerners and the Russian opposition alike as undemocratic, dangerous, and unstable in the 1990s did not, in the end, betray their emergence from the Soviet dictatorship, but actually protected their fragile democracy until society regained its balance. This is only a hope, but as Russia nears the end of a decade of democracy, it seems a reasonable one.

Notes

Introduction

1. Boris Yeltsin, *Zapiski prezidenta* (Moscow: Ogonek, 1994), p. 14.
2. "Yeltsin Disbands Parliament, Calls Elections to 'Federal Assembly,'" FBIS-SOV-93–182-S, p. 2.
3. Numerous examples of such dire prophecies abounded at the time. Robert Daniels charged that "Yeltsin's aim as it has unfolded since 1991 was not to preserve representative government," but rather to establish a "presidential dictatorship," while Lilia Shevtsova warned that Yeltsin was "becoming ever more despotic." See Lilia Shevtsova, "The Two Sides of the New Russia," *Journal of Democracy*, July 1995, p. 66, and Robert Daniels, "Yeltsin, Reform, and the West," *The Soviet and Post-Soviet Review* (formerly *Soviet Union/Union Sovietique*) 20, nos. 2–3, pp. 135–136.
4. I use "democracy" here in its most basic sense, as essentially unlimited pluralism: a polity in which free communication, basic civil liberties, and free association are all part of a system of competitive and meaningful elections through which government is held accountable. It is only possible, as Adam Przeworski has noted, when the competitors for power accept that winning is possible and that losing does not mean political or physical annihilation. See Adam Przeworski, "Democracy as a Contingent Outcome of Conflicts," in Jon Elster and Rune Slagstaad, eds., *Constitutionalism and Democracy* (New York: Cambridge, 1988), p. 64.
5. See Chapter 4 for more on Duma member Konstantin Borovoy's comments on this subject.
6. V. Guliev and A. Kozlov, "Perekraivat' Konstitutsiiu nedopustimo," *Rossiiskie Vesti*, February 5, 1995, p. 2, and "Author Debunks Claims of Yeltsin's Growing 'Authoritarianism,'" FBIS-SOV-95-048-S, March 13, 1995, p. 41.
7. Stephen Holmes, "What Russia Teaches Us Now: How Weak States Threaten Freedom," *The American Prospect*, July-August 1997, pp. 30–39.
8. Lilia Shevtsova, "The Current Russian Political Situation," lecture at the U.S.-Russian Forum, Moscow, July 13, 1994.

9. Holmes refers to this as an "electoral charade" that does not result in accountable government. Holmes, p. 32.

10. Gerald Easter, "Preference for Presidentialism: Regime Change in Russia and the NIS," *World Politics,* January 1997, p. 209.

11. Steve Leisman, "A Mistrustful West Finds It Hard to Grasp Real Change in Russia," *The Wall Street Journal,* September 26, 1996, p. A1.

12. Interview with Anatolii Greshnevikov, Moscow, Russia, April 16, 1997. Greshnevikov did not see this as much of a paradox: he simply believed his voters were more independent than others that might have knuckled under to Moscow's wishes (or been duped by Moscow's machinations). Other legislators, of course, felt the same thing about *their* voters.

13. Interview with Sergei Baburin, Moscow, Russia, April 17, 1997.

14. David Remnick, *Resurrection* (New York: Random House, 1997), p. 367.

15. In an example of this exceptionalism regarding the 1996 election, Abraham Brumberg derides the "squalid bribes" used in the campaign, and excoriates a Yeltsin "television blitz" that tried to convince voters that a vote for Zyuganov was a vote for concentration camps and Stalinist repression. Any American with memories of the chicanery in the 1960 presidential campaign, or of Lyndon Johnson's infamous 1964 ad that suggested that a vote for Barry Goldwater was a vote to risk global thermonuclear war (or, more precisely, to drop a nuclear weapon on a little girl in a field), might well wonder what Brumberg finds so uniquely offensive about Yeltsin's commercials. See "'Struggle for the Kremlin': An Exchange," *The New York Review of Books,* September 19, 1996, p. 77.

16. Philippe C. Schmitter, "Dangers and Dilemmas of Democracy," *Journal of Democracy,* April 1994, pp. 60–62.

Chapter 1

1. Matthew Shugart and John Carey, *Presidents and Assemblies: Constitutional Design and Electoral Dynamics* (Cambridge, UK: Cambridge University Press, 1992), p. 2.

2. Kurt von Mettenheim, "Introduction," in Kurt von Mettenheim, ed., *Presidential Institutions and Democratic Politics* (Baltimore: Johns Hopkins University Press, 1997), pp. 2–3.

3. Stephen Skowronek, *The Politics Presidents Make* (Cambridge, MA: Belknap/Harvard, 1993), p. 4.

4. Edward Corwin, *The President: Office and Powers, 1787–1984,* 5th ed. (New York: New York University Press, 1984), pp. 21–22, 356.

5. "France's Imperial Presidency," *The Economist,* April 22, 1995, p. 49.

6. Harvey Mansfield, *Taming the Prince: The Ambivalence of Modern Executive Power* (New York: The Free Press, 1989), p. xix.

7. See, for example, Arend Lijphart's discussion and typologies in Arend Lijphart, ed., *Parliamentary versus Presidential Government* (Oxford: Oxford University Press, 1992), especially pp. 6–9.

8. Mansfield, p. 296.

9. Although Russia is technically structured as a "semipresidential" system—a relatively rare arrangement where the president appoints a prime minister to act as parliamentary leader—it conforms to the "pure" presidential model in all important respects. Although there have been attempts to present semipresidentialism as a kind of institutional "third way," I remain unconvinced that semipresidentialism, as it has been practiced in the very few systems in which it exists, is anything more than a variant on "pure" presidentialism. Giovanni Sartori has wrestled with the problem of defining which systems are truly "semipresidential," and he rightly points out the messy categorizations that result from definitions based solely on things like a directly elected presidency. While I accept his narrower definition as clearer, I disagree that it describes a system all that different *in practice* from presidentialism, particularly in Russia. See Giovanni Sartori, *Comparative Constitutional Engineering* (New York: New York University Press, 1994), chapter 7. For a thoughtful dissent on this issue, see Eugene Huskey, "Democracy and Institutional Design in Russia," *Demokratizatsiya,* Fall 1996. For more discussion of the question of Russian semipresidentialism, see Thomas Nichols, *The Logic of Russian Presidentialism,* The Carl Beck Papers in Russian and East European Studies, no. 1301 (Pittsburgh: University of Pittsburgh Center for Russian and East European Studies, 1998).

10. Quoted in J. E. S. Hayward, "Presidentialism and French Politics," *Parliamentary Affairs,* Winter 1964/1965, p. 29.

11. Juan J. Linz, "Presidential or Parliamentary Democracy: Does It Make a Difference?," in Juan J. Linz and Arturo Valenzuela, eds., *The Failure of Presidential Democracy* (Baltimore: Johns Hopkins University Press, 1994), p. 7.

12. See Lijphart, p. 19.

13. Alfred Stepan and Cindy Skach, "Constitutional Frameworks and Democratic Consolidation: Parliamentarism versus Presidentialism," *World Politics,* October 1993, p. 18.

14. Donald Horowitz, "Comparing Democratic Systems," in Lijphart, ed., p. 203.

15. Scholars of the American presidency are not immune to this kind of nonfalsifiable description of presidential aggrandizement. Consider Arthur Schlesinger's 1973 discussion of the enlargement of presidential war-making powers: "It was as much a matter of congressional abdication as of presidential usurpation. As it took place, there dwindled away checks, both written and unwritten, that had long held the Presidency under control." Arthur M. Schlesinger Jr., *The Imperial Presidency* (Boston: Houghton Mifflin, 1973), p. ix.

16. S. E. Finer, *The Man on Horseback: The Role of the Military in Politics,* (New York: Praeger, 1962), p. 2.

17. These presumptions reflect the influence of the "new institutionalism," which treats institutions as "political actors in their own right" that can then "assume a life of their own, extracting societal resources, socializing individuals, and even altering the basic nature of civil society itself." See James March and Johan Olsen, "The New Institutionalism: Organizational Factors in Political Life," *The American Political Science Review,* September 1984, p. 738, and Stephen Krasner, "Approaches to the State: Alternative Conceptions and Historical Dynamics," *Comparative Politics,* January 1984, p. 240. I use the term "institutions" in its common understanding as the formal and informal patterns of behavior and structures that are, in the words of Douglass North, the "rules of the game in a society or, more formally . . . the humanly devised constraints that shape human interaction." See Douglass North, *Structure and Change in Economic History* (New York: Norton, 1981), p. 201, and *Institutions, Institutional Change, and Economic Performance* (Cambridge, UK: Cambridge University Press, 1990), p. 3.

18. The attribution of power as a generic goal is a variation on so-called "thick" rational choice approaches. For a discussion of problems associated with positing such broadly similar goals across cases, see Donald Green and Ian Shapiro, *Pathologies of Rational Choice Theory* (New Haven, CT: Yale University Press, 1994), pp. 17–20.

19. Linz makes this comment in the context of noting that the only presidential democracy with a long history of constitutional continuity is the United States. Juan J. Linz, "The Perils of Presidentialism," in Lijphart, ed., p. 118.

20. Valerie Bunce, "Comparing East and South," *Journal of Democracy,* July 1995, p. 99.

21. See R. Kent Weaver and Bert Rockman, "When and How Do Institutions Matter?" in R. Kent Weaver and Bert Rockman, eds., *Do Institutions Matter?* (Washington, DC: Brookings Institution, 1993), p. 451.

22. Stephen Holmes, "The Postcommunist Presidency," *East European Constitutional Review,* Fall 1993/Winter 1994 double issue, p. 37.

23. See Linz, "The Perils of Presidentialism," p. 123.

24. Holmes, "The Postcommunist Presidency," p. 39.

25. Al'bert Plutnik, "V Dume b'iut zhenshchinu," *Izvestiia,* September 12, 1995, p. 1.

26. Terry Moe, "Political Institutions: The Neglected Side of the Story," *Journal of Law, Economics, and Organization,* vol. 6 (special issue) 1990, p. 240.

27. Weaver and Rockman have noted an obvious flaw in the parliamentary alternative, namely, that the out-party has a particular incentive to undermine the party in power by not cooperating and depicting the performance of the ruling party as poorly as possible. Weaver and Rockman, eds., p. 24; also see R. Kent Weaver, "Are Parliamentary Systems Better?," *The Brookings Review,* Summer 1985.

28. Peter Ordeshook notes, correctly, that from a technical standpoint the Russian constitution reflects "an extremely shallow understanding of the separation of powers." Elena Mizulina, one of the Duma's leading judicial experts, believes that the system is flawed not only in terms of legislative-executive relations, but even in the balance of power between the upper and lower houses of the legislature itself. See Peter Ordeshook, "Institutions and Incentives," *Journal of Democracy*, April 1995, p. 50, and interview with Elena Mizulina, Moscow, Russia, July 12, 1994.

29. Barbara Mizstal, *Trust in Modern Societies: The Search for the Bases of Social Order* (Cambridge, UK: Polity Press, 1996), p. 229. A recent study of Russian social opinions put it more succinctly: "Distrust is a pervasive legacy of communist rule." Richard Rose, "Postcommunism and the Problem of Trust," *Journal of Democracy*, July 1994, p. 19.

30. For a more detailed discussion of sovietism and social capital, see Thomas Nichols, "Russian Democracy and Social Capital," *Social Science Information*, December 1996.

31. Kenneth Jowitt calls these the phases of "transformation" and "consolidation." See Kenneth Jowitt, *New World Disorder: The Leninist Extinction* (Berkeley: The University of California Press, 1992), pp. 56–57.

32. See Sarah Terry, "Thinking about Post-Communist Transitions: How Different Are They?," *Slavic Review*, Spring 1993, pp. 335–336.

33. John Lowenhardt, *The Reincarnation of Russia* (Durham, NC: Duke University Press, 1995), p. 6.

34. V. Zamkovoi, *Stalinizm: stalinskaia model' totalitarizma* (Moscow: Institut Mezhdunarodnogo Prava i Ekonomiki, 1995), pp. 18–19. Zamkovoi calls this "open or latent sadomasochism," but in a sociopolitical rather than sexual context.

35. Zamkovoi, p. 20. In his book about the final days of the USSR, David Remnick recounted a small, sad anecdote that illustrates this kind of cruelty. Remnick was sitting in a courtyard speaking to an elderly man when they were suddenly interrupted: a woman hurled a cat out of a tenth floor window, yelling "Animal! No room for you here! Be gone!" The cat, Remnick writes, "hit the pavement, and it sounded like the soft pop of an exploding water balloon. Now the two of us, the old man and I, were watching: the woman at the window, her face twisted into an angry knot, the cat struggling to get up on its broken legs. 'Ach,' the old man said, turning away, 'our Russian life!' . . . He [then] went on talking." David Remnick, *Lenin's Tomb* (New York: Vintage, 1994), pp. 26–27.

36. Gennadii Khokhriakov, *Russkie: kto my?* (Moscow: VIEMS, 1993), p. 82.

37. As Niklas Luhmann puts it, "Familiarity is an unavoidable fact of life; trust is a solution for specific problems of risk." See Francis Fukuyama, *Trust: The Social Virtues and the Creation of Prosperity* (New York: The Free Press, 1995), Chapter 1, and Niklas Luhmann, "Familiarity, Confidence, Trust: Problems

and Alternatives," in Diego Gambetta, ed., *Trust: Making and Breaking Cooperative Relations* (Oxford, UK: Blackwell, 1988), p. 95.

38. Rigby notes that this set the pattern of Soviet life into the 1970s. T. H. Rigby, "Stalinism and the Mono-Organizational Society," in Robert Tucker, ed., *Stalinism* (New York: Norton, 1977), p. 62. My colleague Sergei Baburkin of Yaroslavl' University dissents from this view, suggesting that many of these activities (particularly sports clubs and the like), although state-sponsored, provided "escape" from political life, which he argues represented a kind of voluntary association among nonpolitical citizens.

39. Jacek Kuron, "Overcoming Totalitarianism," *Journal of Democracy,* October 1994, p. 72.

40. "Memorandum from the KGB Regarding the Planning of a Demonstration in Memory of John Lennon," *Cold War International History Project Bulletin* no.10, March 1998, p. 219.

41. Jonathan Grant has detailed the "elaborate process" through which the Soviet regime "socially reconstructed the hobby of stamp collecting," a process undertaken mostly by midlevel bureaucrats who could not tolerate the idea of a hobby as "an autonomous realm of social activity." See J. Grant, "The Social Construction of Philately in the Early Soviet Era," *Comparative Studies in Society and History,* Spring 1995, p. 495. By chance, I experienced the effect of the meddling in this particular hobby in a small way in 1987. My father, a lifetime philatelist, accompanied me to the Soviet Union, where he visited a state-run Soviet stamp shop (a small and cheerless place filled only with stamps from socialist nations), and found—after giving one of the collectors there a book of U.S. stamps as a gift—that the shop itself was not really part of the hobbyists' community but merely a meeting point. American stamps in hand, the collectors quickly gathered *outside* the store in a hushed knot to divvy them up. By owning American stamps, which were apparently considered the equivalent of hard currency, they were now pursuing their hobby in violation of Soviet law.

42. See Timothy Colton, *The Dilemma of Reform in the Soviet Union* (New York: Council on Foreign Relations, 1986), p. 54; see also Donna Bahry and Brian Silver, "Intimidation and the Symbolic Uses of Terror in the USSR," *American Political Science Review,* Winter 1987.

43. Richard Lotspeich, "Crime in the Transition Economies," *Europe-Asia Studies,* Winter 1995, p. 571.

44. See John Dunlop, *The Rise of Russia and the Fall of the Soviet Union* (Princeton, NJ: Princeton University Press, 1993), p. 73; for a more detailed listing of the actual organizations and a brief picture of how they changed and mutated in so short a time, see *Neformal'naia Rossiia* (Moscow: Molodaia Gvardiia, 1990), and *Novye politicheskie i obshchestvennye organizatsii (1987–1991),* part 2 (Moscow: Ministerstvo Kul'tury i Turizma Rossiskoi Federatsii, 1992) and part 3, (Moscow: Gosudarstvennaia Istoricheskaia Biblioteka Rossii, 1993).

45. See Victoria Bonnell, "Voluntary Associations in Gorbachev's Reform Program," in George Breslauer, ed., *Can Gorbachev's Reforms Succeed?* (Berkeley, CA: Berkeley-Stanford Program in Soviet Studies, 1990).

46. Dunlop, p. 76.

47. Richard Rose, "Russia as an Hour-Glass Society: A Constitution without Citizens," *East European Constitutional Review,* Summer 1995. p. 35.

48. Ivan Rybkin, *Duma: piataia popytka* (Moscow: Znanie, 1994), p. 47.

49. E. N. Danilova and V. A. Iadov, "Kontury sotsial'no-gruppovykh identifikatsii lichnosti v sovremennom rossiiskom obshchestve," in V. A. Iadov, ed., *Sotsial'naia identifikatsii lichnosti* (Moscow: Rossiiskaia Akademiia Nauk, Institut Sotsiologii, 1993), p. 130.

50. Edward Banfield, *The Moral Basis of a Backward Society* (Glencoe, IL: The Free Press, 1958), p. 86.

51. Judith Shklar, *Ordinary Vices* (Cambridge, MA: Harvard/Belknap, 1984).

52. Gabriel Almond and Sidney Verba, *The Civic Culture* (Princeton, NJ: Princeton University Press, 1963), p. 490.

53. Fukuyama, p. 11.

54. One of the vexing issues of Russian survey research has always been the high proportion of "don't know" or "hard to say" answers, but in a recent study Ellen Carnaghan has done an admirable job in showing that these answers are not only decipherable but do not in themselves represent a danger to democratic stability in Russia. See Ellen Carnaghan, "Alienation, Apathy, or Ambivalence? 'Don't Knows' and Democracy in Russia," *Slavic Review,* Summer 1996, pp. 325–363.

55. The H. J. Kaiser Foundation, *Why Don't Americans Trust the Government?* (Menlo Park, CA: The Kaiser Family Foundation, 1995). The study is summarized and interpreted in a series in *The Washington Post,* January 28 - February 1, 1996, and February 4, 1996. For the study of West Germany, see Kendall Baker, Russell Dalton, and Kai Hildebrandt, *Germany Transformed* (Cambridge, MA: Harvard University Press, 1981).

56. Interview with Konstantin Borovoy, Hanover, New Hampshire, March 28, 1996.

57. The notable exception here among antisystem parties is Vladimir Zhirinovsky's Liberal Democrats, who have supported the institution of the presidency, a position that reflects Zhirinovsky's belief that he can actually win the Russian presidency at some point. There is some evidence, however, that Zhirinovsky has come to see the virtues of parliamentarism in direct proportion to his slowly dawning understanding that he will almost certainly never be president of the Federation. Conversely, the communists now seem to accept the reality of the presidency and are changing their tactics toward capturing, rather than abolishing, the office.

58. Attila Agh, "The Experiences of the First Democratic Parliaments in East Central Europe," *Communist and Post-Communist Studies* 28, no. 2, 1995, p. 205.

59. Agh, p. 207.

60. Thomas Baylis, "Presidents versus Prime Ministers: Shaping Executive Authority in Eastern Europe," *World Politics,* April 1996, p. 308.

61. Sergei Shargorodsky, "Russia-Revolution Day," AP North American Wire, November 7, 1995. Tiulkin added that working people "cannot come to power by parliamentary means."

62. In a striking example of the way in which the system channels opposition legislators into responsible campaigning, one Russian legislator—a member of a bloc allied with the RWP who considers himself to this day to be a member of the Communist Party of the *USSR,* not Russia—told me directly that rather than try to capture first place in every region of his district, he quietly let the other contenders commit fratricide, splitting the vote among themselves while he rode into office as a kind of compromise candidate. Interview with Vladimir Grigoriev, Moscow, Russia, April 17, 1997.

63. Leonid Nikitinskii, "Iavlenie Gorbacheva," *Izvestiia,* July 16, 1994, p. 4.

Chapter 2

1. See, for example, I. M. Stepanov, "Parlamentskaia demokratiia i vybor formy pravleniia" in *Konstitutsionnyi stroi rossii,* 2nd. ed. (Moscow: Institute of State and Law, 1995), and V. N. Suvorov, "Institut prezidentsva: rossiiskaia konstitutsionnaia model' i zarubezhnyi opyt" in *Ispolnitel'naia vlast: sravnitel'no-pravovoe issledovanie* (Moscow: Russian Academy of Sciences, 1995).

2. Among the best documentary accounts of the final days of the USSR in English are a trio of works by journalists: David Remnick, *Lenin's Tomb* (New York: Vintage, 1994), David Satter, *Age of Delirium* (New York: Knopf, 1996), and Michael Dobbs, *Down with Big Brother: The Fall of the Soviet Empire* (New York: Knopf, 1997).

3. V. N. Grigor'iev and Iu. Rogov, *Fenomen "perestroiki:" Cherezvychainoe polozhenie* (Moscow: Verdikt, 1994), p. 8.

4. Dmitrii Volkogonov, *Sem' vozhdei: galareia liderov SSSR* (Moscow: Novosti, 1995), pp. 317–318.

5. See Stephen White, *Gorbachev and After* (Cambridge, UK: Cambridge University Press, 1992), pp. 241–244.

6. White, p. 242.

7. Volkogonov, p. 317.

8. As Vera Tolz pointed out in 1990, despite the growth of autonomous social "circles" and hidden discussion clubs in the 1970s, "the creation of unsanctioned groups with specific sociopolitical goals . . . almost inevitably continued to provoke persecution" until at least 1988. See Vera Tolz, *The USSR's Emerging Multiparty System* (Munich: Radio Liberty, 1990), p. 5.

9. Robert Sharlet notes that the legal and constitutional changes enacted between 1988 and 1990 were nothing less than an attempt at "fundamentally redrafting the 'social contract' governing relations between the citizen and the party-state." Robert Sharlet, *Soviet Constitutional Crisis* (Armonk, NY: M. E. Sharpe, 1992), p. 92.

10. John Dunlop, *The Rise of Russia and the Fall of the Soviet Union* (Princeton, NJ: Princeton University Press, 1993), p. 72

11. Z, "To the Stalin Mausoleum," *Daedalus,* Winter 1990, p. 333.

12. V. Boldin, *Krushenie p'edestala* (Moscow: Respublika, 1995), pp. 189–190.

13. Leon Onikov, *KPSS: anatomiia raspada* (Moscow: Respublika, 1996), pp. 66–67.

14. Arbatov and Yakovlev, in consultation with each other, each tried to stop Gorbachev's panicked rightward turn in early 1991. See A. N. Yakovlev, *Gor'kaia chasha: Bol'shevizm i Reformatsiia Rossii* (Yaroslavl': Verkhne-Volzhskoe, 1994), p. 263, and Georgii Arbatov, *The System* (New York: Random House, 1993), p. 332.

15. Andrei Grachev, *Dal'she bez menia: ukhod prezidenta* (Moscow: "Progress-Kultura," 1994); Mikhail Gorbachev, *Memoirs* (New York: Doubleday, 1996), p. 255.

16. Several reviewers have noted the disappointingly evasive nature of the Gorbachev memoirs. See Jack Matlock, "Gorbachev: Lingering Mysteries," *The New York Review of Books,* December 19, 1996, especially pp. 38–39, for a pointed dissection of the memoirs, including Matlock's charge that an incident involving Matlock himself is "breathtakingly inaccurate, and Gorbachev certainly knows that it is."

17. Quoted in John Morrison, *Boris Yeltsin: From Bolshevik to Democrat* (New York: Dutton, 1991), p. 15.

18. As one ditty of the time ran, "'Acceleration', it's a complex factor; next thing you know, they blew up a reactor; submarines sank, airplanes crashed; Russia's been dirtied with AIDS, the junkies brought it . . . There's no cheese, there's no sausage, there's no vodka, there's no wine, there's only radiation." See V. Pechenev, *Vslet i padenie Gorbacheva* (Moscow: Respublika, 1996). p. 267. Other jokes that used the buzzwords of perestroika such as *uskorenie* ("acceleration") and *chelovecheskii faktor* ("the human factor") were in common Soviet usage in the late 1980s—and which due to their rather frank content are unprintable here.

19. White, p. 249.

20. Institute for Social-Political Research of the Russian Academy of Sciences, *Reformirovanie Rossii: mify i real'nost'* (Moscow: Academia, 1994), p. 27.

21. Volkogonov, p. 318.

22. Yegor Ligachev, *Inside Gorbachev's Kremlin* (New York: Pantheon, 1993) pp. 345–346.

23. "Deputies Analyze Debates at Congress," FBIS-SOV-90–026-S, February 7, 1990, p. 37.

24. See Andrei Melville, "An Emerging Civic Culture? Ideology, Public Attitudes, and Political Culture in the Early 1990s," in A. Miller et al., eds., *Public Opinion and Regime Change* (Boulder, CO: Westview, 1993). Although the 1995 Kaiser-Harvard-*Washington Post* study in the United States found only 35 percent agreeing that most people can be trusted, the only other option on the Kaiser study was a tepid "you can't be too careful," and at least half of those surveyed *also* believed that most people try to be "fair" and "helpful." See "Americans Losing Trust in Each Other and Institutions," *The Washington Post,* January 28, 1996, p. A1; When broken down by educational levels, Robert Putnam found 40–45 percent positive responses to the question of whether "others can be trusted" among Americans with at least a high school education. Robert Putnam, "Tuning In, Tuning Out: The Strange Disappearance of Social Capital in America," *PS: Political Science and Politics,* December 1995, p. 668.

25. A. Kiva, "Bogatstvo—ne porok," *Izvestiia,* June 1, 1990, p. 4.

26. These and following data from "Opinion Poll Reveals Soviet Attitudes," FBIS-SOV-90–065, April 4, 1990, pp. 41–42.

27. Perceived increases in violent crime, for example, even if untrue will drive up pessimistic responses about trust.

28. For crime statistics in this period, see *Reformirovanie Rossii,* pp. 30–33.

29. See Gordon B. Smith, *Reforming the Russian Legal System* (Cambridge, UK: Cambridge University Press, 1996), Chapter 5.

30. "Supreme Court Members View Needed Reforms," FBIS-SOV-90–139, July 19, 1990, pp. 85–86.

31. See Richard Rose, "Russia As an Hour-Glass Society: A Constitution without Citizens," *East European Constitutional Review,* Summer 1995.

32. Yakovlev, p. 346.

33. *Reformirovanie Rossii,* p. 29.

34. Yakovlev, pp. 211–212.

35. Mikhail Gorbachev, *Perestroika i novoe myshlenie dlia nashego strana i dlia vsego mira* (Moscow: Politizdat, 1987), pp. 31–32.

36. See Thane Gustafson and Dawn Mann, "Gorbachev's First Year: Building Power and Authority," *Problems of Communism,* May-June 1986, pp. 2–3.

37. Cameron Ross, "Party-State Relations," in Eugene Huskey, ed., *Executive Power and Soviet Politics* (Armonk, NY: M. E. Sharpe, 1992), p. 75.

38. White, p. 253; *Reformirovanie Rossii,* p. 27.

39. Nicolai Petro, "Perestroika from Below: Voluntary Sociopolitical Associations in the RSFSR" in Alfred Rieber and Alvin Rubenstein, eds., *Perestroika at the Crossroads* (Armonk, NY: M. E. Sharpe, 1991), p. 124.

40. "Poll Expert on People's Attitudes to CPSU," FBIS-SOV-90–045, March 7, 1990, p. 65.

41. Remnick, p. 371.

42. Satter, p. 72.

43. Quoted in Donald Murray, *A Democracy of Despots* (Boulder, CO: Westview Press, 1995), p. 41.
44. "Yakovlev Interviewed on Presidential System," FBIS-SOV-90–084, May 1, 1990, p. 57.
45. "Results of Opinion Poll on Post of President," FBIS-SOV-90–051, March 15, 1990, p. 76.
46. "Poll on Republic Secession, Presidency Cited," FBIS-SOV-90–080, April 25, 1990, p. 67.
47. "Poll Shows Yeltsin Has Highest Approval Rating," FBIS-SOV-90–175, September 10, 1990, p. 84.
48. "Nuzhen li nam prezident?," *Rabochaia Tribuna,* February 24, 1990, p. 1.
49. "Prezident neset otvetstvennost' . . . ," *Rabochaia Tribuna,* March 18, 1990, p. 1.
50. S. Kondrashov, "Mnogopartiinost'—fundament demokratii," *Izvestiia,* March 9, 1990, p. 3.
51. "Presidential Power Discussed," FBIS-SOV-90–049, March 13, 1990, p. 61.
52. For a good overview, see B. M. Lazarev, "Ob izmeneniiakh v pravovom statuse prezidenta SSSR," *Sovietskoe Gosudarstvo i Pravo,* August 1991, pp. 32–33.
53. See Satter, pp. 73–75.
54. "Beseda c zhurnalistami," *Pravda,* February 28, 1990, p. 2.
55. "Presidential Debate Begins," FBIS-SOV-90–040, February 28, 1990, p. 33.
56. "Deputies Offer Amendments," FBIS-SOV-90–040, February 28, 1990, p. 34.
57. "Prezident v SSSR: tochki zreniia," *Argumenty i Fakty* 9, March 3–9, 1990, p. 2.
58. "Yakovlev Interviewed on Presidential System," FBIS-SOV-90–084, May 1, 1990, p. 57.
59. "Justice Minister Yakovlev on Presidential Power," FBIS-SOV-90–042, March 2, 1990, p. 49.
60. "O vnesenii izmenenii i dopolnenii v Konstitutsiiu (Osnovnoi Zakon) SSSR i ucherezhdenii posta Prezidenta SSSR," *Pravda,* March 13, 1990, p. 1; see also "Lukianov on Election of President," FBIS-SOV-90–048, March 12, 1990, p. 54.
61. Quoted in Satter, p. 75, and in Gorbachev, p. 321.
62. "Gavriil Popov Interviewed on Presidential Role," FBIS-SOV-90–047, March 9, 1990, p. 45. Gorbachev recounts the same concerns by deputy (and historian) Yurii Afanasiev, who asked why the USSR needed a president at all. In a rather bizarre passage Gorbachev tried to link Afanasiev's opposition to his expertise on the French Revolution, suggesting Afanasiev had some sort of subconscious desire to be a latter-day "Robespierre of perestroika." "According to Freud," Gorbachev says, "this kind of thing happens." One might add that Freud wrote a word or two about denial and projection, too. Gorbachev, p. 320.
63. Likhachev, a survivor of the Gulag, appealed to his fellow deputies in a televised session to "trust him as an old man and one of much experience" that

electing the president directly, or "depriving him of party support" would lead to war. "Deputies Debate Presidency," FBIS-SOV-90–051, March 15, 1990, p. 56. See also Satter, p. 76.

64. Arbatov, p. 333.

65. *Vneocherednoi tretii s"ezd narodnykh deputatov SSSR, stenograficheskii otchet,* vol. 1 (Moscow: Izdanie verkhovnogo soveta SSSR, 1990), pp. 193–214, and vol. 3, p. 55.

66. *Vneocherednoi tretii s"ezd . . . ,* vol. 3, p. 233.

67. "Results of Opinion Poll on Post of President," p. 76.

68. Kondrashov, p. 68.

69. Eugene Huskey, "Legislative-Executive Relations," in Huskey, ed., p. 83.

70. T. Samolis, "Net, ne s demokratiei my proshchaemsiia," *Pravda,* February 21, 1991, p. 1.

71. "Gorbachev Aide Views Need for 'Emergency' Powers," FBIS-SOV-90–187, September 26, 1990, p. 26.

72. Quoted in Satter, p. 73.

73. "Yakovlev on Concept of Executive Presidency," FBIS-SOV-90–040, February 28, 1990, p. 40.

74. E. Mal'kova, "Terpimost' i otvetstvennost'," *Trud,* February 25, 1990, p. 1.

75. *Reformirovanie Rossii,* p. 42.

76. Huskey in Huskey, ed., p. 98.

77. *Vneocherednoi tretii s"ezd . . . ,* vol. 3, p. 56.

78. "Gorbachev's 16 Nov State of Union Speech," FBIS-SOV-90–223, November 19, 1990, p. 21.

79. "Ukazy, priniatye Prezidentom SSSR," *Argumenty i Fakty* 39, September 29–October 5, 1990, p. 1.

80. Sharlet, p. 95.

81. Gorbachev, pp. 319–320.

82. Morrison, p. 85.

83. Cited in Morrison, p. 81.

84. Morrison, p. 83.

85. Gorbachev, p. 271.

86. Quoted in Morrison, p. 98.

87. "Yeltsin Interviewed, Backs 'Strong Union'," FBIS-SOV-90–123, July 26, 1990, p. 36.

Chapter 3

1. Iurii Levada, "Credibility Crisis," *Moscow News,* June 3–10, 1990, pp. 8–9. The exact numbers were 37 percent for the country's former leaders, 29 percent for the current leadership, and 17 percent for the Party itself.

2. "Poll Shows Lack of Trust in Leaders," FBIS-SOV-91–071, April 12, 1991, p. 38.

3. Institute for Social-Political Research of the Russian Academy of Sciences, *Reformirovanie Rossii: mify i real'nost'* (Moscow: Academia, 1994), p. 53.

4. Michael Urban, "Boris El'tsin, Democratic Russia, and the Campaign for the Russian Presidency," *Soviet Studies,* Summer 1992, p. 191.

5. Urban, p. 188.

6. L. I. Dobrokhotov, et al., eds., *Yeltsin-Khasbulatov: edinstvo, kompromiss, bor'ba* (Moscow: Terra, 1994), pp. 3–4.

7. "Vlasov on RSFSR Presidency, Sovereignty," FBIS-SOV-90–093, May 14, 1990, p. 116.

8. Boris Yeltsin, *Zapiski prezidenta* (Moscow: Ogonek, 1994), p. 34.

9. Yeltsin aide Lev Sukhanov claims that a run at the Moscow city government was also considered but rejected. Lev Sukhanov, *Tri goda s El'tsinym* (Riga: Vaga, 1992), pp. 240–241.

10. The elections themselves took months to complete because of low turnout in several districts. This, in part was due to the sheer number of candidates: in the first round of voting, 6,700 candidates vied for 1,068 seats in a new Russian Congress of People's Deputies (in some cases, with up to 28 nominations for a single seat). Only 121 seats were won outright, and even after a runoff the following month several seats remained empty since turnout in those districts often fell below the mandated 50 percent to make it a legal election. See Stephen White, *Gorbachev and After* (Cambridge, UK: Cambridge University Press, 1992), p. 59.

11. See, for example, V. S. Kladchikhin, *Ne poslednie piat' let iz zhizni nesoglasnogo politika* (Kemerovo: Kemerovo AO Press, 1994), p. 54, in which Yeltsin answers questions about whether Union institutions are needed with a reasonable defense of the need for a national government.

12. John Dunlop, *The Rise of Russia and the Fall of the Soviet Union* (Princeton, NJ: Princeton University Press, 1993), p. 54; see also pp. 50–52. John Morrison has correctly noted that the more strident nationalists foolishly entered into a kind of unholy alliance with communist hardliners, leading to a trouncing at the ballot box so severe that they called for the results to be annulled. John Morrison, *Boris Yeltsin: From Bolshevik to Democrat* (New York: Dutton, 1991), p.141.

13. Yeltsin, p. 32.

14. S. Kiselev, "'Ne voevat' so svoim narodom'," *Komsomol'skaia Pravda,* May 31, 1990, p. 1.

15. "Sotsiologicheskii opros," *Argumenty i Fakty,* August 25–31, 1990, p. 3.

16. "Sto dnei Prezidenta," *Komsomol'skaia Pravda,* June 24, 1990, p. 2.

17. T. V. Novikova, "Reformirovanie rossiiskoi izbiratel'noi sistemy v usloviiakh stanovleniia mnogopartiinosti," in *Federal'noe sobranie Rossii: opyt pervykh vyborov* (Moscow: Institue of State and Law, 1994), p. 59.

18. "Deputies Question Yeltsin," FBIS-SOV-90–103, May 29, 1990, p. 113.

19. "RSFSR Poll on Leaders, Republic Ties, Market," "RSFSR Poll on Leaders, Republic Ties, Market," FBIS-SOV-90–177, September 12, 1990, p. 87.

20. "Defitsit zakonov, a ne lozungov," *Rabochaia Tribuna,* June 18, 1990, p. 1.

21. Jonathan Harris, "President and Parliament in the Russian Federation," in Kurt von Mettenheim, ed., *Presidential Institutions and Democratic Politics* (Baltimore: Johns Hopkins University Press, 1997), p. 211.

22. "'Bad-Tempered Debates' Reported Slow Congress," FBIS-SOV-90–098, May 21, 1990, p. 108.

23. "Consensus Urged," FBIS-SOV-90–112, June 11, 1990, p. 99

24. Quoted in Donald Murray, *A Democracy of Despots* (Boulder, CO: Westview Press, 1995), p. 154.

25. Urban, p. 188.

26. "Discusses Draft Constitution," FBIS-SOV-90–171, September 4, 1990, p. 97.

27. See Harris, pp. 213–214.

28. "Poll Shows Support for USSR Preservation," FBIS-SOV-92–055, March 20, 1992, p. 58.

29. "Goryacheva 'Horrified' at Prospect," FBIS-SOV-91–065, April 4, 1991, p. 71.

30. See Morrison, pp. 263–264.

31. Dunlop, pp. 56–57.

32. Quoted in Morrison, p. 265.

33. Urban, p. 197.

34. David Remnick, *Resurrection* (New York: Random House, 1997), p. 293.

35. Russians, when polled in 1992, gave some version of nearly all these reasons, but most believed that the USSR fell because "it was a totalitarian state whose end was predetermined by the victory of democratic forces." "Views Differ on Inevitability of Union's Fall," FBIS-SOV-92–055, March 20, 1992, p. 58.

36. "Parliamentarism 'Failed the Test,'" FBIS-SOV-93–192-S, October 6, 1993, p. 40.

37. Aleksandr Gol'ts, "Konstitutsiia, prezident, parlament: opasnosti podlinnye i mnimye," *Krasnaia Zvezda,* April 11, 1992, p. 2.

38. "People's Deputy Filippov for 'Professional' Parliament," FBIS-SOV-93–115, June 17, 1993, p.33.

39. Alexander Rahr, "The Rise and Fall of Ruslan Khasbulatov," *RFE/RL Research Report,* June 11, 1993, p. 13.

40. Otto Latsis, "S"ezd kak istochnik opasnosti," *Izvestiia,* April 13, 1992, pp. 1–2.

41. Lilia Shevstova, "Russia's Post-Communist Politics: Revolution or Continuity?" in Gail Lapidus, ed., *The New Russia: Troubled Transformation* (Boulder, CO: Westview Press, 1994), p. 11.

42. This was recounted by Mikhail Poltoranin in an interview with Murray, p. 161.

43. See Harris, pp. 22–223, and Murray, p.165.

44. The amended constitution would, among other things, have allowed the parliament to dismiss government ministers "at its own discretion and on its own authority." For Khasbulatov's report to the Congress, see "Doklad R. I. Khasbulatova," *Rossiiskaia Gazeta,* April 18, 1992, pp. 1–2.

45. Rahr, p. 13. Rahr added that for those who were not necessarily predisposed to supporting the speaker, Khasbulatov resorted to Soviet-era inducements, including "subsidized housing, automobiles, and trips abroad."

46. "Yeltsin Wins 'Round Two' against Opposition," FBIS-SOV-92–078-S, April 22, 1992, p. 40.

47. Poltoranin (then the press officer for the government) told Murray that Khasbulatov called him late one night in 1992 and said "Alright, let's close *Izvestiia!* They criticize everything!" Murray, p. 164. Khasbulatov admitted publicly that the paper should be "dealt" with, but presented himself, implausibly, as the paper's fiscal savior. See also "'Izvestiia' obrashchaiutsia k iuristam dlia podgotovka sudebnogo iska k R. I. Khasbulatovu," *Izvestiia,* April 13, 1992, p. 1.

48. Harris, p. 222.

49. Nugzar Betaneli, "Izbirateli predlagaiut svoiu povestku s"ezda," *Izvestiia,* March 23, 1992, p. 3.

50. *Reformirovanie Rossii,* p. 119.

51. D. A. Volkogonov to Boris Yeltsin, "O predstoiiashchei zharkoi oseni i deistviiakh vlastei," September 11, 1992, The Dmitrii A. Volkogonov Papers, Library of Congress, Washington, DC, box 12, folder 2, p. 1.

52. *Reformirovanie Rossii,* p. 142.

53. V. V. Il'in, ed., *Filosofiia vlasti* (Moscow: Izdatel'stvo Moskovskogo universiteta, 1993), pp. 191–192.

54. "Survey Finds Low Confidence in Leaders and Growing Support for Strong Government," *RFE/RL Research Bulletin,* January 19, 1993, pp. 3–4.

55. "Tridtsat' shest' dnei, kotorye potriasut mir," *Moskovskie Novosti,* March 28, 1993, p. 3.

56. Mark Rhodes, "What Do Russians Think about the Constitutional Process?," *RFE/RL Research Report,* July 16, 1993, p. 15.

57. The "worms" comment was heard on television and widely reported on at the time. See, for example, "R. Khasbulatov v epitsentre potriasenii," *Izvestiia,* April 14, 1992, p. 2.

58. Peter Reddaway, "Russia on the Brink?," *New York Review of Books,* January 28, 1993, pp. 30–31.

59. "Move Debated," FBIS-SOV-92–239-S, December 11, 1992, p. 4.

60. Murray, p. 167.

61. "More on Vote; Khasbulatov Sees 'Triumph'," FBIS-SOV-92–235-S, December 7, 1992, p. 3.

62. Yeltsin, p. 290.

63. Shevtsova, p. 18.

64. "Tridtsat' shest' dnei . . . ," p. 3.

65. "Text of Khasbulatov Speech to Congress 11 Mar," FBIS-SOV-93–046, March 11, 1993, p. 21.

66. Shevtsova, p. 20.

67. Vladimir Isakov, *Gosperevorot: parlamentskie dnevniki 1992–1993* (Moscow: Paleia, 1995), p. 298.

68. *Reformirovanie Rossii,* p. 285.

69. See Ruslan Khasbulatov, "Referendum: lozhnye interpretatsii i deistvitel'nost,'" *Rossiiskaia Gazeta,* April 30, 1993, pp. 1, 4. Later, when holed up in the Russian White House, Rutskoi told a Swedish reporter that Yeltsin cheated in April by lying to the people and getting too much television time. "Intends to Fight to the End," FBIS-SOV-93–199, September 30, 1993, p. 19.

70. Isakov, p. 331.

71. *Reformirovanie Rossii,* pp.163–235.

72. *Reformirovanie Rossii,* p. 236.

73. "Poll Shows Yeltsin Favored over Khasbulatov," FBIS-SOV-93–057, March 26, 1993, pp. 41–42.

74. Yeltsin, p. 314.

75. "Komu na Rusi doveriaiut bol'she?" *Kuranty,* June 18, 1993, p. 3. The Supreme Soviet and the CPD were rated "fully" trustworthy by only 6 percent of respondents.

76. "Constitutional Commission Member Notes Political Options," FBIS-SOV-93–047, March 12, 1993, p. 45.

77. "Ob ochevidnom i blizhaishem," *Izvestiia,* May 4, 1993, p. 2.

78. Sergei Chugaev, "Izbirateli Baburina i dr. progolosovali za prezidenta," *Izvestiia,* April 30, 1993, p. 2.

79. "V zashchitu parlamentarizma i demokratii," *Rossiiskaia Gazeta,* August 21, 1993, p. 1.

80. "Work Interrupted by 'Political Disputes,'" FBIS-SOV-93–117, June 21, 1993, p. 38.

81. Iurii Orlik, "Chego mozhno ozhidat' ot sentiabr'skogo nastupleniia prezidenta," *Izvestiia,* September 10, 1993, p. 4.

82. D. A. Volkogonov to Boris Yeltsin (untitled), July 26, 1993, The Dmitrii A. Volkogonov Papers, Libarary of Congress, Washington, DC, box 12, folder 2, p. 1.

83. "Khasbulatov Assails Yeltsin at Conference," FBIS-SOV-93–180, September 20, 1993, pp. 27–31.

84. Nikolai Gulbinsky, "Take-off and landing," *Moscow News,* November 26, 1993, p. 14.

85. "Deputies' Debate Detailed," FBIS-SOV-93–171, September 7, 1993, p. 50.

86. Yeltsin, p. 353.

87. "Yeltsin Disbands Parliament, Calls Elections to 'Federal Assembly,'" FBIS-SOV-93–182-S, p. 2.

88. The actual edict is available in *Lefortovskie protokoly* (Moscow: Paleia, 1994), p. 4, and in *Izvestiia,* September 22, 1993, p. 1.

89. Yeltsin aide and press secretary Viacheslav Kostikov notes that Rutskoi and Khasbulatov, certain of victory and "already talking like they were the bosses of Russia," issued dozens of orders in a matter of days. See V. Kostikov, *Roman s prezidentom* (Moscow: VARGRIUS, 1997), p. 233.

90. "Dom Sovetov: s"ezd nachal rabotu," *Pravda,* September 24, 1993, p. 1.

91. "Seeks Support of Military Units," FBIS-SOV-93–185-S, September 27, 1993, p. 27.

92. "General Addresses White House Rally, Warns 'Traitors,'" FBIS-SOV-93–184-S, September 24, 1993, p. 17.

93. Gulbinsky, p. 14.

94. "Obrashchenie Prezidenta Rossiiskoi Federatsii—Glavnokoman-duiushchevego Vooruzhennymi Silami Rossii," *Krasnaia Zvezda,* September 24, 1993, p. 1.

95. The transcripts of the negotiations can be found in *Tishaishie peregovory* (Moscow: Magisterium, 1993).

96. There were rumors in Moscow in 1994 that Yeltsin's aides had actually called Fujimori's staff for pointers on how to execute the kind of internal coup the Peruvian president had so successfully pulled off, but these remain unsubstantiated.

97. See "Rutskoy Comments on Crisis," 185-S p. 26, and L. Nikitinskii, "U nas vse eshche ostaetsia vybor mezhdu dvumiia demokratiiami," *Izvestiia,* September 23, 1993, p. 3.

98. "Byl li vybor u El'tsina?" *Izvestiia,* September 25, 1993, p. 3.

99. "Justice Ministry Explains Legal Basis for Yeltsin Decree," FBIS-SOV-93–184-S, September 24, 1993, p. 30.

100. During the summer of 1992, 56 percent of Muscovites said the national leadership had actually lost control of the Republic and that the situation was essentially one of anarchy. *Moskovskie Novosti,* August 30, 1992, p. 2.

101. Nikitinskii, p. 3.

102. Il'ia Mil'shtein, "Ocen' 1993: voprosy sotsiologov," in *93 Oktiabr' Moskva: Khronika tekushchikh sobytii* (Moscow: Vek XX i Mir, 1993), p. 130.

103. "Reiting vedushchikh politikov Rossii," *Izvestiia,* September 19, 1993, p. 4.

104. See *Moskovskie Novosti,* September 28, 1993, p. 2, and September 29, 1993, p. 2.

105. "Deistviia Prezidenta i Pravitel'stva podderzhany," *Rossiiskie Vesti,* October 6, 1993, p. 1.

106. "Russia: Election Observation Report," Washington, DC: International Republican Institute, January 27, 1996, Appendix 1.

107. Julia Rubin, "Russia—Anniversary," AP News Wire Service, October 1, 1994.

108. Yeltsin, p. 165.

109. Yeltsin, p. 14.

Chapter 4

1. David Remnick, *Resurrection* (New York: Random House, 1997), pp. 80–81.

2. The regional governments were divided about the violence in October, but many of the local soviet's past resolutions that, unsurprisingly, defended the independence of the national Supreme Soviet, and Yeltsin was being urged by many in his circle to move quickly against retrograde elements at all levels. Most, however, called for neutrality and a return to the status quo ante of September 21. For day-by-day reports on reactions in the regions, see *93 Oktiabr' Moskva: Khronika tekushchikh sobytii* (Moscow: Vek XX i Mir, 1993). Also see "Yeltsin's Regional Policy Assessed," FBIS-SOV-93–194, October 8, 1993, p. 20, and "Roundup of Regional Reactions to Moscow Events," FBIS-SOV-93–192-S, October 6, 1993, pp. 49–50; "Regions Views of Yeltsin, Supreme Soviet Viewed," FBIS-SOV-93–187-S, September 29, 1993, p. 35; "Regions Lean toward Neutrality," FBIS-SOV-93–184-S, September 24, 1993, pp. 45–46.

3. "Public Mood Surveyed Prior to Referendum," FBIS-SOV-93–237, December 13, 1993, p. 47.

4. Institute for Social-Political Research of the Russian Academy of Sciences, *Reformirovanie Rossii: mify i real'nost'* (Moscow: Academia, 1994), p. 293.

5. "Poll on Forthcoming Elections Published," FBIS-SOV-93–195, October 12, 1993, p. 77.

6. *Reformirovanie Rossii,* pp. 287, 300.

7. As Gordon Smith has noted, the danger to the Constitutional Court remains being politicized by factions. Elena Mizulina, the deputy chairman of the Committee on Constitutional Legislation and Jurisprudential Issues in the upper house in the 1993–1995 Duma told me in 1994 that she was less concerned about the powers of the court itself than ensuring that the court remain beyond capture by the presidency. Subsequent events regarding the court have been, as Smith notes, "encouraging," with all sides so far trying to respect the independence of the judiciary. Interview with Elena Mizulina, Moscow, July 12, 1994.

8. For commentary on the constitutional status of the president's powers, see A. I. Kovalenko, *Osnovy konstitutsionnogo prava Rossiiskoi Federatsii* (Moscow: TEIS, 1994).

9. Mizulina unhesitatingly described this as the worst part of the constitution, and even a strong Yeltsin ally like former deputy prime minister Boris Nemtsov has described decrees as "dangerous," especially in the wrong hands. Interview with Boris Nemtsov, Cambridge, MA, February 18, 1999. See also Kovalenko, pp. 14–16 for a more formal legal discussion of the issue.

10. The important difference here, of course, is that American presidents can act with considerable autonomy by reference to previous statutory authority, while the Russian president can act independently and then be defeated only

retroactively by statute. American legislators, however, have not been above passing sweeping acts that then force great powers into the president's hands to achieve the same effect of escaping responsibility. My thanks to Gordon Silverstein for his comments on American practice on this question.

11. Nicolai Petro, *The Rebirth of Russian Democracy* (Cambridge, MA: Harvard University Press, 1995), p. 153.

12. In theory, a candidate can win in the first round by gaining an outright majority, if a majority of eligible voters is certified as having turned out. Given the number of candidates likely to be fielded in a system like Russia's that lacks party discipline, the possibility of an outright win by any one contender is remote.

13. Nemtsov has argued that the ability to hire and fire the cabinet is the real source of the president's day-to-day power over the government, and that even now any discussion of "reducing" Russian presidential power is really just discussion about how to give the Duma more say in creating the government. Interview.

14. Olga Burkaleva, "Dume vlasti malo, i ona khochet peredelat' Konstitutsiiu pod sebia," *Rossiiskie Vesti,* July 27, 1995, p. 2.

15. See *Kommentarii k konstitututsii Rossiiskoi Federatsii* (Moscow:VEK, 1994), pp. 340–343, 364–368.

16. "'Nasha Konstitusiia zasluzhivaet bol'she pokhval, nezheli uprekov . . . ,'" *Rossiia,* December 14–20, 1994, p. 3. When a reporter objected that Italians seem to live fairly well, Tumanov replied that Italy was a wealthier and more stable country, and could well afford the occasional convulsions caused by its legislative institutions.

17. I put the question of proportional representation to a number of Duma deputies and staffers, and the response was almost uniformly negative. Only the most firmly oppositionist deputies like Vladimir Grigoriev were receptive to the idea. When I raised the "Italian problem," Grigoriev smiled quietly and said: "We are not Italians." Interview with Vladimir Grigoriev, Moscow, Russia, April 17, 1997.

18. "Public Mood Surveyed . . . ," p. 47.

19. Lilia Shevtsova, "Russia's Post-Communist Politics: Revolution or Continuity?" in Gail Lapidus, ed., *The New Russia: Troubled Transformation* (Boulder, CO: Westview Press, 1994), p. 23.

20. See, for example, the statements on the constitution by various candidates in *Vybory v Gosudarstvennuiu Dumu, 7 oktiabr'—14 dekabria* (Moscow: Postfactum, 1993), section 8, pp. 7–22.

21. I. Kliamkin, V. Lapkin, and V. Panin, *Mezhdu avtoritarizmom i demokratiei* (Moscow: Fond "Obshchestvennoe mnenie," 1995), p. 16, and "Public Mood Surveyed . . . ," p. 47.

22. A British study argued that the new constitution was the beneficiary of a halo effect, but I would counter that this was in fact support for the general

orientation of a reformist government; there is no escaping the fact that there were no serious challenges to the presidentialist provisions save that of the communists. See Matthew Wyman, Stephen White, Bill Miller, and Paul Heywood, "Public Opinion, Parties, and Voters in the December 1993 Russian Elections," *Europe-Asia Studies,* Fall 1995, pp. 610–611.

23. "Poll on Forthcoming Elections Published," FBIS-SOV-93–195, October 12, 1993, p. 77. When asked if they would vote for their former deputy, or for pro- or anti-Yeltsin candidates, pluralities in both cases reported that their vote "didn't depend on that." Fifty percent wanted early elections in June 1994; only 32 percent wanted to see simultaneous presidential and legislative elections. See *Reformirovanie Rossii,* pp. 291–294.

24. See, for example, the platform and application for membership handed out as campaign literature in Moscow in 1993 in "Obrashchenie Vladimira Zhirnovskogo, Programma Liberal'no-Demokraticheskoi partii Rossii, Ustav LDPR" (Moscow, pamphlet, no publisher). Zhirinovsky's infamous brochure, "Last Dash to the South," was actually one of a three-part series that put forward his political views in detail. See V. V. Zhirinovskii, *O sud"bakh Rossii, chast' II: poslednii brosok na iug* (Moscow: RAIT, 1993). For a short and entertaining compendium of Zhirinovsky's more outlandish remarks, see Graham Frazer and George Lancelle, *Absolute Zhirinovsky* (New York: Penguin, 1994).

25. "Profile of LDPR Voters Outlined," FBIS-SOV-93–249, December 30, 1993, p. 33.

26. "Composition of Zhirinovskiy Base Analyzed," FBIS-SOV-93–246, December 27, 1993, p. 13.

27. For a detailed analysis of the military vote for Zhirinovsky, see Thomas M. Nichols, "An Electoral Mutiny? Zhirinovsky and the Russian Armed Forces," *Armed Forces and Society,* Spring 1995.

28. See Richard Sakwa, "The Russian Elections of December 1993," *Europe-Asia Studies,* Spring 1995, p. 213.

29. Sakwa, p. 213.

30. "It is revealing," one Russian legal scholar has written, "that the [first] State Duma, where there are more than 100 formally independent deputies, immediately ran into difficulties in forming parliamentary factions." Iu. A. Iudin, "Parlamentskie vybory 1993 goda i problemy razvitiia izbiratel'nogo zakonodatel'stva," in *Federal'noe sobranie Rossii: opyt pervykh vyborov* (Moscow: Institue of State and Law of the Russian Academy of Sciences, 1994), p. 34.

31. See Sakwa, p. 212.

32. Valerii Vyzhutovich, "Bez sensatsii," *Izvestiia,* January 12, 1994, p. 1. It should be noted that Borovoy, for one, believes that this moderating influence is to some extent unintentional, the by-product of the Federation Council's overriding preoccupation with regional autonomy.

33. Nemtsov agreed with this characterization, but did not see it, as Grigoriev did, as necessarily a pejorative term.

34. Sakwa, p. 211.

35. Sakwa, p. 213.

36. Pavel Voshchanov, "'Nu vot ia i v Kremle!' A dal'she?," *Komsomol'skaia Pravda,* December 8, 1994, p. 2.

37. David Remnick, *Resurrection* (New York: Random House, 1997), p. 87.

38. Wyman, et al., pp. 602–604.

39. Petro, p. 160.

40. Michael Urban, et al., *The Rebirth of Politics in Russia* (Cambridge, UK: Cambridge University Press, 1997), p. 308.

41. "'Mnenie' ob amnistii," *Izvestiia,* March 12, 1994, p. 4.

42. "Pravda, polupravda, i 'moment istiny'," *Rossiiskaia Gazeta,* November 15, 1994, p. 1.

43. Iurii Vedeneev and Vladimir Lysenko, "Vybory–93: uroki i al'ternativy," *Nezavisimaia Gazeta,* June 28, 1994, p. 5.

44. The comment was attributed to Aleksei Kiva in "Politicheskii terror byl ostanovlen," *Rossiiskaia Gazeta,* September 21, 1994, p. 2.

45. "Chem etot sovet Prezidentu tsenen," *Rossiiskaia Gazeta,* July 23, 1996, p. 2.

46. Grigoriev, for example, claimed that he sat out the 1993 elections in protest, but finally decided to run in 1995 in part to help the Duma overcome what he called "the '93 syndrome," in which legislators were paralyzed by the fear of presidential power.

47. "Chem etot sovet Prezidentu tsenen," p. 2.

48. *Dogovor ob obshchestvennom soglasii* (Moscow: "Iuridicheskaia literatura," 1994), pp. 6–7.

49. Aleksandr Batygin, "Ideia prekrasna, da khrupok mir," *Rossiiskaia Gazeta,* September 21, 1995, pp. 1–2.

50. Anna Ostapchuk and Iulii Lebedev, "Na politicheskom barometre 'iasno,'" *Nezavisimaia Gazeta,* September 15, 1994, p. 2.

51. For details, see Al'bert Plutnik, "V Dume b'iut zhenshchinu," *Izvestiia,* September 12, 1995, p. 1; for more details, see "Draka na zasedanii Dumy," *Segodniia,* September 12, 1995, p. 1.

52. Sergei Shargorodsky, "Russia-Yeltsin," AP Wire Service, September 17, 1994.

53. Iurii Levada, "Trevogi i ozhidaniia," *Moskovskie Novosti,* January 8–15, 1995, p. 14.

54. "Social, Political Developments in First 6 Months of 1995," FBIS Document FTS19970602002322, June 2, 1997.

55. Iurii Levada, "Teper' my bol'she dumaem o sem'e, chem o gosudarstve," *Segodniia,* January 24, 1995, p. 10.

56. Robert Cottrell, "Russia's Parliamentary and Presidential Elections," *Government and Opposition,* Spring 1996, p. 160.

57. "Russia: Elections in Moscow Oblast Analyzed," FBIS-SOV-96–062-S, February 28, 1996.

58. "Dorogie sootchestvenniki! Brat'ia i sestry!," *Duma* 34 (102), 1995, p. 1.

59. These and other figures in this section are from *Vybory v shestuiu gosudarstvennuiu dumu: itogi i vyvody* (Moscow: Voenizdat, 1996), pp. 18–20 and 609–615.

60. Olga Burkaleva, "Parlament—ne rychag dlia partiinykh tselei," *Rossiiskie Vesti,* August 1, 1995, p. 2.

61. Thomas Remington, Steven Smith, and Moshe Haspel, "Decrees, Laws, and Inter-Branch Relations in the Russian Federation," *Post-Soviet Affairs,* October-December 1998, pp. 288–291.

62. V. Kononenko, "Nezavisimo ot resultatov 17 dekabria kabinet Chernomyrdina ustoit," *Izvestiia,* December 16, 1995, p. 1.

63. V. A. Chetvernin, "Vvedenie," in V. A. Chetvernin, ed., *Stanovlenie konstitutsionnogo gosudarstva v posttotalitarnoi Rossii* (Moscow: Institute of State and Law, 1996), p. 7.

64. Russians overwhelmingly "reject the view that a tough dictatorship is the only way out of the current situation." Richard Rose, "Boris Yeltsin Faces the Electorate: Findings from Opinion Polling Data," *Demokratizatsiya,* Summer 1996, pp. 386–387.

65. Kliamkin, et al., pp. 50–60. Rutskoi has since been elected governor in the Kursk region.

66. Interviews with Konstantin Borovoy, Hanover, New Hampshire, March 28, 1996, and Moscow, Russia, April 17, 1997.

67. Baburin claims that this was an important point in his "Narodovlastie" movement's legislative break with the communists.

68. Gleb Cherkasov, "Segoniia Duma budet utverzhdat' kandidaturu prem'er-ministra," *Segodniia,* August 10, 1996, p. 2.

69. Sergei Shargorodsky, "Russia-Revolution Day," AP North American Wire, November 7, 1995. The speaker, Viktor Tiulkin, added the blunt admission that working people "cannot come to power by parliamentary means."

70. "Shokhin Sees Duma Adopting Laws to Provoke Yeltsin," FBIS-SOV-96–098, May 17, 1996. The bill, apparently, died after being bottled up in committee.

71. Anna Kozyreva, "U Dumy dostatochno vlasti. Prosto eto vlast' drugaia," *Rossiiskaia Gazeta,* August 14, 1996, p. 3.

72. A number of Duma legislators and staff members, regardless of party, told me that it was widely accepted in Moscow that Zhirinovsky is a venal man who was materially bought off by the president's administration, thereby collapsing what little credibility or effectiveness he had as a representative of Russia's most discontented citizens.

73. A. Frolov, "Pochemu El'tsinu udalos' vyigrat'?," *Sovetskaia Rossiia,* July 9, 1996, p. 2.

74. As Arturo Valenzuela puts it, unlike presidential systems, in parliamentary systems "crises of government do not become crises of regime." Quoted in Giovanni Sartori, *Comparative Constitutional Engineering* (New York: New York University Press, 1994), p. 94.

75. Irina Savvateeva, "El'tsin sokhraniaet pravitel'stvo i ugrozhaet dume rospuskom," *Izvestiia*, June 23, 1995, p. 1.

76. Juan J. Linz, "The Perils of Presidentialism," in Arend Lijphart, ed., *Parliamentary versus Presidential Government* (Oxford, UK: Oxford University Press, 1994), p. 120.

77. Borovoy related to me that he—like so many of his reformist colleagues—was certain of the fact that a communist president and a communist Duma would be merciless in bringing Chechnya back into the Federation.

78. *Obshchaia Gazeta* called the Chechen war a "generous gift to the architect of the idea of a 'march on the south.'" See "CPRF Rapprochement with 'Party of Power,'" FBIS Document FTS19970626001510, June 6, 1997.

79. See Anatol Lieven, *Chechnya: Tombstone of Russian Power* (New Haven, CT: Yale University Press, 1998), pp. 89–94. Lieven points out that "in the search for 'deeper' reasons for the Russian decision to invade Chechnya, the hijackings are often forgotten."

80. Lev Gudkov, "Vlast' i chechenskaia voina v obshchestvennom mnenii Rossii," *Segodniia*, February 23, 1995, p. 3.

81. "Yabloko's Lukashev on Duma's Confidence Vote," FBIS-SOV-95–125, June 29, 1995, p. 27.

82. The comments were by Duma member Viacheslav Nikonov. See Lee Hockstader, "Anti-Yeltsin Vote Fails in Duma," *The Washington Post*, July 2, 1995, p. 1.

83. Hockstader, p. 1.

84. See, for example, Sergei Chugaev, "Napadaia na pravitel'stvo, duma tsenitsiia vyshe," *Izvestiia*, October 29, 1994, p. 2, and "'Bol'shaia chetverka' prishla k vyvodu o neobkhodimosti ocherednogo obshchestvennogo soglasiia," *Nezavisimaia Gazeta*, October 21, 1997, p. 1.

85. "Lukyanov Denies Government-Communist Contract as 'Bluff,'" FBIS-SOV-97–001, January 1, 1997.

86. Aleksei Kirpichnikov, "Vesna i votum nedoveriia obostriaiut chuvstvo nereal'nosti," *Segodniia*, April 8, 1995, p. 2.

87. Vladimir Isakov, "Vremiia vybora," *Sovetskaia Rossiia*, June 25, 1995, p. 2.

88. See, for example, Sergei Chugaev, "Esli kommunisty pobedaiut na vyborakh, novaia natsionalizatsiia neizbezhna," *Izvestiia*, November 2, 1995, p. 1.

89. A. Yusupovsky, "A Political Portrait of Russia's Upper House of Parliament, 1993–1995," *Demokratizatsiya*, Winter 1996, p. 89.

90. Juan J. Linz, "Presidential or Parliamentary Democracy: Does it Make a Difference?," in Juan J. Linz and Arturo Valenzuela, eds., *The Failure of Presidential Democracy* (Baltimore: Johns Hopkins University Press, 1994), p. 7.

91. "Russians," Rose writes, "are inclined toward government being weaker rather than stronger. When the views of individuals about the rule by decree and parliamentary veto are combined, there is a majority for gridlock." Rose, "Boris Yeltsin Faces the Electorate," p. 387.

Chapter 5

1. Jack Matlock, "The Struggle for the Kremlin," *The New York Review of Books,* August 8, 1996, p. 28.
2. Arend Lijphart, "Presidentialism and Majoritarian Democracy: Theoretical Observations," in Juan J. Linz and Arturo Valenzuela, eds., *The Failure of Presidential Democracy* (Baltimore: Johns Hopkins University Press, 1994), pp. 98–99.
3. Robert Moser, "The Electoral Effects of Presidentialism in Post-Soviet Russia," *The Journal of Communist Studies and Transition Politics,* March–June 1998, p. 72.
4. As usual, the Russian Orthodox Church and the Russian Army posted the best numbers as the most trusted institutions in society. Leonid Sedov, "Boris El'tsin pal zhertvoi Borisa El'tsina," *Segodniia,* April 8, 1995, p. 3.
5. See Richard Rose, "Boris Yeltsin Faces the Electorate: Findings from Opinion Polling Data," *Demokratizatsiya,* Summer 1996.
6. Alastair Macdonald, "Zhirinovsky 'like a virgin' before wedding bash," Reuters North American News Wire, February 9, 1996.
7. See "Priz dostaetsiia odnomu," *Segodniia,* March 22, 1996, p. 5.
8. See Timothy Colton, "From the Parliamentary to the Presidential Election: Russians Get Real about Politics," *Demokratizatsiya,* Summer 1996.
9. Vladimir Krasnikovskii and Aleksei Elizarov, "Kak poluchit' kredit doveriia," *Segodniia,* July 17, 1996, p. 5.
10. Matlock, p. 30.
11. After the elections, journalists would try to compensate for this by making more of a stand against the Chechen fiasco, a press campaign that in the end had little effect. See "Top Editors Vow Antiwar 'Action' in Press," FBIS-SOV-96–160, August 21, 1996.
12. Yeltsin received more exposure than all the candidates combined before the June round of elections; total minutes of coverage of Zyuganov caught up somewhat only the week before the July balloting. See *Vybory prezidenta rossiiskoi federatsii* (Moscow: Ves' Mir, 1996), pp. 62–64.
13. "ORT Official Concedes Channel Is 'Pro-Presidential,'" FBIS-SOV-97–091, April 1, 1997.
14. Boris Nemtsov has described the Federation Council as the bulwark against "communist attempts at a unified state," a description that actually dovetails with opposition legislator Vladimir Grigoriev's objections to the presidential

system: "Power should be unified." See also Gleb Cherkasov, "Za poslednie chetyre mesiatsa regional'nye elity stali bolee blagosklonny k glave gosu-darstva," *Segodniia,* June 1, 1996, p. 2.

15. These and other figures are from "Odin prezident—dve strany," *Segodniia,* July 10, 1996, p. 5, and *Vybory prezidenta Rossiskoi Federatsii 1996 goda: itogi i vyvody* (Moscow:Voenizdat, 1996), p. 15.

16. Quoted in L. N. Dobrokhotov et al., eds., *Ot El'tsina k . . . El'tsinu: prezi-dentskaia gonka–96* (Moscow:Terra, 1997), p. 577.

17. Marie Mendras, "Yeltsin and the Great Divide in Russian Society," *East Eu-ropean Constitutional Review,* Spring-Summer 1996, p. 52.

18. Iurii Levada, "Do vyborov ostalos' 10 nedel'," *Segodniia,* April 4, 1996, p. 3.

19. See, for example, "Optimizm storonnikov Borisa El'tsina vse usilivaetsiia," *Segodniia,* June 1, 1996, p. 4.

20. See Lev Gudkov, "Politicheskie nastroeniia i ozhidaniia pered vyborami," *Segodniia,* June 13, 1996, p. 3.

21. See "Odin prezident—dve strany," and *Vybory prezidenta Rossiskoi Federatsii 1996 goda,* p. 15.

22. "Rossiiane o vyborakh i ikh itogakh," *Segodiia,* July 26, 1996, p. 4.

23. Oleg Moroz, "Osobennosti natsional'noi okhoty za golosami izbiratelei v vesenne-letnii sezon 1996 goda, *Literaturnaia Gazeta,* April 10, 1996, p. 1.

24. Inga Mikhailovskaya, "Russian Voting Behavior as a Mirror of Social-Political Change," *East European Constitutional Review,* Spring-Summer 1996, p. 62.

25. Michael McFaul, "Russia's 1996 Presidential Elections," *Post-Soviet Affairs,* October-December 1996, p. 329.

26. As McFaul notes, Zyuganov's "fiery rhetoric" simply "frightened away the centrist voters." McFaul, p. 345.

27. Ron Laurenzo, "Zyuganov: Hellfire for Yeltsinites," UPI News Wire, June 8, 1996.

28. From January to May, the number of Russians who worried about simul-taneous communist control of both the executive and legislative branches climbed steadily until it reached 40 percent. Vladimir Krasnikovskii and Aleksei Elizarov, "Kak poluchit' kredit doveriia," *Segodniia,* July 17, 1996, p. 5.

29. See T. A. Astrakhankina, "Zakon sodoma i gomorry," *Duma* 26 (128), 1996, p. 2, and "Deklaratsiia," *Duma* 6 (108), 1996, p. 1.

30. "KPRF gotovitsia k bor'be c 'levoi opasnost'iu'," *Segodniia,* January 27, 1996, p. 2.

31. "Priz dostaetsiia odnomu," p. 5.

32. Yeltsin had easily outpaced Yavlinsky by April, thus making the election ef-fectively a two man race by spring. McFaul, p. 331.

33. "Polls Show 'Devotion' to Zyuganov," FBIS-SOV-96–085, April 16, 1996.

34. Iu. Aleksandrov, "Trudno byt' krasnymi, kogda net belykh," *Rossiikie Vesti,* July 16, 1996, p. 2.

35. See McFaul, pp. 334–337.

36. "Boitsia!," *Sovetskaia Rossiia,* May 16, 1996, p. 1.

37. "Kandidaty v prezidenty drug o druge," *Moskovskie Novosti,* June 2–9, 1996, p. 10.

38. "Priamoi otvet," *Sovetskaia Rossiia,* May 14, 1996, p. 1.

39. "Poll—33 Percent Believe in 'Western Conspiracy,'" FBIS-SOV-97–026, February 7, 1997.

40. Aleksandr Zinov'ev made the comments in an interview. See "Chto budet s Rossiei posle vyborov," *Pravda,* July 10, 1996, p. 1.

41. Iurii Aleksandrov, "Kommunisty ispoveduiut filosofiiu grazhdanskoi voiny," *Rossiikie Vesti,* April 18, 1996, p. 2.

42. L. Velikodnyi, "Zhupel grazhdanskoi voini," in Dobrokhotov et al., eds., pp. 309–310.

43. Korzhakov settled some scores with Yeltsin's circle in a disjoint and evidently self-serving recounting of the campaign in his memoirs. See A. Korzhakov, *Boris El'tsin: Ot rassveta do zakata* (Moscow: Interbuk, 1997), pp. 306–386.

44. Even in the 1995 elections, exit polls showed that voters were still more likely to blame Gorbachev (24 percent) or the Congress of People's Deputies (18 percent) or previous Soviet leaders (10 percent) for Russia's troubles than Yeltsin (8.5 percent). "Russia: Election Observation Report," Washington, DC: International Republican Institute, January 27, 1996, Appendix 1.

45. G. Ziuganov, "Otechestvo v opasnosti!," *Pravda,* June 22, 1996, p. 1.

46. G. Zuiganov, "K soglasiiu i doveriiu," *Sovetskaia Rossiia,* June 25, 1996, p. 1.

47. "No Future Elections under the Communists," FBIS-SOV-96–133-S, May 8, 1996.

48. "Prezident pobedil v pervom ture," *Segodniia,* June 28, 1996, p. 5.

49. Gleb Cherkasov, "Kommunisty rassmatrivaiut prezidentskie vybory 'kak poslednii i reshitel'nyi boi'," *Segodniia,* February 16, 1996, p. 2.

50. "No Future Elections . . ."

51. "Yeltsin Seen Providing 'Stability,'" FBIS-SOV-96–133-S, May 8, 1996.

52. A. Frolov, "Pochemu El'tsinu udalos' vyigrat'?," *Sovetskaia Rossiia,* July 9, 1996, p. 2.

53. Aleksandrov, p. 2.

54. "Yeltsin Seen Providing 'Stability.'"

55. Quoted in David S. Mason and Svetlana Sidorenko-Stephenson, "Public Opinion and the 1996 Elections in Russia: Nostalgic and Statist, Yet Pro-Market and Pro-Yeltsin," *Slavic Review,* Winter 1997, pp. 716–717.

56. Vasilii Kononeko, "Boris El'tsin obosnachil osnovu svoei predvybornoi platformy—antikommunism," *Izvestiia,* March 7, 1996, p. 1.

57. Aleksandrov, p. 2.

58. *Vybory v shestuiu gosudarstvennuiu dumu: itogi i vyvody* (Moscow: Voenizdat, 1996), p. 17.

59. "Svobodnoe obshchestvo, spravedlivoe gosudarstvo, obespechennaia sem'ia," *Rossiiskie Vesti,* April 9, 1996, pp. 1–2.

60. "57 voprosov izbiratelei prezidentu rossii," *Izvestiia,* May 22, 1996, p. 2.

61. "Kandidaty v prezidenty drug o druge," p. 10.

62. "B. El'tsin: Mne debaty s Ziuganovym ne nuzhny," *Sovetskaia Rossiia,* May 12, 1996, p. 1.

63. "Veriu, liubliu, nadeius'!," *Rossiiskie Vesti,* July 1, 1996, p. 2.

64. "Vperedi—vtoroi tur," *Pravda,* June 18, 1996, p. 1.

65. "Veriu, liubliu, nadeius'!," p. 2.

66. B. Slavin, "Pochemu B. El'tsin vyigral?," in Dobrokhotov, et al., eds., p. 585.

67. Ivan Rybkin, "Pochemu ia budu podderzhivat' na vyborakh pervogo prezidenta Rossii," *Izvestiia,* March 22, 1996, p. 3.

68. Valerie Bunce, "Presidents and the Transition in Eastern Europe," in Kurt von Mettenheim, ed., *Presidential Institutions and Democratic Politics* (Baltimore: Johns Hopkins University Press, 1997), pp. 168–169.

69. For a more detailed discussion of the flaws in these "East *vs.* South" comparisons, see Dean McSweeney and Clive Tempest, "The Political Science of Democratic Transition in Eastern Europe," *Political Studies,* September 1993, and Valerie Bunce, "Comparing East and South," *The Journal of Democracy,* July 1995, p. 99.

70. Robert Cottrell, "Russia's Parliamentary and Presidential Elections," *Government and Opposition,* Spring 1996, p. 161.

71. Identification of platforms with individuals was so strong in 1994 that one was more likely to call a party by the name of its founder rather than a proper name: "Travkin's Party," "Shakhrai's Party," and so on. Pavel Voshchanov, "'Nu vot ia i v Kremle!' A dal'she?," *Komsomol'skaia Pravda,* December 8, 1994, p. 2.

72. "Egor Stroev: 'Nel'zia orientirovatsiia na togo, kto podzhigaet bikfordov shnur," *Argumenty i Fakty* 22, May 1996, p. 8

73. Duma member and *odnomandatnik* Greshneviikov made it clear that his support from his district gave him a great deal of latitude to join or leave coalitions as he saw fit. His particular positions, he said, were important, but no less so than the fact that he returned to his district as often as possible and that he had never, in seven years, rented an apartment in Moscow.

74. Inga Mikhailovskaia and Evgenii Kuzminskii, "Making Sense of the Russian Elections," *East European Constitutional Review,* Spring 1994, pp. 60–61.

75. An excellent chronological tracking of these political comings and goings from 1989 through 1995 can be found in a compendium assembled by the private "RAU University" research center. See *Rossiia: partii—vybory—vlast'* (Moscow: "Obozrevatel'," 1996).

76. Gordon Silverstein, *Imbalance of Powers: Constitutional Interpretation and the Making of American Foriegn Policy* (Oxford, UK: Oxford University Press, 1996), p. 201.

77. "'Liubaia voina konchaetsia mirom . . . ,'" *Literaturnaia Gazeta,* December 11, 1996, p. 10.

78. Aleksei Kiva, "Proigraiut li storonniki demokratii parlamentskie vybory?," *Rossiiskaia Gazeta,* August 12, 1995, p. 3.

79. As an aside, the behavior of antisystem parties in seeking list seats raises the issue of whether the real matter at hand, at least where elections are concerned, is not parliaments or presidents but rather single-member districts versus proportional representation. While this is an issue for another study, it is interesting to note that the Russian experience seems to confirm the general principle that presidential elections, like races for single-member districts, produce more moderate representatives, while proportional representation produces narrower and more extreme ones. In both the 1993 and 1995, the communists and the LDPR made dramatically more gains in party-list seats than in the individual districts, which were overwhelmingly won by independent candidates—largely on prosaic local issues—and reformers. Antisystem parties were trounced soundly in the upper house elections in both cycles. See Cottrell, p. 167, and Chetvernin, Appendix 1, p. 123.

80. See David Lane, "The Transformation of Russia: The Role of the Political Elite," *Europe-Asia Studies,* October 1996.

81. Giovanni Sartori, "Neither Presidentialism nor Parliamentarism," in Linz and Valenzuela, eds., p. 112.

82. "Chem etot Sovet Prezidentu tsenen," *Rossiiskaia Gazeta,* July 23, 1996, p. 2.

83. Tat'iana Malkina, "Boris El'tsin ukazal nakazyvat' tekh, kto ne vypolniaet ego ukazy," *Segodniia,* June 7, 1996, p. 1.

84. "'Liubaia voina konchaetsia mirom . . . ,'" p. 10.

85. "Presidential Election Lessons Analyzed," FBIS-SOV-96–174-S, August 10, 1996.

86. Mason and Sidorenko-Stephenson, p. 717.

Chapter 6

1. Boris Yeltsin, *Midnight Diaries* (New York: Public Affairs, 2000), p. 387.

2. "A sharp, unexpected, aggressive move always throws your opponent off balance and disarms him," he later wrote, "especially if it is unpredictable and seems absolutely illogical. I have become convinced of this many times over the course of my whole presidential career." Yeltsin, *Midnight Diaries,* p. 275.

3. Roy Medvedev thinks the answer lies somewhere in between, in that Yeltsin was searching for someone who could not only defend the "Family's" interests, but also "Russia's interests, as Yeltsin understood them." Roy Medvedev, *Zagadka Putina* (Moscow: Prava Cheloveka, 2000), pp. 25–26.

4. Yeltsin claimed that Putin's first response, that he "wasn't ready" for the job, made his "heart sink." Yeltsin, *Midnight Diaries,* p. 6; see also Medvedev, p. 27.

5. Yeltsin, *Midnight Diaries,* p. 12.

6. Yeltsin, *Midnight Diaries,* p. 337.

7. In 1974, Richard Nixon positioned Gerald Ford to succeed him after a presidential resignation that left the United States with both the president and vice-president coming to office via succession and appointment rather than election. Ford went on and nearly won election in his own right in 1976. During the 1998 scandal that led to Bill Clinton's impeachment, some commentators suggested that Clinton resign and allow Vice President Al Gore to run in 2000 as an incumbent. Whether Gore agreed or not is unknown, but recent news reports indicate that there was an angry postelection confrontation in 2001 between Clinton and Gore over Gore's perception that Clinton failed to do enough to protect Gore's presidential future.

8. The OSCE Final Report on the March 2000 election is available at www.osce.org. See also Richard Rose, Neil Munro, and Stephen White, "How Strong is Vladimir Putin's Support?," *Post Soviet Affairs* 16 (4), October–December 2000, pp. 294–295; Rose et al. point out that for fraud to matter, it must be "well-organized, consistently [favor] one candidate, and [be] on a large enough scale to reverse what would otherwise have been the result," and that even if the numbers had been tampered with in order to give Putin a first round victory (and there is no conclusive evidence that they were), he would have been a certain victor in the second in any case.

9. To be fair, the makeshift anthem Russians used between 1992 and 2000 was a cumbersome piece of classical music without lyrics, and the Soviet anthem is, to many ears, a fine (and easily sung) tune. Still, the move prompted concern among many in Russia who saw it as a sign of a creeping Soviet restoration. See Aleksandr Porfir'ev, "Staraia pesnia o glavnom," *Segodniia,* July 3, 2000, p. 1.

10. Peter Baker and Susan B. Glasser, "Putin Consolidates Power But Wields It Unsteadily," *The Washington Post,* March 26, 2001, p. 1.

11. Richard Sakwa, "Russia's 'Permanent' (Uninterrupted) Elections of 1999–2000," *The Journal of Communist Studies and Transition Politics* 16 (3), September 2000, p. 86.

12. "'Bol'shaia chetverka' prishla k vyvodu o neobkhodimosti ocherednogo obshchestvennogo soglasiia," *Nezavisimaia Gazeta,* October 21, 1997, p. 1.

13. Yeltsin, *Midnight Diaries,* p. 188.

14. Yeltsin, *Midnight Diaries,* p. 205.

15. Yeltsin, *Midnight Diaries,* pp. 103–113, 274–277.

16. Yeltsin, *Midnight Diaries,* p. 283.

17. Yeltsin, *Midnight Diaries,* pp. 330–331; Putin confirms this account in *Ot pervogo litsa,* pp. 185–186.

18. Marina Ozerova and Irina Rinaeva, "Prem'er, priiatnyi vo vsekh otnosheni-iakh," *Moskovskii Komsomolets,* August 17, 1999, p. 2.

19. Svetlana Babaeva, Vladimir Ermolin, and Evgenii Krutikov, "Territoriia," *Izvestiia,* October 6, 1999, p. 1.

20. *Ot pervogo litsa: razgovory s Vladimirom Putinym* (Moscow: Vagrius, 2000), pp. 132–135.

21. The expression, *zamochit' v sortire,* resists exact translation, but is viscerally powerful and certainly crude. With its scatological crudeness and overtones of a gangland execution, a closer American translation would probably be something more like a threat to "whack them in the can"; whatever the translation, it is indicative of utter contempt. Yeltsin believes that Putin genuinely didn't think his career would last past the Chechen war, and so didn't much care about watching his language. Yeltsin, *Midnight Diaries,* p. 338.

22. See "Chechnya" at www.russiavotes.org. (The site is a joint project of the Center for the Study of Public Policy at the University of Strathclyde and the Russian Center for Public Opinion and Market Research.)

23. See Peter Rutland, "Putin's Path to Power," *Post Soviet Studies* 16 (4), October-December, 2000, p. 322.

24. Dmitrii Koptev and Evgenii Krutikov, "Udar," *Izvestiia,* October 23, 1999, p. 1.

25. Rutland's personal impression is that "the tone of war coverage did not differ substantially among the three main TV channels," to which I would add that my own viewing of Russian television in this period struck me, with the exception of NTV, as verging on jingoistic. If there was a liberal journalistic opposition to the war, it was hard to see on a daily basis—not least because the media moguls supporting Putin made sure to use their own outlets to crowd it out. Rutland, p. 327.

26. See Timothy Colton and Michael McFaul, "Reinventing Russia's Party of Power: 'Unity' and the 1999 Duma Election," *Post Soviet Affairs* 16 (3), July-September 2000, p. 211.

27. "The poll on 19 December," Sakwa correctly noted, "was in effect an opportunity for voters to express their preferences for the future after Yeltsin." Sakwa, p. 86.

28. Colton and McFaul, p. 204.

29. Colton and McFaul, p. 206.

30. Colton and McFaul, p. 220.

31. Colton and McFaul, pp. 209–210.

32. Rutland, p. 325.

33. Rutland, p. 330.

34. This is in contrast, of course, to candidates like Ronald Reagan or Al Gore, who can return to the national stage after defeats in primary elections, which by their nature are fought in staggered regional contests rather than on one single national ballot.

35. Rutland, p. 330.

36. See "Putin's Support," www.russiavotes.org.

37. For official results, see the Russian Central Election Commission site, http://www.fci.ru/prez2000/default.htm.

38. Zyuganov's speech and other opposition commentary can be found in *Sovetskaia Rossiia,* March 28, 2000, p. 1.

39. Leonid Radzikhovskii, "Blestiashchii razgrom," *Segodniia,* March 28, 2000, p. 1.

40. Michael McFaul has pointed out that "Putin supporters had a much more positive assessment of their leader and were much more optimistic about the future," and that the last time polls indicated so much optimism among Russians was in 1991. See "One Step Forward, Two Steps Back," *Journal of Democracy* 11 (3), July 2000, p. 23.

41. See "Putin's Performance in Office," www.russiavotes.org.

42. Baker and Glasser, p. 1.

43. Quoted in Medvedev, p. 40; *Zavtra* 13, March-April, 2000, p. 1.

44. "Putin's Performance in Office," www.russiavotes.org.

45. Quoted in Baker and Glasser, p. 1.

46. See "Public Opinion and the New Duma," www.russiavotes.org.

47. "Putin's Performance in Office," www.russiavotes.org.

48. Vladimir Radyuhin, "Putin popularity rises," *The Hindu* online edition, March 31, 2001.

49. See Marina Volkova, "God prezidenstva Putina: s programmoi ili bez nee?," *Nezavisimaia Gazeta,* March 24, 2001, p. 8, and Igor Bunin, "Ratsional'naia magiia prezidenta," *Nezavisimaia Gazeta,* March 29, 2001, p. 3; and "Is Putin Suffering from Post-Kursk Traumatic Syndrome?," *RFE/RL Russian Political Weekly* 1 (4), February 9, 2001.

50. *Ot pervogo litsa,* p. 163.

51. *Ot pervogo litsa,* p. 162.

52. Shortly before the CPRF's move against the government, the Third Congress of the "Popular-Patriotic Union of Russia"—of which Zyuganov is a member—was held. The rhetoric of the congress was considerably more harsh than that of the new kinder, gentler, CPRF, and may have been a factor in the no-confidence vote. See "My vse u rodiny v dolgu," *Sovetskaia Rossiia,* February 20, 2001, p. 1.

53. See Ivan Rodin, "Bol'shaia politicheskaia igra v dume zakonchilas'," *Nezavisimaia Gazeta,* March 15, 2001, p. 1, and Evgenii Iur'ev, "'Edinstvo' strelialo kholostymi," *Segodniia,* March 14, 2001, p. 1.

54. It is also too complicated. For the most complete discussion of Russian entrepreneurship in the 1990s, see Thane Gustafson, *Capitalism Russian Style* (Cambridge: Cambridge University Press, 1999).

55. Svetlana Babaeva and Georgii Bovt, "Razvod," *Izvestiia,* January 24, 2001, p. 1.

56. Putin claims Gusinsky was jailed by overzealous prosecutors without his knowledge, a claim that as of yet cannot be validated.

57. In an open letter to the president, Berezovsky charged that he was being forced to hand over his controlling interest in ORT television to the government. *Kommersant,* September 5, 2000, p. 1. He has since left the country to escape prosecution. Gusinsky's NTV, the most independent television network in Russia, is also claiming to be under government pressure to dilute Gusinsky's control; CNN's Ted Turner is reportedly interested in buying a major interest in the network.

58. Rutland, p. 347.

59. "[Presidential Envoys] Fail to Win Over Public Opinion," *RFE/RL Russian Federation Report* 3 (9), March 7, 2001.

60. "More 'Resignations' Predicted in Far East Province and Other Regions," *RFE/RL Russian Federation Report* 3 (7), February 14, 2001.

61. Jeremy Bransten and Sophie Lambroschini, "Does Kremlin Reshuffle Augur Real Change?," *RFE/RL Newsline,* March 30, 2001.

62. Egor Gaidar, remarks to the Carnegie Endowment, Washington, D.C., January 29, 2001, available in Johnson's Russia List, 5071, February 3, 2001.

63. Peter Baker, "Putin on a pedestal," *The Washington Post,* February 12, 2001, p. A15.

Chapter 7

1. Edward Corwin, *The President: Office and Powers, 1787–1984,* 5th ed. (New York: New York University Press, 1984), p. 30.

2. Quoted in Roy Medvedev, *Zagadka Putina* (Moscow: Prava Cheloveka, 2000), p. 22.

3. Quoted in David Filipov, "If only to Moscow's mayor, Yeltsin remains relevant," *The Boston Globe,* January 18, 1999, p. 2.

4. Guillermo O'Donnell, "Delegative Democracy," *Journal of Democracy,* January 1994, p. 60.

5. Alfred Stepan and Cindy Skach, "Constitutional Frameworks and Democratic Consolidation: Parliamentarism versus Presidentialism," *World Politics,* October 1993, p. 20.

6. Liliia Shevtsova and Igor' Kliamkin, "Eta vsesil'naia bessil'naia vlast'," *Nezavisimaia Gazeta,* June 25, 1998, p. 8.

7. Corwin, p. 359.

8. Quoted in Corwin, p. 22.

9. "'Bol'shaia chetverka' prishla k vyvodu o neobkhodimosti ocherednogo obshchestvennogo soglasiia," *Nezavisimaia Gazeta,* October 21, 1997, p. 1.

10. These statements, and the chronology of the 1996 referendum, may be found in a series of Radio Liberty reports at http://www.rferl.org/nca/special/election-watch96/.

11. Roland Eggleston, "Belarus: OSCE Report on Movement Towards a Totalitarian State." *RFE/RL Reports,* June 4, 1997.

12. "Only Major Party in Belarus Polls Pulls Out in Protest," Agence France Presse News Wire, March 18, 1999.

13. As one Russian colonel said to me in 1996 when I asked him about the potential of a Russian military coup: "Against whom? For what?" See Thomas Nichols, "An Impending Russian Coup? Nyet," *The Christian Science Monitor,* op-ed, November 6, 1996.

14. Terry Moe and Michael Caldwell, "The Institutional Foundations of Democratic Government: A Comparison of Presidential and Parliamentary Systems," *The Journal of Institutional and Theoretical Economics* 150, no. 1, March 1994, p. 175.

15. Lee Hockstader reported that Russian analysts believe part of the collapse of the July 1995 no-confidence vote could be traced to legislators who worried that dismissal of the Duma would mean the forfeiture of their personal privileges. Lee Hockstader, "Anti-Yeltsin Vote Fails in Duma," *The Washington Post,* July 2, 1995, p. 1. In a similar vein, in interviews in April 1997, legislators as varied in their orientations as Grigoriev and Borovoy felt it was obvious that the CPRF and the LDPR had both been bought off and heavily neutralized as serious opponents with material largesse from the presidential apparatus and its allies. Whether this is true is difficult to ascertain, but the image of venality is one that seems to dog Russian legislators.

16. As Stephen Skowronek has pointed out: "the American presidency has proven itself most effectively as an instrument of negation." Stephen Skowronek, *The Politics Presidents Make* (Cambridge, MA: Belknap/Harvard University Press, 1993), p. 27.

17. See Lidiia Andrusenko, "Kreml' vse eshche ne opredelilsia s partiei vlasti," *Nezavisimaia Gazeta,* February 7, 2001, p. 3. Andrusenko worries that this might lead to a disenchantment with parties in general; despite the argument that this would bring the Russian system more closely in-line with the U.S. or German models, she points out that Russia still lacks an American-style civic ideology, "with its symbols and rituals that draw the nation together more strongly than any religion."

18. "Eto ne po-partiinomu!," *Segodniia,* August 7, 2000, p. 1.

19. Harvey Mansfield, *Taming the Prince: The Ambivalence of Modern Executive Power* (New York: The Free Press, 1989), p. xvi.

Index